A WORKING CLASS
HERBERT
IS SOMETHING
TO BE

By

TIM SMITH

While all the stories in this book are true, some names and identifying details have been changed to protect the privacy of the people involved.

To my mother and all those who stand like Guardians at the Gate of Hell tempering the Rise of the Planet of the Winkles.

CONTENTS

INTRODUCTION 1

ACT 1. STRATFORD (1086 TO 1973) 8

INTERMISSION 178

ACT 2. ROMFORD (1973 TO 1980) 184

ACT 3. A WORKING CLASS HERBERT IS SOMETHING TO BE (2022) ... 271

ACT 4. AN ACORN RUNS THROUGH IT 277

ABOUT THE AUTHOR 281

This may have remained just another untold story
without the support of my wife Georgie Samantha Smith who, it
turns out, is the love of my life.

INTRODUCTION

"As usual there is a great woman behind every idiot." John Lennon

When this manuscript threw itself into the paper shredder, only to reappear as a king-size mattress in my granddaughter's hamster cage, I thought aye aye … here we go again. But why were the Romford Young Conservatives trying to scupper this story … a story no different from a million others?

Well, as Maria von Trapp once said to Al Pacino:

'*Okay Mr Montana put down the flamethrower, and let's start at the very beginning.*'

My name is Tim. I am a fully-certified working-class Herbert and most days you can find me by a slow-moving river eating cheese. That wasn't the plan.

As a kid, I vowed to fight for peace and battle inequality but instead I did forty years travelling the building sites of East London learning a thousand terms for the human genitalia. I'm not complaining. I got a nice little house, three healthy kids and a whole bunch of gorgeous grandchildren.

Then fate gave its velvet ball-bag a shake and now our gutters are blocked, my garden's a jungle and I'm not entirely sure the Jehovah's Witnesses lady isn't working for MI5.

It began in 2012 when my thirty-year marriage came to an end and I was made redundant with knees so knackered I was limping around like Long John Silver. Fortunately, I did my basic training under Val Singleton, and with the help of some duck tape and a toilet roll tube, was soon back skipping up the shops like Bulldog Drummond. Then came the opening day of the 2012 London Olympics and fate delivered one final devastating kick in the nuts.

My mum died.

I always wondered how people cope. Now I know. It's a bastard.

She was one of SEVEN sisters who, throughout the 1960s and 1970s, gathered every Saturday evening to share intelligence and flick through an Avon catalogue while their men played cards, and the rest of us hung from a lamp post like a colony of fruit bats. With a few sister-in-laws, they formed the closest family I've ever known ... and I know at least four if you include the Von Trapps.

Now the only woman to love me unconditionally and provide a never-ending supply of delicious home-made sausage rolls was gone.

When I arrived that morning, my kids were already consoling their 80-year-old granddad and together we crumbled and broke our bloody hearts. By midday, it was standing room only in that little flat behind Witham library. By teatime, it was just me and the old man.

They were married for over sixty years. You know those old marriages: she paid the bills and did all the cooking and cleaning, and he washed up on Christmas day. There were a few tear-ups but the bond was unbreakable. Now, all he had was a pile of her old library books, one empty armchair, and me.

We watched the Olympic opening ceremony in silence. My family come from Stratford so it all felt very close to home. In fact, it was so close, my old secondary school was across the road from the Olympic stadium, and we got our kippers from a fish stall now buried under the long jump pit.

Even the Chinese Olympic Committee said it was the second-best opening ceremony ever, but Kenneth Branagh in a top hat was never going to stop my old man falling asleep, and he was off before Huw Edwards could unscrew his BBC hip flask.

It's funny. I've spent half my life creeping around during my old man's ceremonial evening kips, but this one was different. Good luck to him.

Nature's way and all that.

Then the snoring started! Bloody hell. How my mother shared a bed with him for over sixty years I shall never know. It sounded like a herd of Billy Smart's elephants being chased around the front room by the Coronation Scot.

He eventually woke up during his *Boston Strangler* showstopper, and pointed to the telly where David Beckham happened to be speeding down the Thames with the Olympic flame:

'Is that Beckham?' he enquired.

'Yes, Dad, he's bringing the Olympic torch,' I answered.

'Should've known that ponce would stick his fucking nose in,' he concluded.

It may have been that never-ending line of track-suited Americans, but when the Great Britain team entered the stadium to a fanfare of Bowie's *Heroes* and the crowd sang *I'm Forever Blowing Bubbles,* I cried like a bloody kid.

For the next two weeks, I kept an eye on Claire Balding and the medals table, waiting for the inevitable cock-up. Instead, we smashed the Russians and the crowd blew a collective raspberry at Chancellor George Osbourne. And by the time Ginger Spice and one of the Pet Shop Boys had extinguished the Olympic flame, the entire world knew there was plenty of spunk left in this salty old sea-dog!

Like that Mafia speech in *The Long Good Friday,* it was the perfect rallying cry for a flagging spirit so I decided to chart my journey through the choppy waters of Newham. You know: tell the kids what it was like when Henry Cooper and the Beatles were slugging it out with Muhammad Ali and the Monkees. I could also explain why my family joined the Great Cockney Exodus to Romford, just as Donny Osmond and his family were being wheeled out one by one, like a slow-dripping Chinese water torture.

The thing is I'm no Rudyard Kipling. I'm not even a Jeffrey Archer. And who's gonna be interested in an ordinary family rather than a bunch of dysfunctional nitwits living on a bomb-site inside a walnut cocktail cabinet? We weren't hard up, there was no abuse, and my father was the only man in East London who didn't run with the sodding Kray twins! Nope, if this book was gonna find its way to a Sue Ryder shop and nuzzle between a pair of well-thumbed Nigella Lawsons, I needed to find the *Eye of the Tiger* and become the literary equivalent of Rocky Balbao.

*

Dear reader, before we proceed, I should explain the lifestyle choices available to a young British winkle during those Golden Wonder years. At the top you had entrepreneurial 'geezers' like my mate Dave Stanley. Down the bottom you had your 'berks', 'twerps' and unlikeable 'chancers' like Michael Gove.

Somewhere in the middle, standing quietly at the back, were those of us following a long-standing British tradition of keeping their heads down while others stampede for the finish line. I speak of course of the 'herbert'. Becoming one might mean a few extra holidays on the Isle of Wight, but it's good for the old blood pressure, and nobody notices when you slip away from a wedding reception to go fishing.

So, as finding the *Eye of the Tiger* was taking longer than a training montage with Burgess Meredith, I chucked in the towel on this writing lark. It happened at Oxford University where I was studying the works of Emily Brontë and noticed her rare use of vulgar slang like 'arsehole' and 'bollocks'. I'm not kidding. I flounced out of that gift shop quicker than Scarlett O'Hara with her pants on fire.

I moved into the former chapel of an old Victorian workhouse in

Witham with my eldest son and a new pair of titanium knees; all thoughts of writing a memoir disappearing quicker than David Cameron after the Brexit referendum. But a few months later, a ghostly benefactor reignited those embers glowing dimly on my curly bush of ambition. Was it the spirit of Beatle John? Or was it the mysterious girl who had been haunting my dreams since 1967? Who knows? All I remember is standing in the tiny kitchen dreaming about DCI Jane Tennyson coming at me with some pink furry handcuffs, when a familiar song drifted in from the other room:

'*... a working-class hero is something to be ...*'

That was it! Spending the evening with Dame Helen Mirren, a Cluedo board, and a bottle of Johnson's baby lotion just had to wait, because David Bowie and Bonnie Tyler were right. I needed a Hero.

As a kid, I dabbled with Joe 90, dallied with Dick Van Dyke, and could dribble a football like Georgie Best. Then in 1971, while standing in a blood-stained woodworking apron, John Lennon lobbed a political acorn through my bedroom window, knocking me clean onto my little cockney arse. Anyone who can write a song like *Imagine* but still get his knob out for an album cover couldn't be all bad, and he became my big brother as I prepared to battle the '*yellow-bellied-pig-headed-politicians*', waiting only for a full complement of pubic hair and the midnight call from Anthea Redfern.

What happened? By 1985, I was stretched out on a bunk bed reading *Miffy the Rabbit* while Margaret Thatcher flogged the silver to Rupert Murdoch as the scrawny little fucker span around in his executive chair.

'*...So, this is Christmas, and what have you done?*'

I did nothing and now the latest bunch of public school chancers are driving us off the White Cliffs of Dover like a bunch of patriotic lemmings. Boris Johnson anyone? I know they can't all be Barack Obama, but fuck me!

And it's no good looking to the playing fields of Romford. I've broken biscuits with hundreds of British and Commonwealth Winkles, and in the cosy afterglow of a McVitie's Chocolate Hobnob, most men will agree we're about as much use as Ian Duncan Smith's shower cap. Sure, we're good with the kids and can knock up a decent BBQ, but deep down we're all fighting the urge to put on a cowboy suit or catalogue our mint collection of Razzle magazines. We simply can't be trusted which is no big deal if you're loading an extra roll of roofing felt on the van, but a big fucking problem if you're skipping a Cobra meeting for a Goldman Sachs *'Oooh, look at us, aren't we fantastic'* All-You-Can-Eat Buffet'.

And whereas it's easy to remove a distributor cap from a Ford Transit, how do you make a long streak of rarefied vapour like Jacob Rees-Mogg hang his top hat on a lower peg? The answer, my friend, is blowing behind the billowing net curtains of Great Britain.

'... it's the other half of the sky...'

My mum and her Olympic sized squad of sisters steered some big old ships using a technique based on the FIFA-recognised, Peggy Mount-Alf Ramsey system. My dad had a broken nose and was built like Charlie Atlas. He also had the gambling instincts of the Cincinnati Kid, the athleticism of a young Bobby Moore and the money-making qualities of Raffles the Gentlemen Thief; and a chinless wonder like Nigel Farage would've lasted five minutes before being draped over the bonnet of a Ford Escort. Yet thanks to one woman's ability to drop-kick a casserole dish through a serving hatch, I never once saw my old man plunge the world into financial crisis!

I was lucky. Instead of being sent away to boarding school, I grew up within the sound of a large collection of cockney bosoms, and my formative years were so perfect even Huckleberry Finn would've snapped his fishing pole in half and stormed off to join the Republican Party. So, I've decided to break the first rule of Herbert Club and reveal what effect a battalion of Venus lady shavers had on a little wanker like me, and it is dedicated to all those women who stand like Guardians at the Gates of Hell, tempering The Rise of the Planet of the Winkles.

Will my lack of punctuation make Tory ministers invest more in education? Without overstating the bleedin' obvious, the answer is NO.

But a Herbert's needs are manyfold, so welcome aboard this old Mississippi paddle steamer as we navigate the backwaters of Newham where beautiful sirens will tempt us onto the rocks, and a flotilla of tugboats with names like Dolly, Alice, Polly and Queenie will stop us running aground on every sandbank between Stratford, Romford, and all stations to Southend.

And one day, when my granddaughter grows tired of burying dead hamsters, I hope she'll read this and understand the power inside her unicorn back-pack. Use it wisely, sweetheart, because there's something in the air, and it's definitely not coming from your granddad.

Stay cool, everyone. Power to the People and all that.

Huckleberry Herbert

ACT 1

STRATFORD

(1086 TO 1973)

In the distance, we see The Tower of London under construction and imagine the strangled curse of a stonemason as his thumb gets trapped between two blocks of Kentish ragstone. Four miles to the east, my 10-year-old medieval ancestor Herbert the Unready sits on a wooden bridge over the River Lea, dangling his legs into the clear water and imagining the damage he could do with a size 14 hook and a decent float rod ...

Stratford, My Stratford

In 1086, the manor of West Ham had a recorded population of 130, by all contemporary standards a pretty large village, which gave young Herbert plenty of scope to do a bit of light thieving while his family worked their nuts off in the soggy London clay.

Life wasn't easy but for the next four hundred years, despite revolution, plague, and heavy taxation, Herbert families continued to plough the fields and scatter the good seed on the land. Children played; Herbert larks ascended; everyone was happy. Praise the Lord.

News soon spread of this Secret Garden east of London, and by the 16th century, magnificent country homes began popping up on Herbert land. One of them was owned by a wealthy botanist called Dr John Fothergill, who used its 80 acres to house a collection of flora and fauna that was second only to those at Royal Kew. Time smoked a cigarette and by the 19th Century, London had slid into the smoggy haze of the Industrial Revolution, and that Secret Garden looked more like California during the Gold Rush as a massive influx of workers followed the factories, docks and railways across the River Lea. By 1900, West Ham was the 9th most populated town in England.

Somehow, Fothergill's botanical gardens remained the jewel in the town and after being bequeathed to the Corporation of London, it was given the grand old name of West Ham Park.

Back in 1763, Dr Fothergill planted a tree called a Maidenhair (*Gingko Biloba*), which grew to become the oldest specimen of its kind in the country. Two hundred years later in 1963, a six-year-old descendent of Herbert the Unready took revenge on behalf of his displaced ancestors by having a slash against that famous old tree.

It wasn't much, but that was my first attempt at raging against The Man.

The Stately Home of Dame Polly Moffatt *or* Tufty and the Headless Chickens

Around 1860, when crinoline ladies were not knitted accoutrements for a toilet roll, a terrace of fine-looking houses was constructed overlooking West Ham Park, and named in honour of Prime Minister William (Cheeky Chops) Gladstone after his brother-in-law pulled a few strings at the West Ham Planning Department. By 1945, after eighty years of miserable English weather and one close shave from a V2 rocket, Gladstone Road was looking decidedly ragged and beginning to wish it hadn't fucking bothered. This is where our story really begins.

My maternal grandmother was a short sturdy woman who spent her first forty years living within smell-shot of the horse droppings on Stratford Broadway. Her name was Alice Moffatt (known as Polly) and after receiving an eviction notice from the German Luftwaffe, she gathered her husband and nine children and moved the short distance to Gladstone Road where a street party was already in full swing with bunting strung along the park railings and people in khaki uniforms singing *When The Lights Go On Again*. It was VE Day. Victory in Europe. A few days earlier, Hitler had committed suicide allowing German soldiers to go home to their wives. Of course, Nigel Farage's dad was furious but everyone else was jubilant, especially Britain's greengrocers because now they needn't adopt the metric system until some time in the early 1970s.

As a result, number 54 remained precisely twenty feet tall and fourteen feet wide.

It was a happy home full of the joyous squabbling that comes from seven daughters sharing a single bathroom. Polly kept the place spotless, including a daily regime of polishing the step and washing down the pavement. Once a week, the iron weights in the window frames would clank loudly as the bottom sash flew up and Polly's ample backside edged onto the sill so she could clean the outer glass.

Yep, she kept the place spotless alright but the back garden looked like a battlefield in Flanders. No hollyhocks or pretty rows of delicate pink foxgloves, just a desolate expanse of mud peppered with distress messages from the dog. There were also two scrawny chickens in a coop made from beer crates, whose incessant clucking only stopped on Christmas Eve when they began scratching at the dirt, desperately trying to appear busy.

To avoid the dog excrement and chicken pox, the younger Moffatts played out in the street where the coal man's horse joined in the fun by crapping in the middle of their cricket pitch. There wasn't much traffic so, apart from horse droppings in the shape of large Walnut Whip's, Gladstone Road was a safe place to play. In fact it was so safe that Tufty Club cast members arrived one day to make a road-safety film about Willy the Weasel shoving his bushy tailed co-star under a Tonibell ice cream van. Local children lined the pavement with autograph books waiting for their hero but unfortunately Tufty was 50 miles away filming an episode of *Animal Magic* after being double-booked by his agent who also managed *Secret Squirrel* and a few Beatrix Potter characters.

One by one, Polly's children married and moved away, leaving just the youngest son and three daughters at No. 54. Now, with the queue for the bathroom well under two hours, it was agreed that my future dad could marry my future mum and take two rooms on the top floor.

For over a century, Gladstone Road watched different families change the curtains and different dogs defecate in its back gardens. Everyone agreed it was a wonderful place to live. Everyone except the West Ham Planning Department who demolished the lot in 1975, allowing the ghosts of headless chickens to roam the ground forever.

But hold your horses there, sister. That's not where this story ends for Gladstone Road. First, we must go back to Christmas Eve 1957, when No. 54 became home to yet another descendant of Herbert the Unready *(me, me, me)* and where our story really, really, really, begins.

Behold! Charlie and Jean Have a Boy Child: The Right Honourable Little Lord Herbert

And on that magical night, No. 54 lay empty.

Pifco Christmas lights flickered in the front room window as Harry Belafonte sang *Mary's Boy Child* from inside a large wooden radio. Apart from two cups of warm tea, nothing stirred ... not even a mouse. Where was everyone? Was my heavily pregnant mother being led around the streets on the back of an old donkey? Nope. She was on the back seat of an old donkey – her brother Bill's Austin A35 – being driven screaming to Queen Mary's Hospital.

One moment I'm floating upside down in the warmth, the next I'm being ushered into a cold delivery room without any ceremony apart from the NHS band playing *A Fanfare for the Common Man*. After a quick wash and shave, they weighed me in at 8lbs and the midwife took measurements for my first sailor suit. Five days later, having solved the mystery of the 999 on my scalp *(something to do with print rubbing off the midwife's pools coupon)*, I was gift-wrapped in swaddling and sent home to begin my ordinary life.

As we waited at the bus stop, three men approached wearing middle-eastern robes and asking for directions to Bethnal Green. Dad thought they might be Asian shepherds ... or even German spies, but they turned out to be *(drum roll)* ... Shepherds' pies!

Britain was repaying the monthly instalments on its massive war debt so rationing was still in place, especially on Gold, Frankenstein and Mermaids, so the three wise men clubbed together and bought me a knitted panda with a wavy woollen line for a mouth.

Mum's brother Bill fashioned me a cot from an old wooden sleigh, and each night at least four Moffatt ladies would gather around my wooden crib to sing their little heads off:

'The stars in the night sky looked down where he lay ... at little Lord Herbert asleep on his sleigh.'

Meanwhile in 251 Menlove Avenue, Liverpool, a 15-year-old short-sighted Teddy Boy was pulling on his Elvis pyjamas after a long day back-combing his quiff with two pals called Paul and George. And across town at 10 Admiral Grove, little Richard Starkey was creeping downstairs with eyes only for the drumsticks on the Christmas turkey.

Vice Admiral William Moffatt VC and The Unsinkable Polly Thompson

I never met my maternal grandad but a grainy image of him stared down from above the fireplace dressed in a naval greatcoat like an officer in the Royal Navy who sailed the Atlantic convoys alongside Noël Coward, on the bridge of HMS Torrin in *In Which We Serve*.

No. 1: (played by William Moffatt) *Cocoa, sir?*

Captain: (played by Noël Coward) *Thank you, No.1.*

No.1: *Pretty sky, sir.*

Captain: *Yes, it's the dawn of a new day and I shouldn't be surprised if it's a perfectly uncomfortable one.*

No.1: *Look, sir* (pointing to the horizon). *The Germans are jumping overboard in full marching order.*

Captain: (using binoculars) *Hmm, I think they may be penguins No.1?*

When I was old enough to handle the truth (age 55), Dad told me that Vice Admiral William Moffatt VC was actually a jobbing builder from Bethnal Green.

When Bill first met Polly, she thought he was all at sea, but after watching how quick he could repoint a chimney stack, she accepted his marriage proposal and they set about making their nine children. It was a happy and loving partnership.

Everything rattled along swimmingly until 1939 when a man called

Neville Chamberlain declared war on Germany. Operation Pied Piper swung into action, and before you could say *Goodbye Mr Tom*, four of Polly's noisiest children were bundled onto a train and evacuated out of London with labels tied to their coats like little cockney Paddington Bears.

Jean (my eight-year-old mum) and her elder sister Eileen lived with a butcher's family in Penzance and enjoyed paddling in the sea and scoffing extra lamb mince. The two brothers weren't so lucky. They stayed on a windswept farm and wrote home complaining about having to share a bath with a herd of sheep. Without further ado, and with no money for the return fare, Polly caught the first train south and brought them all back to Stratford to wave rolled-up newspapers at the German Luftwaffe. This fierce maternal instinct not only taught her children how to dodge fares on public transport, but also forged a family bond so strong, it can be heard arguing to this very day.

Wild Bill Moffatt died young (aged 56) but he left his mark on this world. Nine of them to be exact, along with a well-thumbed book on family planning. Without Bill's input I might never have got to draw intricate patterns with a Spirograph, or be traumatized by Donny and Marie Osmond looking into each other's eyes singing *I'm leaving it all ... up to yooo ... oo ... ooou*. Thanks a bleeding lot Granddad.

Polly died in 1962 (aged 62) and my abiding memory is sitting on her lap sipping Guinness and watching *Squiddly Diddly* play his drum kit in Bubbleland. I wonder if my own grandchildren will have similar memories of eating my sausage sandwich while watching *Peppa Pig*?

Polly left seven daughters, Alice, Dolly, Eileen, Jean (Mum), Pat, Christine and Lynda, and two sons, Derek and Bill, along with their respective partners, Charlie Vaughan, Bill Godfrey, John Adlam, Charlie Smith (Dad), Brian Jupp, Gordon Milne, and Jean and June Moffatt, who became the new and improved Moffatts, and the closest family since *The Waltons, The Munsters* and of course *The Jetsons*.

Polly's youngest daughter, Lynda, was still a kid when Polly died, so it was decided she would become my big sister. Today, she's a doting great-grandmother but in 1962 she was making more of an impact on the neighbourhood than a V2 rocket. Known locally as *'that little mare from Gladstone'*, her formative years were spent leaving a trail of broken hearts around the valleys and billiard halls of Stratford. She also left her mark in the hallway of No. 54 by carefully pricking every bubble on the anaglypta wallpaper. Yep, those Freudian warnings of her man-eating nature were there for all to see. More of our lovely Lynda later.

The Boy Who Would Be Caligula

Being the first grandson after a run of five granddaughters meant I was courted, cosseted and serenaded like a young Roman Emperor, and the only way to avoid being smothered in pink lipstick was to keep crawling around like a little royal train. It was hard work but – *drum roll* – it kept me off the streets! Anyway, it was while scooting around polishing the lino that I earned my family nickname.

According to legend, I liked to take regular pit-stops under the dining table where the Moffatt sisters (collective noun: a slander) were usually discussing the rising cost of a pint of whelks. Sitting amongst those nylon clad legs, I would apparently remove their high-heeled shoes and enjoy a good chew upon those stockinged toes. Now. I love them loads but surely it must say more about my aunts letting me do it rather than any fledgling stocking fetish (see Dame Helen Mirren and, to a lesser extent, Juliet Bravo). In my defence, each one of those Moffatt ladies did have very shapely legs. Anyway. That, M'lud, is why I was sitting cross-legged under a table in the Romford Waterstones, and why my aunts still call me Timmy Toenails.

Being fussed over by large groups of beautiful women only reinforced my Roman Emperor complex, and quite honestly, I was having the time of my bloody life.

This all came to an abrupt end with the arrival of my annoying little cousin Jeff, closely followed by Mark, Billy Boy and a whole bunch of other winkles who stole my limelight, my Dinky cars and most importantly, a brand new box of Farley's rusks.

A Day in the Life

Mum worked as a seamstress in a mattress factory so, with Lynda at school and my aunt Christine up a ladder replacing roof slates, I was strapped into a high-chair and parked in front of the upstairs window with some bacon rind. From there, like a captain in a ship's wheelhouse, I could look across Gladstone Road towards the gentle swell of West Ham Park where brightly coloured figures were chasing footballs.

And that's my earliest memory. Not one for the vegetarians, but it did instil a passion for sitting with a tray of food while other people run around for my amusement.

Actually, because of the high-chair thing, I did briefly consider becoming a professional tennis umpire, as it would not only provide unlimited access to Robinson's Barley Water but also allow my ongoing research into Ladies Wimbledon Champions and their relationship with frilly knickers. It was a lofty ambition which never materialised. Instead, I ended up pushing wheelbarrows around building sites. More from Old Wheelie later.

While sucking upon delicious strips of crispy bacon, a BBC Light Programme was usually playing in the background. It was called *Woman's Hour* and it must have made a deep psychological impression because even today. I love listening to women rabbiting... even when I don't have a clue what they're going on about.

However, I do know that ladies love Milk Tray, and only the crumbliest flakiest chocolate tastes like chocolate never tasted before.

Pavlov's Dogs and the Little Indian Prince

Thanks to the regularity of the Greenwich Time Signal and the precision of the BBC Radio schedules, I soon developed a decent working knowledge of Pavlov's conditioning experiments. For example, the opening bars of *Listen With Mother* became my cue to bounce down the stairs and catch a lift on a passing dog towards the scullery, where a well-spoken female voice welcomed me from deep inside Nan's radio:

Are you sitting comfortably, little Herbert? Then I'll begin.

My afternoon chaperone was Derek's fiancée, Jean. She was a trainee nurse and practised triage by strapping me to the high chair and wrapping white bandages around my head until I looked like a little Indian prince. Then it was time for an early BBC children's TV programme designed to give trainee nurses ten minutes alone with a KitKat. It was called *Watch With Mother,* and began with a slow, faltering animation of a delicate lace flower slowly unfurling, accompanied by a drunk Scotsman playing a xylophone.

Each day was a different show. Mondays, a matronly lady played piano while a naughty sausage dog pestered the fucking life out of her. Tuesday was a soap opera about a struggling family of wooden actors, and on Wednesday two flowerpot men talked complete bollocks for fifteen minutes. On Thursday, two glove puppets called Ragtrade and Bob Tailor calmed everything down before it kicked off again on Friday with a puppet called Andy Pandy. Andy was a contrary little fellow with an early form of ADHD, who was easily distracted by a rag-doll called Looby Lou who danced and sang her little head off in an effort to impress the producers and get her own show.

The psychological effect of all those puppet shows and the received pronunciation of the lady narrator made a profound impression on a generation of young telly watchers. Personally, I like nothing more than to sit down and dream of a prudish lady in a 1950's dress, scolding me for being a *silly sausage.*

Uncle Derek and The Tight-Fisted England Fast Bowler

Before Polly died and while John Lennon was stomping around the Star Club in Hamburg with a toilet seat around his neck, I was sharing a bedroom with Mum's youngest brother. Derek was a kind man with an infectious laugh and a spiky quiff giving him the appearance of Elvis Presley doing a Stan Laurel impression. Every night I laughed excitedly as my cot dragged itself across the bedroom, desperately trying to escape his thunderous bloody snoring.

He was a decorator on West Ham Council and an absolute wizard with a set of marbling combs. But his big passion was Sunday league football. It was a passion so big that he kept a jar of football studs on his bedside table alongside a photo of his fiancée. Each stud had three vicious nails protruding from it and Sunday mornings Derek would bang them into the thick soles of his football boots with a toffee hammer. Each lace was approximately three quarters of a mile long and had to be wrapped underneath the soles before being tied off with a huge sheepshank. Soon after kick-off those laces were cracking like whips and the loosened studs were tearing bloody holes into the calves of opposing players. And that's why Derek was known throughout the league as Del the Impaler, strolling around the pitch like an early incarnation of the German midfield general, Franz Beckenbauer.

After a match, it wasn't uncommon for Derek to come home supported by team mates, staring blankly ahead as if he had witnessed some dreadful sporting tragedy. It was those old leather footballs, you see. Caked in mud, they weighed the equivalent of a medicine ball pumped full of cough mixture, and anyone silly enough to put their head on one was left staggering around like a shell-shock victim. Yep, football was a tough old game in the late fifties, and no place for an Elvis Presley impersonator.

Living in a house full of women meant Derek and my dad knew their place ... and they retreated to that place at every opportunity. It was the downstairs front room, where lived a half size snooker table, a dartboard, a shove halfpenny board, bar skittles, a piano and some corporate boxes for spectators to watch the fun while enjoying a brown ale.

Every Saturday night that front room filled with male decathletes, moving between events and laying off bets. And as the stack of beer crates grew taller and the ladies got busy discussing the lady above the bike shop, the kids were set free to go outside and beg passers-by for their spare change. Which brings me to the tale of Sir Freddie Trueman.

It was just an ordinary Saturday evening and we were outside playing with a large pile of horse dung when we noticed a large gentleman peering through our downstairs window. Dear reader, I've no wish to disparage the famously stingy Yorkshire cricketer, but it is no coincidence that ten years later Fred would replicate the sporting atmosphere of our front room with his hugely successful 1970s TV show, *Indoor League*. When asked to comment, Sir Fred drew on his pipe, zipped up his chunky cardigan and replied:

"Aye lad, it strikes me as bein' queer at fowk at's allus buyin' bargains dooan't get rich hauf as fast as them 'at sell 'em."

No nonsense, our Fred.

Those Saturday gatherings would rattle on, in one form or another, for two decades. A place for men to go all-in with the housekeeping, and for ladies to share the kind of fruity gossip that would've made Katie Boyle run screaming to the outside toilet. It was also a good place for young boys to hear off-colour jokes, and for young girls to hear heart-stopping tales about surprise pregnancies. A weekly institution that would bind four generations.

At 10 pm, the kids were crammed into temporary beds like sardines covered in an Ovaltine sauce. Two hours later, with the moon casting dark shadows across West Ham Park, a dwindling proportion of men continued playing cards while tea cups and ashtrays were stashed away for another week. Inevitably, a hush would descend upon No. 54, broken only by Derek's thunderous snoring and one last mournful postern blast from Uncle Brian stretched out under the snooker table.

Goodnight, children everywhere.

Jean Florence Smith or The Way of the Dragon

When Mum was busy rustling up five-course meals or practising her Sarah Vaughan impressions, I was left doing press-ups and ten-piece puzzles in our upstairs front room. Heated by a single paraffin stove, it was like an isolation cell in Alcatraz. The linoleum floor was simply furnished with two armchairs and a small telly. Between the chairs was a wedding present from Dad's brother Jim: a small, circular coffee table with a walnut veneer lid hiding a secret compartment where Mum kept her knitting needles and a half-finished admiral's uniform for her little sailor (*me, me, me*). There was also an oak sideboard displaying four brass ashtrays, six Babycham glasses, and a bottle of Stones Ginger wine, which nobody drank except me when I went off the rails during my Billy Bremner phase in 1965.

Money was tight but not as tight as Dolly's husband Bill, whose arms were notoriously short when it came to reaching down to the padlocked money box sewn into his fireproof trousers. In other words, we weren't awash with the young queen's newly minted coinage, but we weren't skint either. However, this didn't stop Mum from converting her three rooms into the height of fifties chic. Of course, it helped having a brother who could pilfer from the council stores, so, while Uncle Derek got to work, Mum could choose from the most exotic wallpapers that Young & Martens on Stratford Broadway could offer.

My parent's bedroom had a Grecian theme with stone columns, lutes and harps, entwined with grape vines. The kitchen paper was a vinyl affair with perfectly symmetrical lines of assorted root vegetables. But it was the living room where Mum gave full vent to her inner Pistachio. It was a shimmering black wallpaper dotted with elderly Chinese gentlemen in rowing boats, each with a lantern and a cormorant diving off the back. Now remember, this was ten years before Karl Douglas and *Hong Kong Phooey* so she was way ahead of her time.

This interest in the Orient continued with her Kung Fu, which she practised on her husband whenever he came in late after spending the evening discussing Greek mythology with the landlord of The Bay Tree. I'm told her Praying Mantis was a thing of beauty, which could reduce my hard-as-iron father to a quivering wreck.

Nelson, Lord of the Admiralty, and Little Aunt Lynda

Mrs Miller was from Barbados and she lived next door with three grown up sons, a German Shepherd and a parrot called The Great Mizundo. I was always intrigued by the parrot's brightly coloured exotic plumage and her stories of it being able to read minds. I believed her because whenever I made a move for its peanuts, The

Great Mizundo began sharpening its beak on a piece of cuttlefish.

We had a Corgi called Nelson and one day Mrs Miller's German Shepherd tore a large chunk from its side. Poor Nelson died where he fell – on the poop deck – and was buried in true naval fashion behind the chicken coop. Little Aunt Lynda was so upset that she swore upon Mr Mizundo's sandpaper bible to hunt down Mrs Miller's three sons. The youngest brother copped it first, and came home with Lynda from a Georgie Fame concert staggering like a zombie from *Night of the Living Dead*. Realising they were under attack, the other two quickly got themselves confined to Parkhurst on the Isle of Wight for robbery with firearms, hoping this would somehow deter my little aunt. They were mistaken. Lynda was a determined little lady who knew plenty of sailors.

Our other neighbours were known as the Woodsies, having dropped their more formal title The Woods of Gladstone. Mr Woods was a small man who carried the world on his shoulders, and his wife was a large lady who carried his eight children on hers. Having no brothers or sisters, I used to play with the Woods children like Little Lord Fauntleroy until one of them stole my Dinky Rolls Royce. Diplomatic relations broke down until Dad came home from work, went next door, and hung Mr Woods from the first-floor window.

Reunited with my Dinky status symbol, and after a supper of cod roe à la pomme frites served with a chilled bottle of Cow & Gate, my mum serenaded me with her favourite Sarah Vaughan song: *Little Man You've Had a Busy Day*, about a boy losing his marbles.

Life couldn't get better. Surrounded by lutes, harps and Grecian pillars, with a beautiful lady in glasses singing only for me. Like the infant Caligula, I burped, crapped my nappy and drifted off to sleep.

Man, I was living the dream.

My Perfect Cousin

When I could change my own nappies, I was sent off to play with the blonde-haired offspring of Mum's sister, Eileen. Denise was five years older than me but made up for it by having some brightly coloured Gonks, and a 'Push the Magnetic Filings onto the Head of a Bald Beatle' game. We got up to all the usual stuff like hop scotch, randy brandy, and Hergé's *Adventures of Gin Gin*. But her favourite pastime was miming to Beatles records while playing incredibly difficult chord progressions on a Slazenger tennis racket. To give a dash of realism to proceedings, she had me smashing her mum's saucepans with a wooden spoon like the famous Ringo. Happy days.

Denise had a goldfish which gave up its troubadour lifestyle with a travelling fair to live in a butler sink in their garden. It was called Lucky, and when Den was having some alone time with Paul McCartney, Lucky and I fought with plastic frogmen or enjoyed a threesome with Troy Tempest and the enigmatic Marina. You could say we got along swimmingly until the big freeze of 1962 when I decided to smash the thick ice on Lucky's sink with a house brick. For the next few days, my concussed playmate remained motionless ... even when Troy offered him the keys to Stingray. Yep. The little golden vagabond was dead.

Luckily Denise had another pet – a white terrier called Pip who, sensing I was a danger to the animal kingdom, sank its teeth into my ankle like a four-legged Christopher Lee. I showed my aunt the blood pouring from two puncture wounds but instead of administering Pip with a lethal injection she gave the little white fluffy bastard a brand new rubber bone! From then on, whenever I saw Pip sprawled in its basket licking its own genitals, he always gave me a big smug toothy grin.

Denise's bedroom was like Aladdin's cave, full of Bunty annuals, coloured pencils, and a Pelham puppet of a Dutch girl hanging lifelessly from her bedhead. The best thing was a collection of twelve-inch dolls dressed in national costumes, kept on a shelf above her bed. I used to spend hours bouncing up and down on her mattress, admiring those national stereotypes. There was a Welsh lady with a stovepipe hat; a Scotsman with kilt and bagpipes; and an English policeman with tiny helmet, bra and panties. There was even an Irishman with a butane gas bottle and barrow full of tarmac.

Dear reader – I'm ashamed to say that one day I helped myself to a miniature revolver from the holster of a Royal Canadian Mountie, leaving him defenceless against the vampish lady flamenco dancer. I'd like to take this opportunity to formally apologise to that little Canadian law enforcer. It must have been hell in there during those long Spanish nights, without your .44 Magnum … the most powerful handgun in the world.

This petty thieving remains a blemish on my otherwise perfect childhood and was something I wouldn't repeat until the story below … and then continue on a regular basis until sometime in 2005.

The Beano, The Dandy and The Amityville Road Horror

Mr Silburn ran the newsagents like Kevin Costner in *The Bodyguard*: ready to throw himself between the comics and any light-fingered little cunt who fancied their chances. Every Thursday, Den and I made the pilgrimage to collect that week's Bunty (Britain's most popular girls' comic, and only one letter away from the taste of paradise). Denise couldn't wait to wallow in a warm bubble bath and read tales of Shetland ponies and valiant sheep dogs, and she caused quite a stir one day when she prematurely stripped down to her vest and knickers behind the ice cream cabinet. But every cloud has a Lyons Maid lining, and while Mr Silburn had a mild heart attack, I was able to swipe a roll of explosive caps for my toy Winchester to help me control the outbreak of Eamonn Andrews on telly.

For a young gentleman on a tight budget, choosing a boys' comic was like some diabolical torture. There were dozens: The Hornet, Hurricane, Hotspur, and Britain - Valiant, Victory, Cupid and Blitzen, each with the mission of teaching boys how to wedge a bucket of water over a classroom door while bayoneting a Japanese footballer with one leg chained to a swarthy German spy. Interestingly, most stories ended with the hero enjoying a large bag of piping hot fish and chips ...

This weekly dilemma was made easier whenever Alf Tupper was stapled to a brown paper Wacker, or Captain Hurricane was supplemented by a two-inch plastic submarine propelled by baking soda. Yep, free gifts! Code-breaking kits, football league charts, whistle balloons, tattoo transfers, clickety-clackers, super squirt rings, plastic cigars, boomerangs, balsa aeroplanes, and the 'Modern Miss, Comb and Mirror Set', for those wanting to look their best over the debris.

One popular give-away was the three-inch plastic paratrooper which came supplied with its own polythene parachute. There wasn't a boy in Greater London who could resist one of those little blighters, even though we all knew it would soon be dangling helplessly from the nearest telephone wire. Come to think of it, I spent much of 1964 standing in silent vigil under a lamppost in Gladstone Road, waiting for those thin cotton lines to degrade so my little green paratrooper could finally plummet to his inevitable and very painful death.

Across the road from Silburn's was a launderette, a bike shop, and the local Spar, offering treble Green Shield stamps on tins of Ye Olde Oak ham. Green Shield stamps were at the height of their popularity, collected and exchanged for household items from a gift catalogue. Eileen was a big fan and often found draped across her chaise lounge like Zsa Zsa Gabor, deciding between six lager glasses and a record rack, or whether to go for broke and exchange all thirty books for a Kenwood Chef. Around this time, stories began circulating about local men exchanging their stamps with the lady above the bike shop who, for three books and the price of a cream horn, would provide an executive massage and complimentary facial!

Looming over this small parade was a pub called The Park Tavern where wealthy Victorians once rested after a long day promenading around West Ham Park. In Victorian times, the road would have been a muddy quagmire, churned up by horse drawn traffic. But in 1964 it was smooth tarmac with a new zebra crossing and a pair of blinking Belisha beacons, named after The Right Honourable Leslie Hore-Belisha, first Baron Hore-Belisha, who I'm pretty sure was a toff.

For some reason, my old man, The Less Honourable Straight Up and No Mistake Charles Robert Smith Esq, was banned from that distinguished old pub and when I asked him forty years later if there was any particular reason, my father sucked on his one good tooth before replying:

"Yes, boy … the landlord was a fucking ponce, that's why!"

Which put my mind at rest somewhat. (My father was also banned from The Pigeons and The Bay Tree, suggesting some kind of conspiracy by the Bass brewery).

As the medics loaded Mr Silburn into the ambulance, Den and I walked home along Amity Road, past a small independent dairy selling cheese, eggs and freshly sliced ham. Outside was a blue vending machine dispensing cartons of flavoured milk from a steel drawer which snapped shut on your fingers like a short-tempered mechanical fly trap. Thanks to the enterprise of the Milk Marketing Board, I now flinch like Herbert Lom if I'm ever asked to root around inside a lady's handbag.

Behind the shop window, looming over the white marble counter, was a large bacon slicer. We were told told never to stick out fingers inside the bacon slicer because (*drum roll*) it was an old joke that shouldn't be touched with a ten-foot tickling stick.

Behind the dairy was a cobbled yard and some disused stables where war horses once slept after a long day between the shafts. By the 1960s, the clip-clop of horses' hooves was mostly replaced by the whinnying sound of motorised milk floats made from captured Messerschmitt engines. This new efficiency allowed milkmen to finish their rounds and be upstairs swapping their Green Shields stamps with the lady above the bike shop while the coalman was still downstairs adjusting his horse's nose bag.

Our milkman was Glaswegian and for some reason he wore a white ARP helmet to accompany the leather money satchel dangling from his midriff like a sporran. Every Christmas, he stood with frozen snot hanging from his hooter, hand outstretched, waiting for his Christmas bonus. And only after his bony little fingers had closed safely around a few coins would he offer a cheery:

"Och thankyaemissus... and a HappyChristmastoyaetoo."

What happened to all those old war horses? Did they take voluntary redundancy and go on the pull with Jack Hargreaves, or did they end up in the local pie and mash shop?

I guess we'll never know.

Billy Bunter Meets Eamonn Andrews

Denise's house was crammed with all the luxuries available to a well-heeled 1960s working class family. Things like a pale blue Formica dining table, a chrome table lighter, and a twenty-inch telly living its own showbiz lifestyle behind the concertina doors of an oak-effect wooden cabinet. Den had to use every ounce of her strength to turn its huge ON button and crank it's three-inch tuning dial, but once it was crackling away nicely, we were free to share a few snatched moments away from killing goldfish and enjoy some early children's TV.

We watched ground-breaking programmes like *Billy Bunter,* where grown men dressed up as private schoolboys to show us the cheating and gluttony required to become a high-ranking Tory minister. It made for addictive viewing, mostly because it was absolute fucking crap. On Tuesdays, Ollie Beak (an owl) and Fred Barker (a dog) joined Muriel Young (a lady) and Wally Whyton (a guitarist) to play pop tunes with two pigs wearing dungarees who lip-synched to Dusty Springfield songs. On Wednesdays, an old music hall act called Mr Pastry fell over his trombone for twenty minutes, and on Thursdays a glove puppet called Sooty developed an act using mime and magic props while Harry Corbett was terrorised by a squeaking dog covering him in custard. It was all very exciting. On Fridays, an ex-boxer called Eamonn Andrews handed out pencils on a long-running children's variety show called *Crackerjack.* I'm afraid Eamonn's perspiration and fixed grin had me reaching for my plastic Winchester and a full set of those caps, ready to put him out of his misery.

Even more traumatic than Eamonn Andrews trying to interact with young children were shows featuring dead-eyed marionettes like *Torchy the Battery Boy* about a boy who flew through space with a glistening torch poking from his helmet. *Twizzle* was another one, about a boy with ratcheting extendible legs suitable only for cleaning gutters. Not forgetting *Sara and Hoppity,* starring a young girl who looked like Amanda Holden and a little bastard called Hoppity. Thanks to Amanda and Hoppity, my cousin Den still sleeps with a Bowie knife under her pillow!

Who knows what damage those glass-eyed devils did to our young British psyches? I only hope that other young 1960s TV viewers turned out normal.

I know I did ... praise the Lord.

Steve Zodiac and The First Day at School

As the Beatles put the finishing touches to their second album, my mother, with a mouthful of pins, was putting the finishing touches to a British Infantry uniform ready for her little soldier's first tour around the battlegrounds of the British education system. Me? I was sitting cross-legged watching *Fireball XL5* starring my space hero, Steve Zodiac. I always felt an affinity with old Stevie boy mostly because he also had enormous blue eyes and bits of thread dangling from his uniform. But that Sunday evening in September 1963, all was not well. I was very worried about my first day at school and needed some of Steve's vim and pep to help get me off to sleep. Eventually, thanks to some reassuring words from a one-eared panda, I managed to drift off, dreaming about Steve Zodiac being my school chaperone. Yep. Everything would be okay with Stevie Zee by my side.

Next morning, I bravely set about my boiled egg and soldiers before being dragged screaming to school by a team of Shire horses. Ten minutes later, we arrived to find the playground full of screaming children in various states of undress and I'm afraid it was a bit too much for this five-year-old space cadet and I wet myself.

Thanks a fucking lot, Steve (so-called) Zodiac.

Park Primary School

Park School was one of those old Victorian, darkly Gothic three-storey institutions with bell towers, turrets and mysterious mezzanine floors where naughty children disappeared to another dimension. Among its distinguished alumni was the nephew of Des O'Connor and a boy called Nigel who could pass wind in time with popular show tunes.

After prising my fingers from Mum's overcoat with a crowbar, Mrs Fasbin led me and the other first years into her classroom where the floorboards shone like brown glass and the smell of varnish washed over us like a coat of satin Ronseal. It was all very evocative; so evocative, that I ran straight into the Wendy house, drew the curtains, and refused to come out.

No amount of gentle persuasion could tempt me onto the wooden slide or to join the little girl boiling bunnies on the pretend cooker. Fortunately, Mrs Fasbin had experience with raggedy arsed intransigent cockneys, and after an offer of semolina and a dollop of strawberry jam, I was tempted aboard a dappled grey rocking horse, where I placed my feet in the stirrups, held the reins between my teeth, and began rocking with a frenzy unbecoming of an infant genius. So began my ten years of schooling.

Every morning we gathered for communal nose blowing which was so loud that the caretaker's toupée was often seen hanging precariously around his ears before giving up completely and falling to the floor during *All Things Bright and Beautiful*. (The Health and Safety Executive eventually banned this practice as the implications of loosened bogies in three hundred light-headed children was way too big a chance to take).

Morning worship continued with everyone rattling through the Lord's Prayer like a collection of Commonwealth parrots. It was 1963, so multiculturalism was still in short trousers, but we already had a decent smattering of West Indian, Pakistani, Muslim and Sikh children happy to join the rest of us chasing the German boy around the playground. Many suspected he was a Nazi spy and, quite honestly, he didn't help matters by tapping out Morse code during silent reading.

I made a few new friends so the old man was happy because this time they weren't imaginary. When I first saw Colin Zamboozu, he was doing a soft shoe shuffle and singing *Little Eliza Jane*. It was his finest moment, and I'm afraid it was all downhill from there. Amjad was from Pakistan and a fine cricketer who gave everyone our first exotic whiff of garlic. In return, he was followed everywhere by over-dramatic children wheeling in circles, clutching their throats.

But it wasn't all hands-across-the-water. There was an Italian boy who liked to piss himself without warning which wasn't great if you shared a bench seat with him. We never got on but in case he's now head of the Corsican Mafia, may I humbly say, 'Don Palumbo, I always thought of you as a true friend, and hope that your first child was a masculine child with above-average bladder control.'

One indigenous Numbskull family fulfilled all trouble-maker duties. Mrs Numbskull used her deep growling voice to direct her eldest son towards any teacher, parent or child who displeased her. She called him Noddy, and he was a vicious bastard who most definitely didn't have a cheeky bell on top of his blue felt hat. They were obviously complete nutters, and during an otherwise low-key harvest festival in 1964, I distinctly remember Mrs Numbskull calling across the playground:

"You keep on, my darling … and I'll get Noddy up here to kick your fucking brains in!"

To a young space cadet, those classrooms felt pretty huge. The gigantic windows reached up to the twenty-foot ceilings, and had bottom sills that were just far enough from the floor to stop me gazing wistfully towards West Ham Park … even in my Cuban heels. Yep, it seems those Victorian architects had thought of everything to keep pupils on task, everything except offering protection when the summer sun zapped us like tiny ants under a giant magnifying glass! What was it like? Well, imagine doing a complex country dancing routine with Janet Freshwater in the tropical section of Kew Gardens! Luckily my mum knocked up a Foreign Legion uniform so I could sit there like Gary Cooper in *Beau Geste*, watching the German boy evaporate slowly before sliding under his desk.

With the tall ceilings, steel girders and hard-rendered walls, our voices would echo and swirl around the classroom like sound effects from the BBC Radiophonic workshop. Morning register took ages, and old Colin Zamboozu was still waiting to answer his name while the rest of us were outside in the playground enjoying a carton of free milk. Colin's mum complained to the Department of Education, but Margaret Thatcher missed the point completely, and sent back a letter promising to remove free milk. Truly the people's princess.

A bench under the window stood as a grim reminder of nature's vulnerability amongst my class of eco-warriors. Spread out upon brown paper were dried worms, wrinkled leaves, and birds' eggs, still warm from being nabbed that very morning. I sat beside it and was particularly taken by a dummy bar of Cadbury's chocolate and replica cocoa pod, and made complex plans to smuggle it past the armed guards. I never did. It was the infra-red laser beams which did for me.

But the headline act on the nature bench was two Victorian glass taxidermy cases. One had a stuffed fox inside with two glass eyes which followed you everywhere like Dick Van Dyke's *Laughing Cavalier*. No matter if you were scratching your bum or picking your nose, old Mr Fox was always there … giving you the death stare. The other case contained a Barn owl nailed to a log. We called it Vernon after the pools' coupon because its eyes pointed in different directions, one home and one away. I thank you.

Tea is Taken with Florence Smith and Topo Gigio

Like testicles, every boy is entitled to two, and my other nan lived in Forest Gate.

Every Sunday I travelled there on Flying Angel Airlines, cruising at an altitude of six feet along Forest Lane before stowing away the drinks table over Forest Lane near a pub called The Golden Horse.

The original Golden Horse was destroyed by the Luftwaffe so this was a prefabricated replacement quickly erected to stop my granddad wandering down to The Coach and Horses by Forest Gate station. A white flag pole in the pub forecourt stood proudly erect with two white beer barrels either side of the base, sending a defiant two-fingered message to Herman Goering and his drug-fuelled cronies.

No. 49 Wellington Road. A handsome Georgian town house, once home to a respectable middle-class family. From the pavement it had six steps down to a basement and another six up to a brown front door. For some reason, the middle-class family fucked off, leaving my great grandparents to move in, change the locks, and set about avoiding the landlord.

My nan was born there. Her name was Florence Reed. Little Florence lived there for twenty years until she married a man called Bert, when she became medium-sized Florence Smith. Florence and Bert would live happily there for another thirty years, raising six children. The first was a daughter called Bertha, followed by Harry who was six foot one and built like a small kitchen extension. He was followed by Bill, George and Charlie (my dad), each one increasing in size until the arrival of Little Jim, whose shoulders were wide enough to support three daughters and the entire West Ham United reserve team. By the time I was born, little Florence Smith was six feet tall and built like a professional wrestler.

Grandad Bert was a short, stocky man who fought in World War I. Take away his Woodbine, add false teeth, and he bore a striking resemblance to Sir Anthony Hopkins with a touch of Ralph Fiennes. He raced greyhounds and had a fruit and veg stall, which he pushed to and from Stratford market every day. So, he had some muscles and liked to impress his grandchildren by crushing walnuts between his fingers. If he had a good weekend with the greyhounds, he would buy everyone a drink down The Golden Horse, earning him the affectionate nickname of Bert Monday.

Nan and granddad had a lodger – a Scotsman called Sandy, whose Sunday newspaper had a strip cartoon called The Broons with a ginger boy called Oor Wullie who sat on a bucket and bore a striking resemblance to Ginger in *The Beezer*. For Christmas 1963, I gave Sandy a yellow Bakelite ashtray which turned out to be particularly generous considering he gave me fuck-all in return. Nonetheless, Sandy was well-liked, and when he died in 1966, the Smiths sent a crate of whisky to his family in remembrance, which I believe is somewhere north of Glasgow.

Nan's front room was rarely open to the public and its heavy velvet curtains kept the watery Forest Gate sun firmly in its place. Dead family members were laid there prior to burial, giving them every opportunity to rise again as zombies. None did apart from Uncle Reg and we don't talk about him. The back room was simply furnished with a small dining table, two armchairs, one granddad, and a four-inch wooden penguin. A door behind Nan's armchair hid a staircase to the bedrooms, and protruding from the back was a tiny kitchen with thin wooden walls and a corrugated tin roof. When I say tiny … it was just big enough for a sink and a bar of Lifebuoy. That's why the gas cooker stood in the living room between two armchairs, and was the only thing to ever come between Bert and Flo.

Every Sunday afternoon, while the Smith ladies wrestled shellfish and the Smith gentlemen discussed the abstract impressionism of Jackson Pollack, the Smith grandchildren, risked our little cockney lives by negotiating seven uneven concrete steps down to the garden where a cobblestone path led to a lopsided shed that survived two world wars but now smelt of creosote and decay. Dad told me that when they were youngsters, his brother George speared Dad's hand to the shed roof with a garden fork. George was a cruel boy … but fair.

Inside the shed was granddad's workbench, and strewn across it were metal heel protectors and assorted boot-mending paraphernalia. It looked like a scene from *The Mystery of the Mary Celeste*, where the owner had fucked-off mid cobble. Fixed to the bench was Granddad's only vice (apart from a mud-wrestling fantasy about Ena Sharples and Minnie Caldwell), which held an anvil shaped like a small child's prosthetic foot. For some reason, that iron foot resulted in many cobbler related nightmares.

In the garden, on a bench under a rose arch, was an old wind-up gramophone left to collect rainwater in its trumpet-shaped bell. One crank of the handle and it roused itself like an old war hero to send a crackly slowed down version of *We'll Gather Lilacs* floating around the garden like the beginning to a ghost story.

Seven more uneven concrete steps led down to the basement and two green doors. The first was a lavatory big enough to swing a cat in … as long as the cat was the size of an apple and the swinger had extremely short arms. Its walls were painted working-class (white distemper) but the toilet was definitely upper middle-class (with an intricate blue flower pattern inside the bowl). Hanging on a nail beside the square mahogany toilet seat was some medicated toilet paper and a small calendar for Nan to monitor her loved-ones' bowel movements. This was the only toilet in the house, so any nocturnal visit meant descending three flights of stairs – two under the twinkling stars. As a result, my father and his brothers shared an enamel chamber pot in their bedroom. Come to think of it, one pot, five men? It would've been the size of a witch's cauldron!

The other door led to a scullery lined with tin baths, washboards and wooden tongs bleached white from years of soap flakes and boiling water. On the floor stood an old cast-iron, green mangle. Unlike the Green Lantern, who swanned off to America to become a comic book hero, this green mangle stayed in Forest Gate, tempting children to stick their fingers between its wooden rollers and take a lucky turn on the handle.

Tucked under the front pavement was a coal store which smelt of smoky-bacon crisps. Twenty years before, Bert had reinforced that store with heavy railway sleepers so his children could hide there while the Luftwaffe bombed the shit out of local pubs. Now it was our turn to huddle in that black hole of coal clutter, waiting for the call that would herald The Great British Winkle Race of 1963.

Mule Train and the One-Legged Ghost

Apart from *Strangers on the Shore* by Acker Whelk, is there any song more suited to eating shellfish than *Sing Something Simple* by the Cliff Adams Singers? Glorious melodies, warm voices and beautiful harmonies which guided us up from the basement, through a squally haze of pepper and a downpour of vinegar, towards a table laden with winkles, shrimps, cockles, brown bread, tomatoes and celery.

One of Nan's high tea's lasted about as long as *Mother Kelly's Doorstep*, one *Red Sails in the Sunset*, and two verses of *Down by the Old Mill Stream*. Then the table was set with tea cups while the kids toasted crumpets on the open fire using bone-handled forks. It was an interesting few minutes. A trial by fire. The offer of a hot buttered crumpet in exchange for your right arm crackling like a nice bit of pork!

Trial accomplished, and our faces glowing like partially cooked lobsters, Bert's old Bakelite telly was turned on and Efrem Zimbalist Jnr flew in from Burbank Studios Hollywood. Everyone loved *77 Sunset Strip,* and I suspect most of my uncles were imagining the damage they could do with a shoulder holster and an FBI badge.

After one final round of tea and cakes, a man called Tarby introduced a variety show from the London Palladium, with high-kicking chorus girls, international cabaret stars, magicians, tumblers, clowns and acrobats riding tiny bikes. Every few weeks, somewhere between Judy Garland and Frank Sinatra, a bald Englishman would appear on stage and sing *Mule Train* while crashing a drinks tray over his head. Even as kids we knew his act was crap, but when he bowed towards the royal box with blood trickling from his pate, the cameras showed, Princess Margaret going absolutely fucking bananas.

After a slobbery kiss from Flo and Bert, we were discharged into the cold night air. Uncle Harry off to Forest Gate station for the train to Catford, Bill and George into their cars back to Plaistow. Jim onto his scooter and sidecar, and Aunt Bertha on Uncle Pete's motorbike. Which left my old man pulling down his RAF goggles, hoisting me onto his shoulders and taxiing along Wellington Road. If there was any turbulence, Air Traffic Control walking a few yards behind would moan at her loyal and grinning husband.

"That's not funny Charlie ... I'm bloody ashamed to go anywhere with you!"

Approximately one hour later and I'm well into my first, cobbler-related, nightmare where a ghostly one-legged child emerges from Granddad's shed singing:

"Mule train, clippity clopping, clippity clippity clopping, clippity clopping ..."

Ah, they don't write lullabies like that anymore.

Bethnal Green Children's Hospital

One day I found my mother wrapping a box of Airfix mini-soldiers for cousin Jeff. Apparently, he was recovering from a circusprism, whatever that was. The thing is, I'd seen that little shyster skipping around the garden with a rubber ring around his midriff, and he wasn't fooling me! If it meant me getting a David Nixon Magic Set, I wanted a circumspection too. And when my turn came for an all-expenses-paid trip to Bethnal Green Children's Hospital, it was for something a little more serious than having bits of my winkle chopped off. Oh Yes.

It was for a bone spur on my ankle, and after pleading with the consultant to let me wear house slippers for the rest of my life, it seemed the only option was to have it removed. A week later I was loaded onto a wheelbarrow and pushed through the streets of Bethnal Green before being dumped outside the Swallows and Amazons Ward for Criminally Insane Boys with Rickets, where a nurse from Ireland marked my left ankle with black felt tip from W.H.Smiths.

There were twelve beds in the ward, each surrounded by tall, white-painted steel bars. Escape seemed impossible so I met up with John Mills and Richard Todd to arrange a counterfeit passport and travel permit to Switzerland. With luck, I could be at the border in time for Val Singleton's legs on Friday. Alas, they informed me that the escape committee were already focussing on a network of tunnels from under a wooden horse in the play area. It was all very hush hush. Each tunnel had its own name. No.1 was Tommy Cooper. No.2 was Arch Deacon, and No.3 was Harry Worth. Collectively known as Tom Deacon Harry. I thank you.

During the day, everything was fine – pretty nurses fussing around while we coloured in pictures like extras from *Curse of the Mummy*. It was at night, when the nurses disappeared to watch *Emergency Ward 10*, that things took a turn for the mental with another patient taking it upon himself to drench everyone with jugs of water and talcum powder. He was an absolute nutcase and more importantly, he was in the bed next to mine. Every night, I hopped away like Robert Newton in *Treasure Island*, with that maniac two yards behind. He definitely wasn't the full ticket but could look forward to a successful career as a US Army interrogation officer.

After four sleepless nights, Doctor Kildare and Nurse Killarney said I could go home and Dad arrived with the wheelbarrow, unaware that his only son had spent five nights in a snow blizzard like the Norwegian resistance in *The Heroes of Telemark*. Meanwhile the Night Stalker was in the next bed, sketching out some sleep deprivation techniques for the new arrival, and for some reason my old man gave him a brand new sixpence. Fuck me. Who said crime doesn't pay?

Back home, sitting on an upturned bucket in the servants' quarters, I waited for the arrival of David Nixon and his magic set. Did he show? No. It seems I had risked my life for a bowl of Heinz tomato soup. So be it. I smeared Marmite on my face and held my breath like Violet Beauregarde until we reached a compromise and Mum allowed me to move my bucket closer to the paraffin heater. Result!

It was later that evening, while enjoying ten minutes with Huckleberry Hound and a pack of ginger nuts, that I watched the old man go outside and lean into a Ford Zodiac where a heavy-set man in a trilby handed him something wrapped in newspaper. Was it my slice from the 1963 Great Train Robbery? Nope, it was a set of lead soldiers in the green livery of the British Commando. A nice gesture from Dad's mate which gave me a decent head start in the lead poisoning race, popular in the early 1960s.

The Freddie Mills Punch Bag

With no elder brothers to trap my head in a wardrobe door, there were few opportunities for a young gentleman to learn unarmed combat. So, when I kept asking for a new butterfly net Dad grew increasingly concerned about my ability to engage in the local custom of 'looking after yourself' (formerly known as fisticuffs). So instead, he got me the most precious gift a young butterfly collector could ever wish for … a pair of red boxing gloves and the British Light Heavyweight Champion of the World. Or, to be precise, the life-size foam rubber head of Freddie Mills on a spring-loaded pole.

In white underpants and a pale blue vest, I set out to become the new Henry Cooper, building up some steam by landing evermore extravagant hay-makers on the side of Fred's grinning face before going downstairs for a bowl of Sugar Puffs drenched in sweat like I had spent the night white-water rafting. My little size three knuckles regularly collided with the metal pole and it became obvious I would never appear at The Royal Albert Hall playing Mendelssohn's violin concerto in E minor Op. 64. None the less, I carried on bobbing and weaving with old Freddy boy, who became my go-to toy after a frustrating morning on the Spirograph.

For two years, Fred's yellow waxen head loomed over my bedroom like a warning posted on a castle battlement until it was thrown away in 1965 when the real Freddie Mills died. Of course, the old man was right, and thanks to my training with an unarmed rubber head, I never had any problems looking after myself … especially when allowed to stand on my opponent's toes and they promise not to punch back.

West Ham Park, an 18th Century Playground for a 20th Century Schizoid Boy

Did you know that the German Luftwaffe dropped five 1000kg bombs, two parachute mines and over one hundred incendiary devices within the curtilage of West Ham Park, but never managed to stop old Mrs Mills from opening the tea rooms?

West Ham Park's western boundary was just a few steps for mankind and one giant leap for Steve Zodiac away from our front door. Every day I sat astride its fence like a cowboy searching the prairie. And with no testicles to speak of, let alone lose on those spiky concrete tops, I then jumped down into that ancient magical world, ready to spend a day tearing around like a complete fucking nutcase.

There was a large pile of stones from Doctor Fothergill's original Ham House, along with an ancient stone bridge and an old Victorian bandstand where lady suffragettes once rallied their sisters by blowing raspberries at men in top hats. Goldfish cavorted under a fountain in an ornamental pond, while a family of Great Crested Newts looked on from inside a discarded Sanatogen bottle.

Order was maintained by a squadron of First World War veterans in pressed green uniforms, who wielded the same authority as Jack Warner in *Dixon of Dock Green*. No walkie talkies, just brass whistles and forearms strong enough to break a young man's neck. One moment they were scampering after Alfie Bumble when he exposed himself on the pitch and putt, next they're stepping between two warring factions on the tennis courts. And if any boy had the temerity to shout '*Oi Parkie … you old cunt!*', well, that mouthy young jester would soon find himself in a well-practised pincer movement and being shown to the gate in a vicious head-lock.

West Ham Park had six football pitches, a pitch and putt course, ornamental gardens with some of the rarest trees in the country, and a dozen greenhouses where flowers were grown for use by the entire city of London. It also had the world's most dangerous children's playground.

On summer mornings when the dawn chorus was broken only by the echo of milkmen coughing up their own lungs, an ethereal mist would swirl around the playground equipment giving it the appearance of scrap metal left on the beaches of Dunkirk. They were painted in rainbow colours but, make no mistake, those killing machines were endorsed by the child catcher from Chitty Chitty Bang Bang. Take the Maypole. Instead of gaily coloured ribbons blowing gently in the breeze, this thing had heavy link chains clanking against an industrial steel pole. There was also three tons of flying metal known as the Witch's Hat, which swayed dangerously in a haphazard arc, while another looked like a medieval battering ram swinging to and fro with little white-faced cockneys clinging on to it for dear life. Most of which explains why, by the tender age of seven, I had bigger forearms than Popeye.

Despite the good chance of being chinned by a large lump of flying metal, the playground was packed every day until the smell of a Heinz Toast Topper tempted a crocodile line of bloodied children to limp home, clutching bundles of broken teeth. And when dusk fell and the old park-keepers blew last orders, the playground grew quiet again … empty apart from a large black crow picking over a decapitated head, and a little cowboy with his head stuck under the drinking fountain.

Trauma in the Park or Howard Woolly's Dad …Was He All Bad?

Like anyone aspiring to become Tory Party Chairman, being a good liar is absolutely essential. So, wearing these claret and blue tinted glasses and pretending my early years were perfect means sailing perilously close to Jeffrey Archer territory. So, join me in the psychiatrist's waiting room as I drop my trousers, touch my toes, and reveal two traumatic events which helped shape me into the witty, urbane, well-rounded twat that I am today.

The first came when I was a five-year-old freewheeling pyromaniac who set fire to his parents' bedroom before running into the park and hiding under an oak tree. Plumes of smoke billowed from the upstairs window as I stood in a puddle of wee waiting for the fire engines. My smoke-damaged father eventually found me amongst the damp acorns and listened carefully while I explained my experiment on the combustibility of quilted eiderdowns. He took my point, and led me by the point to clean up his smoke-damaged bedroom.

The second event was the result of a nightmare display as an eleven-year-old goalkeeper. A week before, at a trial for a new team, I spent two hours plucking the ball from the air, diving at the feet of strikers, and generally impressing the ass off the team's well-regarded manager – Howard Woolly's dad. With smiles all round, he handed me the goalkeeper's kit and sent me home to prepare for my first match. Proud and happy, I curled up with a Topical Times football annual and studied some of the techniques of Peter Bonetti, aka The Cat, who looked well pleased with himself standing alongside a brand new Ford Granada.

The big day arrived and I set off to West Ham Park in green shorts, green shirt, green socks and a green cap – Herberto Bonetti, aka The Green Hornet. During the warm-up and while taking extravagant practice dives in the dusty penalty box, I noticed a large black crow watching intently. Was it a warning? Yes. The first ball pumped upfield, bounced off the rock-hard pitch, right over my outstretched arms onto the crossbar and down onto the goal-line. The Russian linesman confirmed the ball *had* crossed the line.

"Caw," said the large black crow.

"Bollocks," said Herberto.

For twenty years, I pondered that manager's decision to substitute a young goalkeeper so early in his first match, and came to the conclusion that Howard Woolly's dad was a bit of a prick. Actually, he wasn't just a bit... he was a whole one!

Lord Herbert of Tennyson

No. 54 Gladstone Road wasn't the same after Polly died, so my parents handed back the rent book, laced up their climbing boots and weighed down by two bits of excess luggage, began their long climb up the social ladder. The journey would take fifteen long minutes but that did include a brief stop in Vicarage Lane to buy a sliced loaf. Their destination was a long terrace of cramped houses named after that crazy-haired dreamer, Alfred Lord Tennyson.

No. 100 Tennyson Road was a two-up, two-down, and I was to share one of the two-ups with Mum's littlest sister, Lynda. Twenty years before, a 500lb German bomb had arrived by air mail and landed directly opposite our new home. On its metal casing was a handwritten chalk message: *Up Yours, Ze Cockney Herbert Bastards.* It blew a dozen homes to smithereens, and some as far as oblivion, and left a crater the size of a five-a-side pitch. When we arrived in 1964, council workers were still leaning on shovels waiting for a skip to arrive.

So instead of manicured lawns, I now lived opposite something called *a debris*. These were extremely popular in the 1960s and consisted of broken bricks, jagged concrete, and twisted metal. The perfect place to smash ten green bottles and re-enact *The Guns of Navarone*, before wandering home for a bowl of sugar puffs and a lie down.

Behind our back fence was West Ham Recreation Ground, so I still had access to a see-saw and a sand pit.

Our stay in Tennyson Road would correspond exactly with the rise of Beatlemania, Indian Maharishis, Sergeant Peppers, Magical Mysteries, Apple roof tops, a Gibraltar marriage and Beatle break-ups. While I laid in bed reading the Sparky annual, Neil Armstrong walked on the Moon, Bobby Moore lifted the World Cup and a bracelet in Bolivia, and an eleven-year-old *Opportunity Knocks* winner called Neil Reid would make every boy in the country feel very uncomfortable by crooning to his mother while wearing a frilly shirt and bow-tie like a tiny Doug Mountjoy.

By the release of the Beatles' final album, the old man was a devout follower of the Vesta boil-in-the bag curry, *The Golden Shot* was in colour, and I had a healthy sprinkling of pubic hair. More importantly, another bombshell would have landed outside our house. It would be blonde and mysterious and keep me in a heightened state of alert for most of my young adult life.

The Women and Pretty Young Things of Stratford

While Jane Asher and Patti Boyd were charging around the West End, stepping out of Mini Coopers in a haze of LSD and Beatle boyfriends, my big sister was stepping out of her navy-blue knickers after a long week at the Clarnico factory. The weekend started here. No more Creme Tangerines or Savoy Truffles. Bring on the Mary Quant eye gloss.

On Saturday, the Twiggy eye lashes were on before breakfast. By tea-time, Lynda had applied the last layer of heavy black mascara, and after knocking back a handful of contraceptive pills, she headed off for a night on Broadway – Stratford Broadway – to dance above the Two Puddings, drink three port and lemons, smoke twenty Embassy, preside over two fist-fights, and share a snog with the keyboard player from the Dave Clark Five. Don't get me wrong. Lynda was no good time gal. On the contrary, she was always home before midnight, waking me up as she got into bed with a Horlicks and a Melody Maker (and definitely not the keyboard player from the Dave Clark Five).

Meanwhile, her elder sisters were dashing away with a smoothing iron, kick-starting industrial washing machines or flashing smiles at Charlie Ward for some extra mince. Most worked full-time yet still managed to conjure up three courses while Fanny Craddock was downing her first bottle of wine in the ITN green room.

Our new kitchen was the size of a small hamster cage, yet Mum still managed to produce a never-ending supply of dishes to warm the deep-fried cockles of a vegetarian's heart. Stuffed hearts, liver and bacon, lambs' kidneys, pigs trotters, and her signature dish, Mothers Pride with beef dripping, fava beans, and a chilled bottle of Tizer.

Friday night was fish night which meant doing the danse macabre with a grilled bloater whose tiny bones sprang open in your throat like a Viet Cong booby trap, and leaving me and dad coughing up fur-balls like Top Cat and Benny. Even our cat had its own saucepan of evil smelling coley bubbling away on the stove and when Dad came home, he would always remonstrate with his beautiful and loyal skivvy:

"Bloody hell, Jean, can't you give the poxy thing Kit-e-Kat like everyone else?"

Like most working-class women, my mother managed these flare-ups like a non-compliant East London version of *The Stepford Wives*, using an instinctive balancing act of pretend subservience. For example, if a new sideboard was required, a selection of home-made sausage rolls and a few careless whispers were laid before her alpha male. Come harvest moon, my father, almost blind from the stinging tears, could be found bent over a credit agreement in the Co-Op furniture department.

The Moffatt sisters were all accomplished knitters and every Saturday night, with Lynda on a dance floor somewhere recreating the Battle of Monte Cassino, they sat in a circle, passing *Woman's Realm* sewing patterns between them like prison contraband. The speed in which they knocked out some racy swimwear would've left Morris McWhirter scrambling for his record book. Indeed, he would've probably shat himself if he ever put the stopwatch on my aunt June, who could knit an entire family of crinoline lady toilet roll covers during a single episode of *The Cilla Black Show.*

Because Mum was a champion seamstress (Light Heavyweight Mattress Division), she was always first choice for big production numbers like curtains or wedding dresses. When an order was placed, out would come 'Pearl', her trusty Singer, and she'd climb aboard and build up some speed using a prototype wah-wah pedal. All very well for the bride-to-be, but even Matt Monroe singing into a megaphone through the Olympic stadium PA system couldn't compete with the noise from that fucking sewing machine. I'm not kidding. Me and dad had to stand outside and watch *It's a Knockout* through the front room window.

Occasionally, I got roped into being her mannequin, and I can assure you that standing on a chair under a 100-watt bulb wearing your cousin's bridesmaid's dress is an experience no young gentleman should ever have to endure! Colin saw me once and it took years to shrug off a reputation for being a right little wanker.

A Number Two on The Coral Island

Though it meant dragging my satchel an extra mile, I stayed at Park Primary School, learning fluent cockney and making good use of its extensive toilet facilities. The playground toilets had no roof which left us open to sun, rain and plenty of wind. In theory this should've helped in the old ventilation department, but it never seemed to make much difference when some young blighter expelled a large turd and left it floating in the pan to stare up at the next visitor.

Personally, I found it quite inspirational looking at the blue sky while dropping off my own number twos … especially when working on a romantic poem or sonnet. Come to think of it, some of my best work was left on the back of that cubicle door, and my only witness was a stool pigeon looking down from the high-level cistern.

A glazed channel in the floor served as a primitive urinal but wasn't much use because most boys liked to spin around in circles firing piss everywhere like little garden sprinklers. Christopher Rhodes had such exquisite bladder control, he could urinate right over the eight-foot wall into the adjoining girls' toilets, which always earned Christopher a big Bronx cheer from his pals.

The main school toilets were at the top of each staircase inside the roof where a row of dormer windows allowed pupils to gaze romantically across the clay roof tiles while standing in a fresh puddle of piss supplied by the Phantom Slasher (possibly Colin Zamboozu, but more likely Christopher Rhodes). It was up here that I had my mouth washed out by a teacher for bad language. Chomping on that bar of Lifebuoy taught me a valuable lesson and I have never repeated the sentence 'Howard Woolly's dad is a prick' to this very day.

Don't get me wrong. Park Primary School wasn't just about the eye-watering smell of Zammo. With its long corridors and wide granite staircases, it felt like a council-approved prototype Hogwarts. The tall corridor ceiling was decorated with a magnificent multicoloured compass, each inter-cardinal point painted in different colours. I used to sit below it, about north by northwest, rattling through the Janet and Johns, and generally improving my chances of becoming chief librarian at Romford Library. By the age of seven, I had launched myself upon the entire Ladybird catalogue. Then it was onto Eagle annuals and *The Coral Island* by R.M. Ballantyne where shipwrecked schoolboys dived for pearls in shimmering lagoons. By thirteen, I was devouring Sgt Pepper sleeve notes, and by 1975 it was NME articles on Toyah Wilcox, and an off-colour magazine I found behind the sandpaper in Dad's shed.

And if I had to choose just one book to take onto my desert island, it would have to be that 1975 Fiesta Readers' Wives Christmas Edition, a versatile little companion which would keep me warm at night and could always be exchanged with the natives for a nice tin of peaches.

Fists of Fury, The Big Boss, and Enter the Testicles

One day a large telly burst into the classroom followed by Mr Perryman who spent the next ten minutes fumbling heroically with the leads. We never did see that BBC schools programme about Jethro Tull and his girlfriend Spinning Jenny, because the lesson was interrupted by the school nurse herding us up the granite staircase towards one of those mysterious mezzanine rooms. Rumours spread down the line. *Interjections.* To be specific, *rolio interjections.*

The boy in front had scabby knees and appeared to be using both ears to cultivate a crop of King Edward potatoes. He was also scratching his head furiously, so I was just making a mental note to give the old beer shampoo its weekly run out when Janet Freshwater rushed from the medical room with a bottom lip quivering like she was auditioning for lead singer of The Trembeloes. Like a herd of cockney wildebeest, the queue of children became restless. I'm not kidding. My knees were knocking louder than Woody Woodpecker trapped inside Dracula's coffin.

Mr Potato Head was next and disappeared into the medical room. Seconds later, a scream came from inside followed by the school nurse, who insisted the walking farm shop be taken outside for a good hose down. None of this was doing me much good and, quite honestly, I nearly shat myself when the nurse crooked her finger and beckoned me inside.

Nurse: *And what's your name, young man?'*

Herbert: *Lord Herbert of Tennyson. And there seems to have been some terrible mistake!*

Dear reader, when she plunged that chrome needle deep into my upper arm, I let out a blood curdling scream so loud, that when Colin Zambuzoo peered around the door, he looked like Casper the friendly ghost!

My ordeal over, I was getting up to leave when, without warning, she released my elasticated snake belt, blew on her right hand, and reached down to cup my seven-year-old testicles.

Nurse: *I'm making sure they've dropped!*

Herbert: *Where from?*

Fortunately, they had. So may I introduce to you, the act you've known for all these years, my two testicular friends: Buster and Little Jocky.

Buster is a gregarious little chap in charge of temperature regulation who looks like Bruce Willis in *Die Hard II* and enjoys anything by Erich Von Däniken. Little Jocky is more like Uncle Mort from *The Adam's Family*, and is very interested in the Goth movement.

After being rudely awoken, those two little rascals went back to their sacks and have remained close at hand ever since. More from Buster and Little Jocky later.

The Man in the Number Six Shirt

Saturday 2nd May 1964, and a nicely pissed Maurice Chevalier was found sprawled outside Wembley Park Station, naked apart from his signature straw boater and a West Ham United scarf. Asked by the ticket lady if he had been to the game, his response was typical for its Parisian warmth and wit:

'Ah yes ... Ronnie Boyce last minute winner ... I remember it well.'

Sunday 3rd May 1964. West Ham Lane was packed from the Granada Bingo down to West Ham Police Station. Derek had his cine camera, and an old man with a tray strapped to his chest was offering for sale claret and blue rosettes, each with a tin replica FA Cup and a piece of card stapled to it with the words WEST HAM UNITED. One was pinned to my coat and it spent the next ten years in Mum's glass cabinet.

A commotion outside Queen Mary's Hospital heralded the arrival of an open-top coach and two police horses. I remember it being a chilly and overcast day, but as the coach drew level, a shaft of sunlight shone down upon a blonde gentleman holding aloft a large silver trophy.

Fucking hell.

The next time we met was on a Boxing Day at my inaugural home game. After sweeping along Green Street in a rip-tide of slush and overlarge home-made wooden hammers, I was pushed through a turnstile where Dad's brother Bill clicked us through using his Golden Ticket, before I was parked behind a low wall next to a large expanse of mud and sand called The Pitch, where track-suited players were sharing a pre-match cigarette with members of St John's Ambulance.

From what I could tell, two men were in charge. One was a man called Percy Dalton, who was selling hot peanuts and telling everyone to fuck off. The other was called Hugh Cowson who had a white face, black shirt, white socks, black shorts and a white cat dyed black. At eleven o'clock, Hugh blew a whistle, threw his hands in the air, and fell flat on his arse. The game was afoot.

Soon afterwards the ball rolled off the pitch and came to rest in front of me. Guess who came to collect it? Yup, the gentleman from the coach, minus the mohair suit but plus White Horse liniment on his thighs. With a friendly wink, he took the ball from my outstretched hands.

And that, ladies and gentlemen, was my first, up-close and personal encounter with His Supreme Royal Highness, Sir Bobby Moore.

Eighteen months later, that same man led the West Ham reserve team into the World Cup final, and before the German FA could interrogate the Russian linesman, Jules Rimet was standing alongside the FA Cup, the European Cup Winners Cup, and a box of old

Christmas decorations in the chairman's garage.

All that success hadn't come by chance; there was a good reason. God had sent down his only son to grow up in Barking, live in Chigwell, swap shirts with Pelé, and occasionally play in goal for the mighty Hammers.

So why, why, why did Colin Zamboozu insist on supporting Chelsea FC with their Peter Osgoods, Peter Bonettis and Peter McTamblings? I'll tell you why. Because Colin was a contrary little fucker, that's why.

Well, if he wanted to relinquish a lifetime of sweet contentment that would surely come from following London's most well-managed club, then so be it.

Chaining myself to the Boleyn gates, I called towards his departing figure:

"It's no good, Colin, I'm trapped – you'd better go on without me."

Squashed Rats, Copulating Dogs, and Noel Coward

Nowadays, I forget what I had for breakfast, but I'll always remember scooting around Thorpe Park and Alton Towers with my three kids and a rucksack of Marmite soldiers. We even flew to Disney's Magic Kingdom and threw up on Mr Toad's Tea-Cup ride! But this next story tells of a time when a good day out didn't require a fifty-pound note and a token from a cornflakes box. And it's all thanks to the Germans.

God knows what the Mayor of West Ham said to upset them but the German Luftwaffe dropped 1493 high explosive bombs, 32 parachute mines, 1130 incendiary bombs, 65 oil bombs, 16 phosphorous bombs, 68 V1 flying bombs, and 33 V2 long range ballistic missiles onto my little part of London, and did more damage than Boris Johnson pretending to be mayor.

Local builders arrived, estimates were given, and a battalion of Commer vans swung into action as the reconstruction of London began. It was a massive job and, twenty years later, there were still plenty of partially demolished buildings for children to rip themselves a new arse by sliding down a mountain of brick rubble, or collect a length of steel reinforcement up the jacksie. These deconstructed playgrounds were so popular that, Queen Mary's outpatients looked more like a military field hospital as broken children came through the doors like toys on The *Generation Game* conveyor belt.

But you can't put a price on fun, and wasn't it Rudyard Kipling who said:

You're a man my son when you can smash an old toilet pan with a fully loaded engineering brick.

We took the dangers in our stride but there was one thing guaranteed to make a young man lift his skirt and run away like Charles Hawtrey.

Mr Rat.

Disturbing their underground lairs made the rats scurry up into the daylight and boldly give us the beady eye. One little fucker called Ben lived in a broken drain and was always chasing me across Tennyson Road, nipping my heels like a foot-long furry piranha. He finally met his match when our old neighbour used the back of her coal shovel to smash him into the tarmac. Ben's high-pitched screaming stayed with me for many years and I still remember his rattling death throes whenever I hear Marie Osmond singing *Paper Roses*.

Talking of copulating dogs.

I once saw that same old lady throw a bucket of water over two greyhounds who got themselves stuck together outside the off-licence. How they managed it and why the one on top was staring off into space remained a mystery until I met Sir Noël Coward in a little shop on Stratford Broadway.

The shop was Stockdales Sports & Leather Goods, a few doors down from the snooker hall and across the road from where Hussain Bolt would notch up three Olympic gold medals fifty years later. It sold everything from snooker cues and football socks, to leather purses and handbags, and I was in there perusing a pair of Ron Springett goalkeeping gloves when in strolled that international star of stage and screen. He was in town visiting Joan Littlewood at the Theatre Royal and had popped over to buy some billiard balls. What a gent. Not only did he sign the shin pads but he also explained what those two greyhounds were up to. Apparently the one on top was pushing the other one up the shops like a wheelbarrow. What a relief.

Since then, I've always had a soft spot for people called Noel. Noel Gordon, Noel Gallagher, Noel Fielding, Noel Cantwell. In fact, all of them apart from Noel Edmunds, who always comes across as an insincere cheesy prat.

Dustin Herbert is the Marathon Man

In the 1960s, the National Health Service was so well funded that as soon as the tooth fairy reported any sign of tooth decay, a team of dentists would strip to the waist and begin pumping up a series of height adjustable chairs ready for any little Herbert who couldn't be resuscitated by a lump of cotton wool soaked in tincture of cloves.

Luckily, the day that happened to me I was in the unflappable hands of Aunt Maureen who calmly made arrangements for the NHS Rolls Royce to be readied. Ten minutes later, me, Aunt Maureen and a small bottle of tincture of cloves were on our way to one of the world's leading dental clinics, just behind Plaistow Station.

A poster on the waiting room wall showed a smartly dressed young Mod standing beside a Dansette record player, a pile of records, and a brand new Vespa scooter. The slogan suggested he could afford those luxuries because he didn't smoke. A quick calculation proved he would've been on sixty-a-day since he was three, but the point was well made so I stubbed out my sweet cigarette, popped in a raspberry ruffle, and waited for help in my long battle against tooth decay.

The dentist was a friendly old soul called Mr Ryan. He was an Irishman with silver hair and gold spectacles, and in his white coat he looked like Laurence Olivier in *Marathon Man*. His assistant was a West Indian lady called Mrs Toto who, after greeting me with a friendly "*Hello*" then said "*Goodbye*" as she filled my lungs with cold nitrous oxide.

Ten minutes later, I'm leaning over a blood-spattered sink surrounded by smiling faces. Auntie M was there and so was the friendly Mr Ryan and Mrs Toto. I didn't know where I was, but judging by the sink full of broken teeth, I'm pretty sure it wasn't Kansas.

As Auntie M signed for her complimentary NHS bouquet, and Mr Ryan grabbed his *Racing Post*, I stared at the blood-stained instruments strewn on a silver tray beside me. You know the kind of stuff: needle-sharp prongs, mirrors on sticks, and six-inch tungsten drill bits. All the things you wouldn't allow in your mouth unless they were in the capable hands of a drunk Irishman who liked to gamble.

Hands up, Buddy Boy, for You the War is Over

It was alright for John Lennon – he was on a plain in Spain filming *How I Won the War*. Me? I was in Stratford and under attack from a nest of Japanese snipers! The attacks were relentless and dehumanising – like my old man's flatulence – and most days were spent hiding behind parked cars as more shots rang out from the prefab roof. Those square-headed-sausage-eaters never stopped with their blood curdling cries of *Banzai British Tommy!* or *Hands up you, cunt!* or *Lie down, Ringo, you're dead!* I had no choice but to saddle up and head those little motherfuckers off at the pass. Which, in our case, was down Whalebone Lane opposite the public toilets.

Charlton Athletic Heston and those nutters at the National Rifle Association must have been so proud of British boys patrolling the streets with Winchesters, Tommy guns, Webley air pistols, space guns, six shooters, Johnny Sevens, spud guns, pop guns, Hans Solo cap guns, water pistols, sparking laser guns, and plastic Bazookas that fired ping-pong balls around corners. Yep. Whether you were off to the park or popping out for a gallon of paraffin, a full ammo belt was absolutely essential.

However, it's one thing to carry a loaded firearm around your local Spar, but try going to the swimming baths with a Luger stuffed down your trunks! *No Firearms Allowed in the Big Pool* read the sign, which meant us having to tip-toe through the verruca bath totally unarmed.

But young British winkles are nothing if not resourceful, and an index finger became an acceptable replacement firearm. Not mad enough? Those same index fingers were then fitted with imaginary silencers, which meant the last sound Colin heard was a low 'pop' as we shot him clean through his Levi cut-downs. God knows how many times we watched Colin fall lifeless into the pool after staggering along the spring board. His 'dying swan' was a masterpiece of dramatic acting, only spoilt when he resurfaced like an Olympic diver with strands of snot hanging from his hooter.

As you can probably tell by now, the London Borough of Newham was a fantastic place to grow up. Every day an opportunity to frolic under the East London sun. If it did rain, it was only to allow rainbows to dance briefly over the pie and mash shop before directing punters to the pot of gold in the nearby William Hills.

And because everything was so bloody perfect, our guardians had no qualms in kicking us out of the home after breakfast. No packed lunch. No spending money. Free to hob-nob with men exposing themselves, or fly our kites near electricity pylons. Honestly, the whole day could pass in a flash! *Hooray!* Looking back, I reckon our parents were preparing us for life under Margaret Thatcher and then to be regularly fucked by a succession of Tory governments.

On days when the rain was too heavy even to play by a railway inside an abandoned fridge, I stayed home alone, killing time until Val Singleton arrived at five o'clock. With nothing on telly and no parental supervision, I could turn our front room into a Second World War battlefield and myself into a laconic gum-chewing US Marine communicating with comrades via a *The Man from U.N.C.L.E* walkie-talkie. I even put Georgie Fame's *Ballad of Bonnie and Clyde* on the record player and used the final ten-second burst of gunfire to spray the mantelpiece with bullets. Of course, you had to replace the needle every ten seconds ... but it was doable when you're a borderline psychopath.

But you know what? Some days Georgie Fame and a replica Tommy gun just didn't cut the mustard, and because the Army and Navy Stores in Manor Park were clean out of US Army flame-throwers, I got myself an Action Man 45 rpm record. The A side was a marching song extolling the virtues of a nine-inch man with no genitalia, but the B side was five minutes of full-blown military madness packed with the sound effects of machine guns, tanks and explosions. My very own crossfire hurricane. With that playing in the background, I was perfectly content to be pinned down under the dining table as bullets ricocheted off the chrome ashtray and the smell of cordite hung heavy in the air. What more could I do except sit tight, squint my eyes, and smoke the old man's doofers.

One day, in the middle of the spring offensive in Italy, I heard Mum's key in the front door so I slumped to the floor and pretended to be seriously wounded, hoping for some evidence that she loved me more than the fucking cat. Without saying a word, she stepped over my dead body and continued into the kitchen to slam a few drawers. Then it went quiet. Was she rustling up a pancake to dress my wounds?

"I'm going up the Spar. Can you give me a hand?" she called.

What a way to treat a dying soldier! Should I break character, or remain dead and miss the chance of a pack of Dairy Maids? Even though we were out of banana Nesquik, I decided to stay dead until the front door slammed and I could hear the opening bars of *Blue Peter*. How much thigh would Val reveal today?

Like Tiny Tim at an Our Lady of Dollars Evangelical Meeting, I threw away my crutches and limped towards the telly, only to find Val dressed head-to-toe in a deep-sea diver's outfit.

Dads New Wardrobe

It all began when EMI agreed to pay the electric bill and release Sgt Pepper from the confines of Abbey Road Studios. This became the green light for young men to breeze along Carnaby Street wearing vintage military clothing and colourful feather boas. Of course, the old guard scoffed at the prancing kaftans and dancing Chelsea boots, and war was declared, which left pockets of middle-aged London men paralysed with fear in a no-man's land of fashion.

Men like my papa. Until then, his dress code had been simple: plain shirt, plain tie and plain trousers held up by a sturdy pair of plain braces. Perfect for work, the beach, and to go pike fishing. Now the writing was on the urinal wall as wives made plans to drag their husbands through a hedge backwards towards a new dawn of haute couture.

Shirts were first. I remember him slamming the front door and hurrying towards the half light of the snooker hall where he could safely unveil his new snazzy shirt with collars the size of ten bob notes to his mate Charlie Brown, who was already setting up the balls in a lime green paisley number.

Braces were next to go, allowing my father's trousers to be lowered from a starting position five inches above the belly button to now hang provocatively on the hips. As a concession for good behaviour, his wife would allow him to jack them back up and stand proudly at the bar displaying three inches of sock and a sexy dash of lower calf while she rolled her eyes and sipped her tomato juice.

All the Moffatt men went through similar experiences. I don't know how June convinced Uncle Bill to emulate Hollywood heart throb Tony Curtis by attempting the cravat, but to his credit Bill continued wearing one for a few weeks until someone pointed out the folly of sporting a loosely tied silk scarf during an important darts match. Derek was another trendsetter and caused quite a stir when he arrived one Saturday night looking like Val Doonican in tartan golf trousers, mustard polo-neck and a beige short sleeve safari jacket. Derek was a trend setter, alright. More to the point, he didn't give a fuck.

Item by item, those cockleshell heroes found their favourite garments heading out to the bins, and the refrain '*Oh, don't throw them away, love, they'll be alright for decorating*' became the mantra of the common man.

Some, like those brave souls charged with hiding Anne Frank's drum kit, would retrieve items at the dead of night, hoping they might one day roam the streets of London as free men. But deep down they knew it was a lost cause, and within a couple of years sensible slacks and roll neck jumpers became the order of the day.

With regards to the old man's underwear drawer, he was never tempted by the home-made sausage rolls cleverly planted beside the new, brightly coloured jockey shorts. No way, San José. He continued with his white string-vests and matching underpants, whose knotted symmetrical mesh was surely a throwback to Britain's proud nautical heritage.

A Pantomime at the Famous London Palladium

I promise to tell the truth, the half-truth, and nothing like the truth about my role in the genesis of the West End blockbuster *Phantom of the Opera,* which would eventually culminate in Sir Andrew Lloyd Webber getting his leg over the beautiful Sarah Brightman.

It was early December when Cousin Jeff dropped one of his casual bombshells:

"You know there's no Sanity Clause, right?"

Little cousin, say what?

To be honest, I had my suspicions, but didn't care as long as an Action Man Snow Patrol Kit arrived before Boxing Day.

It was a few days later while I was stripping down a plastic Enfield rifle that mum burst in waving two pantomime tickets. Up yours, Cousin Jeff, because there *was* a Father Christmas, and what's more, he owns a mattress factory on the Romford Road!

Southdown Mattresses was just a few yards from a pub called The Pigeons, where for two hundred years weary travellers spent Friday nights knocking seven shades of shit out of each other. But on that chilly evening in 1967, its forecourt was the rallying point for two dozen dolled-up employees and excited children waiting to be delivered to the London Palladium where the cool fizzin', sideburn-wearing, heart-throbbing, bow-tie using Englebert Humperdink was giving one of the finest performances of a ship wrecked entertainer since Oliver Reed threw up on Desert Island Discs. Yep, those Robinson Crusoe pantomime tickets were the hottest in town and *Please Release Me,* was even keeping *Penny Lane/Strawberry Fields* from becoming the Christmas No.1.

The coach arrived and in the twinkle of a reindeer's eye we were up to our necks in Babycham and orange-flavoured Matchmakers, crawling along Regents Street, *oohing* at the Christmas lights and *aahing* at the miniskirted mannequins in Selfridges. London! Christmas! *Magic!*

Thirty minutes to kick off and the coach driver removed his ear defenders as a large group of working-class ladies (collective noun: a racket) rushed into the theatre to powder their noses (possibly Yardley's *Lilly of the Valley,* more likely *Mona Lisa Blush* by Avon). Meanwhile, I checked in my top hat and cape, and sprinted up those thirty-nine steps to the toppermost of the poppermost: the Upper Circle.

For an eagle-eyed theatregoer with 20/20 vision those seats were tough! For a short-sighted knoblet in bow-tie, spats and an oxygen mask, well, let's just say my heart sank lower than a snake's armpit. But wait. Was that a dagger I saw before me or a small pair of opera glasses chained to the seat in front with a coin operated lock?

Like most working class Herberts, I rarely carried cash, and with Mum busy limbering up for a session with Englebert, I asked her friend, Eileen Rhodes, (mother of The Phantom) for help. After a quick look both ways, Eileen produced a junior hacksaw from her handbag and a few moments later, those little binoculars were checking out the gold leaf chandeliers and the stitching on the crimson stage curtains.

And that's when I felt a buzzing from my Batman utility belt. A quick check confirmed it was coming from my STD (Smarmy Toff Detector). Like Kenneth Moore in *Sink the Bismarck!,* I began scanning the theatre until I saw the culprit, a funny little chap in the royal box who was watching *me* through his own, jewel-encrusted binoculars.

Ladies and gentlemen. I may have been no match for his untamed wit but I once sat through an entire episode of *Play School* without blinking, so if that boy fancied a staring competition, then my answer was *'Go for your guns, big nose'*.

Who won? We never found out, because Eileen saw him too and began waving at him, making the boy slink down behind his glossy programme quicker than Boris Johnson scurrying into a walk-in freezer. Eileen was a big girl, you see, who could have easily broken the young toff's spine over her knee.

The lights went down, the overture struck up, the audience sat down, and the curtains went up as Robinson Crusoe set sail. It was very exciting. So exciting that I dropped a brand new pack of blackcurrant Spangles and could only watch helplessly as they made a run for it to hide under the seats in front.

Arthur Askey, Jim Logan and comedy double act Hope and Keen were supporting Englebert Humperdink, who looked totally exhausted after spending the year battling Tom Jones for the right to catch my mother's flying knickers. The show was magnificent and the only boring bit was before the interval, when Englebert stripped to the waist and sang *The Last Waltz*. I'm not kidding. For three minutes you couldn't get an Opal Fruit for love nor money.

My personal footnote in the Palladium's illustrious history came just after the interval when Jim Logan did some shtick with an electric sporran. When it lit up, we had to tell him, and for bonus fun, sections of the audience were asked to compete. And because my competitive juices were fully honed after West Ham's recent dramatic World Cup victory, when it came to the Upper Circle, I bellowed so loud and for so long that Jim insisted the lonely goat herder got his very own round of applause. Yep, ME! The entire audience of the London Palladium clapping the noisy little bleeder in NHS glasses.

And that's when I spotted Richie Rich once again, staring jealously from inside the royal box. Fuck him. From the safety of the crow's nest and on behalf of working-class Herberts everywhere, I picked up my opera glasses and stared right back like some kind of four-eyed phantom.

Honestly, if looks could kill.

The Boy in Striped Pyjamas or A Glow in the Dark, Christmas Day

It was still dark as a little robin redbreast began chirruping outside my bedroom window, perfectly in tune with the tinkling sound of Papa using his en-suite chamber pot. I tugged my pyjama cord, and downstairs in the servants' quarters Buster and Little Jocky pressed record/play on what was to become an absolute *joyeux noël*.

'Hooray, Hooray, it's Christmas, Christmas Day!'

I reached for my bedside light, but weeks of stumbling around like Blind Pew had taught me to first put on my Chad Valley welder's mask. You see, the lamp's 100-watt bulb was so powerful it had already scorched the plastic lampshade and could easily send a shaft of light across East London to illuminate the glistening tip of Nelson's column. But this was CHRISTMAS DAY and no time to fuck about. So, squinting like Charlie Chan, I switched on the lamp and looked towards an interesting, if thrifty, pile of three presents.

The first was a pack of glow-in-the-dark putty which smelt of almonds and left my hands glowing like two bowls of Ready Brek. Fuelled by this early dose of radioactivity, I unwrapped the second present which turned out to be a Reeves painting-by-numbers. For some reason, Santa had chosen the adult version of *The Laughing Cavalier* by Dutch master Franz Hals. None-the-less, I popped open the miniature paint pots and began colouring in all the number fours like Dutch Master Johan Cruyff.

The smell in my bedroom was like a witch's brew of linseed oil and burning plastic, doing the Gay Gordons with the aroma of radioactive almonds.

There came a scratching noise from the window. It was our cat, who used it for after-hours access. "Merry Christmas, Mr Cat!" I called as it spat out some red feathers and lifted its tail to reveal a little brown starfish, before disappearing downstairs for some turkey giblets and a seasonal bowl of fresh milk.

Rightio. Time for the last present!

What looked like a giant Terry's Chocolate Orange turned out to be a Dunlop 'Wembley' football.

Gloria Estefan in Adidas Excelsis!

Was it my best Christmas present ever? Well, let's just say it certainly opened a few doors at the St Johns Church Sunday School.

I wonder why my memories of that particular Christmas morning have lingered longer than a scrounging brother-in-law around a Christmas buffet table? Did the smell of virgin rubber, almonds, linseed oil and the acrid pong from scorched plastic, combine to make a psychedelic episode so perfect that it remained safely inside my Yuletide Memory Bank: account No. 25121967? Probably.

Sixty miles away in his Surrey mansion, John Lennon sat at his own Christmas present: a keyboard with a cabinet full of weird and wonderful tape loops. Tentatively, he pressed middle C and smiled as a mysterious sound filled the room.

"Gloria Gaynor in Mellotron Excelsis!" he said while dipping into the Quality Street.

Inspired by the Quality Street and the new keyboard, he began a brand new Beatles song with the working title *Strawberry Fondue Forever.*

A true story by Herbert (aged ten).

East End Girls and Backward Boys

It should've been easy impressing eleven-year-old girls but I was seriously overestimating any advantage gained by wiping bogies on their satchels. None-the-less, I persevered, hoping at least one of those little dolly mixtures would go all-in with the dashing young Herbert in Joe 90 glasses.

I never missed a chance to show off my wrist action with a pair of plastic clackers, or to knock out a Scooby Doo keyring while engaging in a robust session of British Bulldog. Surely, I shone out like a shaft of gold when all around was dark? Nope. My invisibility cloak worked perfectly and the best I got was a ripple of interest when I stripped to my vest to retrieve a tennis ball from the playground shelter roof.

I wasn't alone in these failures. The playground was full of complete or partial bell-ends who, like Richard Dreyfuss in *Close Encounters of a Third Kind,* sensed something was up, but just didn't quite know what.

So instead of offering furtive glances from behind their fluttering fans, girls continued singing their complicated rhymes and slapping each other's hands while I developed my skills as a wit and raconteur.

Gambling with the Confederate Commander Robert E. Lee

Although Park School didn't have a gaming licence, you could always guarantee clusters of raggedy arsed children would be risking their dinner money on the flick of a coin or the toss of a card. Unsurprising I suppose when our role models spent half their lives studying horse and dog form, filling in pools coupons, or enjoying a candlelit game of three card brag. Even my nan scanned her *Racing Post* like a master criminal before placing her one shilling each way, upside down, two way family favourite, eight horse accumulator.

Of all the talents available to a young gunslinger, God gave me the gift of Throwing Coins Nearest to the Wall. If I say so myself, I was a bit warm, and enjoyed scooping up my winnings like Cool Hand Luke before sauntering down to Vicarage Lane to purchase the most desirable contraband known to a Paul Newman look-a-like. I refer, of course, to A&BC Bubble Gum cards.

While more studious boys pondered stamp collections, and others ran full pelt into brick walls, I had joined the most noble fraternity of collecting bubble gum cards. Every penny went to feeding our addiction to those slim packets containing a few cards and a brittle sheet of dusty chewing gum that tasted like shrapnel from a downed Messerschmidt. Nothing could stop us swapping, gambling and fussing over those precious cards like day-traders at Golum & Partners.

A big favourite was the American Civil War series, where each card carried an illustration of extreme violence, torture, or full-blown war atrocity. My best friend Colin had one I needed – No.56 Painful Death – and after offering two Batmans, one Man From U.N.C.L.E and two Monkees, I was finally swanning around the playground with the eighty-eight card set bulging in my trouser pocket. For a young psychopath, life couldn't be any better.

That's when Mr Wyatt swooped out of the sun and confiscated the lot on some trumped up charge. In theory I would get them back at the end of term. In reality they were gone forever. With no recourse to British justice, I visited a man who shared the school basement with two hundred rolls of antiseptic toilet paper.

The caretaker.

There were rumours about him being a member of the New York Mafia, over here on an FBI witness protection programme. I wasn't so sure. The Bronx accent was one thing but I watched him mop up Janet Freshwater's sick, and he was pretty convincing. Anyway, he listened while I explained the injustice. When I was done, he recounted his own story about a friend called Moe Greene, who ran a gambling empire in Las Vegas and died on a masseur's table with a bullet in one eye and a casino chip on each shoulder:

"No one knows who gave the order. I knew Moe, I knew he was headstrong, loud talking, saying stupid things. So, when he turned up dead, I let it go. I didn't ask who gave the order, little Herbert. This is the business we've chosen. People say caretaking is a two-bit job, but we're now bigger than US Steel. So, on your way little man while I sort out the dinner lady rota."

Mr Corleone taught me a valuable lesson. "Keep your cards close to your chest and let Lord Karma settle things on your behalf." Sure enough, Mr Wyatt came to school nursing a black eye from his big sister, who didn't think confederate soldiers being impaled on wooden poles was an appropriate gift for her son's bar mitzvah.

Bobby the Bastard v The Right Honourable Lord Herbert

Batman had the Joker, and Michael Portillo had Stephen Twigg. My nemesis was a boy called Bobby the Bastard who had a blonde, pudding basin haircut and strutted around like he was lead singer of the Hitler Youth. He was a bit tasty with the old fisticuffs, and did most of the heavy lifting from the cockpit of an orange Raleigh Chopper. I had no idea why he picked on me because I had it on good authority that I was absolutely and totally adorable!

I suppose it could've been my football prowess?

Whereas I had the poise and timing of a young Georgie Best, Bob the B had only the violent shoulder charge and almighty toe punt in his footballing repertoire. More importantly, we both knew it was only a matter of time before girls would be throwing themselves at my dancing boots and not at his overpriced Adidas trainers.

One evening at football training, Bob was outside, gripping the railings and gnashing his teeth, while we dribbled around the plastic cones faster than Harry Redknapp racing towards a microphone. From the ranks came a shout of "Oi, Bobby ... you wankaarrrr!"

Oh, how we laughed as he skulked away, and oh, how we shat ourselves when he cornered us in Vicarage Lane and ran through his collection of stinging seal-necks, Chinese burns, and his speciality ... a good old-fashioned dig-in-the ribs Hong Kong style.

This couldn't go on.

I must have been reading too many *Valiant* annuals because I challenged him to a boxing match. Ten one-minute rounds – or whenever the dinner lady stubbed out her cigar to break it up.

He agreed.

Bollocks.

Next day, during the school lunch break, while Bob warmed up by smashing his head against a cast iron rainwater pipe, I slipped a 10oz horseshoe inside my 2oz boxing gloves before entering a makeshift boxing ring of satchels and rounders bats. My plan was simple: dazzle old fancy pants with some nifty footwork, clump him with a few body shots, and while he was wheeling around like a demented country dancer, switch to southpaw, pop one on his chin and leave him sparko. Yep, that should put this big-headed Aryan tosser to bed.

We stood nose-to-nose, eyes locked in a steely gaze. The bell went and he duly beat the fucking crap out of me.

The Easter Fair or Lynda Moves Away

During the reign of King George II, two friends, Herbert the Poacher and Richard the Turnip, liked to wander the Royal Epping Forest, snaring rabbits and collecting mushrooms. Herbert was a simple chap who wanted only to find a nice girl and poach eggs for a whole brood of little Herberts. But Richard was more ambitious and, after meeting pop impresario Mickey the Most, rearranged his surname to become a

Dandy highwayman and go on to record a string of hits including *Stand and Delivery*, *Antsie Music* and *Goody Two Boots*.

But, like Halal butchery, the 18th century music scene was a cut-throat business, and Dick Turpin's life would eventually end hanging from a tree in York, and the only member of the Turnip family to bear witness was his little brother, Terry Turnip, who was himself already resigned to being a vegetable all his life.

From that day on, to commemorate the life and music of Dick Turpin, a travelling fair set up camp on Wanstead Flats every Easter holiday to play loud pop music and shake down the locals.

And that's how I came to be getting off a bus in Forest Gate opposite a pub called The Eagle and Child. The child (me) was accompanied by two birds of prey (Aunt Lynda and her best friend, Lynda Vincenti) who were both fully blonded and beehived up, and definitely not wearing sensible walking shoes, because those girls were going ahuntin' and I was just the decoy.

Across the dried grass we hurried, towards the feint whiff of coconut and glue and the sound of Alan Price belting out *Simon Smith and His Amazing Dancing Bear*. Once inside the circle of caravans, we were instantly surrounded by the smell of fried onions and diesel fumes from hidden generators. From every stall hung scores of polythene bags, each with a goldfish waiting for the promised land of shiny bowls and multi-coloured gravel.

And as we stepped carefully over the trailing power leads and muddy puddles I began noticing my chaperones were scattering men before them like Hollywood starlets!

Before long, two teddy boys invited them onto The Waltzer, and I had to wait on the steps while they had the time of their bloody lives. I was rewarded afterwards with a ride on a fibreglass duck rattling around a circular track at 3mph while the girls flashed past on the ghost train chased by screams, whistles, and two sharply dressed zombies. For the next hour, they were preoccupied by a long-haired oaf on the crooked air-rifle stall, so I tried my luck on the 'Get the Hoop over a Large Jar of Sweets with a Five Pound Note and a Watch Strapped to its Side' stall, before exchanging my last sixpence with an old woman with red hair for a once in a lifetime opportunity to throw three plastic darts at some playing cards. Finally, with the evening drawing in, I got to sit in a stationary bumper car while Lynda (1) and Lynda (2) sparked past with another bare-chested ruffian standing over them, miming to *There's a Kind of Hush*. All things considered, a grand day out.

Then it struck me like a freshly caught lobster snapping its claws around a fisherman's testicles – Dad's last words:

"I'm warning you, Lyn … be home before it gets dark!"

Yet here we were, surrounded by ten thousand coloured bulbs twinkling in the Forest Gate twilight. Oh boy, was she in trouble.

Alas, my little aunt Lynda had a selective memory and decided to selectively spend our bus fare home on one final attraction: the Freaks and Wonders tent.

Honestly, there were more thrills on our school nature bench. We ambled past two grubby old fish tanks, containing a lonely pot-bellied piranha toying with the remains of a pork chop, and the other with just a handwritten card reading 'Dinosaur Bone'. It was all very underwhelming. Underwhelming, that is until the ghost of Dick Turpin stepped up with the final exhibit.

Move over Elephant Man. Jog on Lady with the Bearded Clam. Standing before us was a life-size Wolfman staring menacingly out from inside an iron cage. As we edged closer, it suddenly came alive, shaking the cage and taking the opportunity to goose Lynda and her mate.

Bloody hell!

I rushed outside with my Action Man underpants clinging on for dear life, leaving the two girls laughing hysterically.

The fourth official held up a board saying VERY LATE, and breathless and penniless, we began the long trek back across Wanstead Flats to the dying strains of *I Was Kaiser Bill's Batman*.

Meanwhile, the family were going nuts, and out scouring the streets. When the three of us turned into Tennyson Road, oh my, how they reprimanded Lyn for scaring the life out of everyone. And oh my, how we all laughed when she told them to jolly well fuck off.

Yep, Lynda was now a paid-up member of the Stratford and District Screaming Diva Society. A Queen Bee stomping about, inviting spotty drones to hang around outside our house on buzzing Lambrettas (I tried shooting them from the upstairs window but the old man eventually dispersed them using sarcasm, wit, and an extra-large cricket bat).

Lynda was a handful, alright, playing Dave Clark Five at four in the morning and The Four Tops at five in the afternoon. The final straw came one evening as we watched Ray Reardon and Eddie Pullman grind out a thrilling 0-0 draw on *Pot Black*. A noise from the front door turned out to be rhythm and blues legend Georgie Fame posting her knickers through the letter box. Enough was enough.

Next day, Lynda and her Pifco Princess hair dryer were off to share a bedroom with Cousin Denise, from where she continued working through the young men of Stratford before branching out to Forest Gate, Manor Park and Romford.

I cried real tears as Lyn clip-clopped away, right up to the exact moment she disappeared down Whalebone Lane, when I ran upstairs and tipped out a Quality Street tin full of Dinky cars before dancing around them cackling like The Riddler.

I would live happily in that bedroom until 1973, alone apart from a dozen cat fleas and an Aurora glow-in-the-dark model of *The Hunchback of Notre Dame*.

Meet the Beatles

In 1965, if a person stood on a bus shelter roof on a quiet Sunday afternoon, they could just hear the far-off sound of the Spanish holiday boom. The Moffatts were some of the earliest British holidaymakers to spend a week abroad, searching for a Marks & Spencer, before flying home like they had just witnessed a nuclear test with only a sombrero and a pair of flipflops for protection. My young cousins didn't fare much better, falling in behind like little barbecued prawns.

Unfortunately, mum's fear of flying meant we never got to see Lynda work her way through her I Spy Book of Latin Lovers (she got as far as P for Pedro. Not bad for a little girl from Stratford). Instead, our summer holidays began with a trek through the backstreets towards Maryland Point where a line of coaches was already under siege by Pac-a-mac raincoats, white flat caps, and twisted wooden tennis racquets. There were lost children, lost grandparents, and wives struggling with suitcases while their husband's spearheaded the way through the crowd, shouting:

"Follow the beach ball, Maureen, follow the beach ball."

Inevitably, those same men wore the uniform of great British explorers like Dr Livingstone: long khaki shorts, reaching down to brilliant white knobbly knees and a brand new pair of white socks who were busy introducing themselves to an old pair of brown leather sandals. Apparently, it's what everyone was wearing that season during the construction of the Burma Railway.

My father wore his usual holiday attire of work trousers, work jacket, shirt, tie and *Daily Mirror* as he checked the handwritten destination cards sellotaped to each coach: Isle of Wight, Walton on the Nose, and the very exotic sounding Island of the Hayling. Ours was called Clacton-on-Sea, and we clambered aboard while the driver stowed away our two battered suitcases. Ten minutes later, he and his hernia were staring back towards forty expectant faces:

"Right … is everyone here who's supposed to be here?" Baffled silence. *"Then, ladies and gentlemen, you may now smoke."*

There followed an urgent flurry of petrol lighters as the coach disappeared inside a holiday haze of nicotine and Opal Fruit confetti.

Squeezing into his seat, the driver adjusted his cap, coughed, farted, and switched on the ignition. In perfect symmetry, the diesel engine coughed, farted, and dragged itself from the pavement, accompanied by ironic cheers and a quick rendition of the working man's favourite song:

"We're all going on a summer holiday, no more shirking for a week or two."

Dad unfurled his *Daily Mirror*, Mum retrieved her Knitting Patterns of the Second World War, and I opened my *Beano Sea-side Special* ready to drive myself into an uncontrollable frenzy, something I wasn't to repeat until the onset of puberty some twenty years later.

By mid-afternoon, we were inside a holiday camp reception, swearing allegiance to Sir Billy Butlin. Then, with one caravan key and a Butlins Beaver Badge, we set off for the final leg between lines of identical caravans followed every inch of the way by those non-ommittal stares that British holidaymakers reserve for newcomers.

Every caravan had its own name and ours was called No. 1765. To the welcoming applause of rain hammering on the roof, me and dad made ourselves comfortable while Mum unpacked the suitcases, brewed a pot of tea, disinfected the cooker, cleaned the windows and disappeared behind a pile of her own fresh linen.

"Ah, she's a great little woman," Dad said.

"Yes, and she's getting smaller all the time," I replied. *(Thanks, Spike.)*

Whether it was the call of East Anglian seagulls or Nancy Sinatra belting out from the speaker system, I developed an overwhelming urge to go exploring. You know. Places to see and an open-air swimming pool to relieve myself into.

But first I had to change out of my travelling clothes (German Panza Tank Commander) and slip into something more appropriate (Neapolitan Ice Cream T-shirt with horizontal bars of cream, beige and delicious dark brown stripes). Only one problem. I'd packed felt-tips and bubble gum cards, but forgotten underpants! Oh well, if Dirk Bogarde could go commando in *A Bridge Too Far*, it looked like Ice Cream Boy was gonna raise a few eyebrows on the monkey bars.

Next morning, me and Papa were up early as our bodies acclimatized to the east coast time zone (GMT +2). Mum was still asleep after spending the night steam-cleaning the curtains, so we set off to get his *Daily Mirror*. A brisk walk around the boating lake, some fisticuffs with two seagulls, and a quick nod to a red-faced man rushing towards the communal wash rooms. Dad said the man was probably on a mission ... and that mission was to defecate within the next two minutes.

Anyway, we left him screaming in trap one, and found our way to the open-air swimming pool where we both stood on the soggy woven rope at the end of the springboard and looked down into the freezing water as the wind rippled the surface and sent an icy finger to tickle my unprotected junior scrotum.

At 8am sharp, the camp shop opened and the camp proprietor welcomed my handsome father with a friendly smile. Two minutes later, the old man's *Daily Mirror* was doing a healthy 60mph towards the sea front where he sat on a bench and did the crossword while I floated over to Holland on a brand new lilo. Those were the days, my friend.

It was the second day when I met the Beatles.

I was coming back from a fancy dress competition (Julius Caesar: beach towel toga, plastic sword ... don't ask), when I passed a large army marquee sandwiched between the shower block and the armed sentry tower. It was a FREE cinema with grass floorboards and wooden benches facing a projector screen. I cracked open a pack of Refreshers and watched the tail end of Disney's *That Darned Cat!* Next up was a film called *Help!* about someone called Ringo being chased across Salisbury Plains by someone called Eleanor Bron. It was brilliant! I watched it three more times that week and began noticing a song called *Eleanor Rigby* playing constantly on transistor radios held to the ears of pretty girls.

I didn't realise, of course, but those mop-topped and dust-panned-up Beatles were battling past a back four of Norman Hunter, Bobby Moore and two female Play School presenters to bury themselves deep within my young English psyche. Like musical time-bombs, they were set to go off a few years later when my big hand was pointing to twelve and my little hand was rooting around inside my nylon underpants.

Jack and Queenie or Pier Pressure on The Island of the White

Before my grandmother became a Moffatt, she was a Thompson (like the sub-machine gun). Polly's youngest brother was a handsome fellow called Tiger, who chaperoned her younger daughters to local dances and to the ice rink behind the Princess Alice. Polly's daughters were all secretly in love with their dashing young uncle and whenever he arrived unannounced, there was always a flurry of drying knickers being stuffed into the piano. If curlers were in, they also had a well-practised routine for hiding under the dining table ... like that scene in *Sense and Sensibility* by Emma Thompson (no relation).

Polly's eldest brother was Jack, a barrel chested, no nonsense, fuck-off Royal Navy hero who only tied away his hammock when the admiral assured him the Germans had ran out of U-boats. Great Uncle Jack lived in Plashet Grove with his wife Queenie, undoubtedly the sweetest and kindest lady in the whole wide world.

Every Sunday, Queenie ironed Jack a clean white shirt and ran a brush over his navy-blue blazer before sending him up the British Legion where other ex-servicemen were waiting to discuss West Ham United and all things new in the Arts and Entertainment Industry.

My father was only seven when the Second World War started, and therefore way too young to put his devastating flatulence to good effect. But in 1950 he got to do his National Service by playing cribbage in the Middle East. When asked if he had ever shot anyone, his reply suggested that at least one Arab may have got on the wrong side of Private Charles R Smith.

My dad thought it important for the two of us to join those old warriors down the British Legion, and by happenchance afford him access to subsidised beer. And that's how a group of war heroes and a twenty-six-year old cribbage champion came to be discussing *The Des O'Connor Show* while the regimental mascot dressed as a Sapper from the 1st Battalion of The Royal Engineers sat outside in the drizzle sucking a damp arrowroot biscuit.

Jack and Queenie would eventually up-anchor and move to Sandown on the Isle of Wight, and in 1968 we caught the train to Portsmouth to pay them a surprise visit. With us were Dad's mum, Flo, and little Cousin Jeff.

Once aboard the ferry, Dad went to see a man about a horse, Mum unwrapped two dozen boiled eggs while nan stood at the rails letting the wind lift her dress like a Mackeson lovin' Marilyn Monroe. With no wish to see her holiday bloomers, me and Jeff disappeared to the back of the ferry where the propeller was whipping the sea into a milky green soup. It was all very exciting. In fact, it was so exciting, we gobbed into the Solent, unaware that our little cockney lives were about to change forever.

Jack and Queenie lived in a terraced house with painted white brickwork and gnomes in the front garden. We kept ringing the doorbell but although the curtains were twitching faster than Herbert Lom dipping into a lady's handbag, nobody answered. It was only after pretending to be Jehovah's Witnesses that we finally gained access to their fridge. Two pints of milk, three pork pies, one ham sandwich, two Penguin chocolate bars and some left-over chicken later, Uncle Jack handed us his old sea fishing tackle and directions to Sandown Pier. Jeff looked across at me and I looked across to him. There we were ... cross-eyed.

As that old natural mystic Sir Izaak Walton once said:

"Welcome, sir, to the brotherhood of the angle."

It was high summer and therefore cold, wet and fucking windy. I borrowed Queenie's see-thru pac a mac and Jeff chose Jack's rather fetching Pierre Cardin bright yellow sou'wester. With the security chain securely fastened behind us, we set off for Sandown Pier, stopping only to buy some lugworms wrapped in newspaper. Lugworms are a versatile sea fishing bait, and, did you know that when cut in half, their bright orange guts can obliterate an entire *News of the World* headline about a vicar in Little Hampton catching his verger inside the collection box? Thought not.

Onto the pier's wooden decking, straight through the amusements, and staring moodily ahead as we passed two teenage girls operating the Tea Cup ride. Finally we reached the end of the pier where we cast our flimsy tackle into the treacherous waves crashing against the steel girders and concrete landings. Move over Mr Crabtree, the boys are back in town.

For five consecutive days, with no buoyancy aids whatsoever, we chomped Dairylea sandwiches with orange-stained fingers as our cork floats dived below the surface with all manner of strange fish grabbing the lugworms. Back then, the coastline of Britain was still packed full of fish and we caught so many we could've easily opened our own Mac Fisheries. And as we returned each night, we shared a knowing glance with those two girls trapped inside a large fibreglass teapot.

Our last night was spent on a mystery coach tour ending in a beer garden near Shanklin. Coloured lanterns nodded in the trees, the smell of seaweed blew in from the sea, and a seagull crapped a detailed map of the British Isles onto the table next to ours. Salt and lugworm flavour crisps never tasted so good as our table disappeared under a tidal wave of beer bottles and lipstick-stained Britvic glasses. As the evening closed, my dad stood up and sang a rousing rendition of *We'll Meet Again*, which brought the entire pub to its feet … only for it to shuffle a few yards nearer the car park before settling down again.

Saturday morning, Mum was up early boiling eggs for the journey home, and the lugworms of Sandown could finally breathe more easily as our young heroes boarded the ferry home. We were still virgo-fully-intacto but those two girls on the Tea Cup ride knew exactly how close they had come to becoming child brides. More importantly, Jeff and I were now full members of the angling fraternity and over the next fifty years would spend thousands of pounds on camouflaged clothing.

Once again, we stood at the back of the ferry (stern), waving towards Jack and Queenie until they were just two tiny dots on the harbour wall. Seizing the moment, my old man offered this fond farewell to our two elderly relatives:

"I'll tell you what, boys … you won't be meeting those two again."

He was right, apart from Lynda's wedding and a Christmas party in 1976.

A Distorted View of the World, or, Playing Soccer at the Highest Level (not altitude)

As the National Health Service celebrated its 18th anniversary, a young man wearing the dress uniform of the Argyll and Sutherland Highlanders sat hyperventilating in the antiseptic atmosphere of Queen Mary's Outpatients. The waiting area was under a glass atrium, built to commemorate those lost in World War I. It was the first memorial of its kind and probably why Queen Mary's became the first hospital to receive a direct hit during World War II.

My own particular drain on the NHS began when I was found discussing Mr Magoo with a cast-iron boy collecting for the Spastic Society. Mum fell to her knees and through loud racking sobs, told me I must've inherited the 'Moffatt Family Curse', otherwise known as acute short sightedness with melodramatic tendencies. And that, dear reader, is how I came to be in the outpatients department with my head strapped into a heavy space helmet while a man who looked like Harry Worth squeezed droplets of burning acid into my eyes.

A pair of heavy-framed NHS spectacles arrived a few weeks later, giving me the exotic appearance of Gerry Anderson's boy-spy, Joe 90. It was a relief, to be honest. Colin Zambuzoo went through the same process and ended up with a bright pink eye patch.

Those new Joe 90s gave me a leg up the education ladder but ended any lingering ambition of captaining England. I could still make a last-ditch tackle but heading meant having to judging the ball's incoming velocity and trajectory before whipping off the glasses at the last moment. Any misjudgement left them dangling askew and a big bruise developing on my little hooter.

After WWI, with high unemployment and very few hobbies, it wasn't uncommon to see thousands of flat-caps watching schoolboy football over West Ham Park. At that time, Park School had seven different teams, with some very talented players including a boy called Billy Murray who is the reason *I'm Forever Blowing Bubbles* is sung by West Ham supporters trying to stave off the crippling disappointment of another fruitless season.

By 1968, due mostly to the heavy demands of stamp collecting, Park School had just one team and this particular Joe 90 lookalike playing right back. I had plenty of stamina but because of the glasses, tended to bottle some of the heavier tackles and instead I skipped away like Peter Pan.

After training, we convened at the famous Cassettari's Café to enjoy a Pepsi and discuss tactics. Using salt and pepper pots as goal posts and a full set of silverware including soup spoons and fish knives for outfield players, we arrived at our most successful formation which entailed every piece of cutlery stampeding towards the ball (ketchup) for the entire ninety minutes.

Home games were played over West Ham Park, so after a high-protein bowl of Ricicles, twelve schoolboy footballers (collective noun: a gallop) would strip off under a conker tree to display a collection of white spindly legs each finishing with a football boot caked in mud. Amongst the Adidas *Santiago*s, Puma *Kings*, and Dennis Law *Mitre*s was a solitary pair of Freeman Hardy and Willis *Generics*, endorsed by the British Army. I'm proud to say those monsters left their mark in the muddy battlegrounds of Temple Mills and the cow pats on Wanstead Flats before ending their life on a bus shelter roof opposite the Bingo Hall in West Ham Lane.

Parents rarely waved goodbye let alone accompany us to away fixtures, which meant catching at least two buses and wandering the outskirts of Newham like *The Warriors* traversing the outer precincts of New York. It wasn't other gangs we were wary of – it was the old ladies who flew from their flats waving baseball bats as we hurried past leaving a trail of Toffo wrappers on the way back to the bus stop. Can you dig it?

Come to think of it, we did have two regular supporters: Mr

McDowell and his girlfriend, Malcolm. But even they couldn't compete with the opposition who had their entire families lining the touchlines with burning spears and snarling dogs, making Howard Woolly fly down the wings faster than Alan Devonshire with his bottom on fire.

After the final whistle, opponents inevitably climbed over the changing room walls to chase us back to the bus stop in a fabulous gesture of friendship and good-natured rivalry. None-the-less, and thanks mostly to the heroics of Little Titch, our three-foot goalkeeper, we finished 19th in the 1967/68 West Ham School League table. Only two behind the Forest Gate Girl Pipers.

I recently found an old black and white photograph of the Park School football team circa 1907. Young men, arms folded, staring dead ahead. There was also a colour photo from 1967 with a bespectacled Boy Wonder standing in the back row. Seven years on from each playground photo-shoot, one group were on the battlefields of Flanders, and the other lot were sodding about in Woolworth's listening to *Drive-In Saturday*.

The Ghostly Girl in the Prefabs

Between Vicarage Lane and Tennyson Road stood two acres of prime real estate so desirable, even the Duke of Westminster was seen measuring for curtains. It was a clutch of single-storey prefabricated homes, with enough sexy accoutrements to tempt any young property mogul. For starters, they had front gardens surrounded by a lovely bit of chestnut fencing, and instead of draughty wooden sashes they had precision-fit crittal windows. Inside, the hard-wearing asbestos walls stood straight and true. And best of all, they had flat roofs perfect for a young man to sit unobserved while finishing off a Cadbury's Flake. Yep, those little homes had everything a young sniper with a tendency for pyromania could ever wish for … including a mysterious girl who would haunt his dreams for over forty years.

My mate Russell lived in one. We called him Sprouty but with his goofy teeth he looked more like Plug from the *Beano*. His prefab also had a canopy over the front door, held up by two metal poles which he hung upside down from while discussing the merits of Glynn Poole, Lena Zavaroni, and the other northern stage school twerps on *Junior Showtime*.

In 1969, a film called *Bronco Bullfrog* was shot in and around Stratford, using local actors from Joan Sutherland's Stratford East Theatre. It drew some acclaim and even Princess Anne was roped into attending the premiere. A boy called John Pitt told us his elder brother appeared in it, and was immediately given the respect due to any sibling of a movie star, especially a skinhead wearing knee high officer boots. One scene was filmed down Tennyson Road in which the main character, Del, had his motor bike crushed by a lorry. It was shot right outside Russell's prefab and I'm proud to say those poles gave a sterling performance, going on to win the 1971 Bafta for Best Supporting Prop. Thirty years later, I got to work with one of those young actors. His name was Trevor Oakley and in the film he played a hoodlum from Forest Gate. Could he act? Nope. Is he available on Blu-ray from the British Film Institute? Yep.

Apart from Russell's blossoming interest in pole dancing, he also had a dog called Lady who wandered the streets at all hours. Inevitably, Lady gave birth to seven multi-coloured puppies and Russell's mum saw an opportunity to top up the old housekeeping. After my enthusiastic story about pink tummies and wet noses, my mum agreed to go take a look.

Unfortunately, Mrs Sprout never studied the art of displaying her wares, and was keeping the puppies in an enamel bath. When we opened the door the puppies were sliding happily around in a sea of brown sludge, covering themselves in poo (shit) and wee (piss).

"What do you think, Mum?" I asked eagerly.

"We'll see," said the back of my mother's head as it disappeared down the road, clutching a lavender hanky.

All of which leads me to a curious episode that would echo through my life like a cockney butterfly effect and make for a decent thirty minutes on Arthur C. Clarke's *Mysterious World*.

It was 1967, and after a long day up Russell's pole, I was spending the last few minutes before tea-time kicking a football against the kerb outside our house. Out of the blue, a girl appeared, pedalling her bike along the pavement. She was beautiful, with straggly blonde hair, blue eyes and dirty knees.

"You live here?" she asked.

Dear reader, by the time Buster and Little Jocky had pulled the correct levers in the signal box, my reply sounded more like a high-pitched cry for help.

"Yes please," I responded.

Without missing a beat, she continued her journey, briefly looking over her shoulder to give a smile which kicked me smack plumb in the solar plectrum.

Seconds later, she disappeared into the evening sun somewhere beyond the prefabs. *What the fuck happened there?* One moment I'm anticipating the delights of fish-finger and peas, now I'm standing knee-deep in concrete. *Bloody hell.*

When I finally went inside, I could hardly raise a forkful of those delicious cod pieces to my lips, let alone answer any of Chris Kelly's questions on *Clapperboard*.

"You alright, son?" asked Mum.

"Dunno, Mum," answered Herbert truthfully.

I had been done up like a right little cockney kipper. A beautiful girl had smiled at me without first being prompted by a large box of Cadbury's Milk Tray.

For the next two weeks, I hung around the prefabs hoping for another glimpse of the mysterious girl who had bicycled into my life and then, just as quickly, bicycled out of it again.

Did I imagine her? Was this a scene from *The Amazing Mr Blunden*, where ghostly children reach out across time? Who was she? Why the enigmatic smile? Were my flies undone? So many questions.

I raised these concerns with Russell as we dangled our legs over the side of his prefab roof.

Herbert: *Well ... what do you reckon? Was she a ghost or what?*

Russell thought for a moment before offering the following advice.

Russell: *Don't be a cunt.*

Wise words indeed.

I Love the Sound of Breaking Glass

Stratford Green Grammar School had stood with its back straight since 1848, a distinguished old building with Gothic spires and Portland stone porticos. A place where grim-faced tutors had once thrown blackboard rubbers at any boy doodling pictures of Queen Victoria having it away with Lord Kitchener. Now, like the British Empire, that old red-brick leviathan waited to be dismantled and its empty corridors echoed to the sound of well-read pigeons. Inside the classrooms, radiators hung off the walls with their lifeblood of rusty water draining between upturned desks and scores of blue-stained, porcelain ink-wells.

If there had been a nearby orchard, we may well have gone scrumping like in a *Just William* story and thrown half-eaten apple cores at girls from the Upper Fourth of Mallory Towers. But there wasn't so instead we scaled the gates of Stratford Green Grammar School, and stood before three storeys of unprotected glass.

The lower panes were dead easy. But lobbing half a brick 30 feet in the air through a third-floor classroom window meant side-stepping showers of jagged glass like a matador, or else be decapitated like David Warner in *The Omen*. It took an entire summer but with indomitable British spirit we did the last pane just as the wrecking ball arrived to finish what Herman Goering and his Dancing Luftwaffe never quite managed.

But worse things can happen than losing your head in a horror franchise, and that's playing Russian roulette with a miserable old bastard taking his last few wage packets before retirement. It was the school caretaker, that rarest of men – a nutcase with an overblown sense of his own importance. Whereas a fictional orchard owner would've smiled ruefully as we ran off with pockets full of apples, this old gentleman liked to yell blood-curdling threats that would've made William Brown shit himself and put him off Golden Delicious for life.

"Oi, you little cunts! If I come out there, I'm gonna rip your FUCKING HEADS OFF!"

Ahh, the wit of the cockney school caretaker.

German Bombers, Silk Camisoles, Stockings and Suspenders

School lunch that day was mincemeat and peas followed by a rectangle of lemon sponge with strawberry custard, all washed down with lukewarm tap water from a copper jug. Delicious. Tummies stretched liked toy balloons, we rushed out to the playground ready for some sexual hijinks and high stakes gambling. Went the day well? No. We were met with a deafening roar and ominous shadows moving across our upturned faces as a squadron of German Bombers flew over the playground, low enough to show us their menacing Nazi insignia.

What was going on? *Daydream Believer* was No.1, yet the German Luftwaffe was making the netball posts vibrate like a pair of tuning forks. The dinner lady took no chances and, after stubbing out her cigar, bellowed:

"Alright kids! RUN FOR YOUR FUCKING LIVES!"

It turns out she needn't have wasted half a panatella because a pack of Spitfires appeared, chasing the German bombers towards central London. Cripes all bleeding mighty! The whole thing lasted no more than two minutes but we stood transfixed and the Phantom Slasher was reduced to a stunned trickle. Even the German boy whispered to his female accomplice:

"Gott im Himmel Sharon! What the fuck vas das?"

Five minutes later, it was like nothing had happened, and a high pitched scream from the girls' toilets confirmed another direct hit from an obviously relieved Phantom.

But how come the children of E.15 could remain so cool in the face of a sky full of German bombers? I'll tell you. Every Sunday afternoon, we gorged upon a diet of British war films where fine actors like Sam Kydd and Albert R.N. made mincemeat of the Germans before Noël Coward and Celia Johnson finished them off with a fluffy potato topping. So why worry about a German invasion when we knew everything would be wrapped up and funky by 5pm, in time for *The Sale of the Century* (from Norwich, apparently)?

I often wonder what our young German counterparts were doing every Sunday afternoon while Richard Todd was straightening out their naughty grandparents. Were they being made to stand in a corner singing Lulu songs? Or were they over the park, queuing in perfectly straight lines, practising penalties? I guess we'll never know.

It turns out those military aircraft were being filmed over London for the 1969 movie *Battle of Britain*. I went to the premiere with Sprouty, Tin Can Tommy, Knock Down Ginger and Ron Goodwin on his rat-tat-tat soundtrack, and chomped merrily through an entire box of Poppets. What a film! My patriotic duffel bag was full to overflowing as we cheered on some of Britain's finest actors in glorious technicolour.

But there was one scene which stood out like a strawberry gobstopper in a packet of Revels. It had the beautiful actress Susannah York stepping out of her WAAF uniform and standing before Christopher Plummer in just her silk stockings and frilly underwear. I'm proud to say that scene instilled in me a lifelong admiration for the RAF, and for any woman dressed in uniform (see Jane Tennyson, Juliet Bravo, and, to a lesser extent, Lynda Carter as Wonder Woman).

Never has so much been owed by one schoolboy to so many actresses.

Nigel Von Trump

There was a block of flats down Vicarage Lane, owned by the Metropolitan Police, for the sole use of its officers and staff. For security reasons, this remained a closely guarded secret and was why the entire neighbourhood knew them as the 'Police Flats'. My mate Nigel lived there. His dad was a copper and when he was out fingering local villains, young men with scabby knees and sticky up hair (collective noun: a helmet) ventured down to those subterranean bin stores where the acoustics were perfect for young Nigel to stand legs astride and share his extraordinary gift.

You see, Nigel could pass wind on demand. Not only that, he would do requests and accompany pop songs, classical favourites or rousing show tunes. It was hugely entertaining and the best thing was, he did it while prancing around like a ballerina.

He gave depth and colour to those bench warmers using techniques such as pianissimo, fortissimo and vibrato, and his showstopper was an homage to the animal impressionist Percy Edwards. Admittedly, none of us could differentiate between his mighty Rooster or red-faced Nightingale, but Nigel's Wind Farm was always an hour well spent, ending with a curtsey and a loud theatrical flourish.

With a decent theatrical agent, Nigel could've become an international cabaret artiste like the great Le Pétomane. Instead, he followed his father into the Metropolitan Police and became known as PC Fartypants, the officer nobody wants to share a squad car with during an all-night stake-out.

In 1969, his father was redeployed to Bexleyheath, and Nigel and I sat on the wall opposite the bakers and swore on a warm chunk of bread pudding to keep in contact and remain friends. And that's why I haven't seen or heard from him for well over fifty years (*parp*).

Brentford Nylons and Radio 1 DJ Alan Freeman

As the Beatles did their second tour of America after turning left at Greenland, the great and good of East and West Ham councils were traipsing up the granite steps of Stratford Town Hall tasked with choosing a new name for the historic joining of those two distinguished London boroughs.

At exactly 10:58am, the two mayors and assorted flunkies, resplendent in ceremonial finery, seated themselves around a polished oak table in the main chamber. At 11:00am, deliberations began. At 11:03, a tea urn crashed through the doors and the tea-lady placed two chocolate biscuits in front of the chairman.

"Ere," she said. *"My old man reckons you should call it Newham."*

A quick glance around the table, and the chairman banged his gavel.

"Okay, that's it! Lunch everybody."

And as they piled down the granite steps and turned left into The Two Puddings, a young man dressed as a corporal in the Royal Gurka Rifles happened to be passing. That young Gurka was me, armed only with my ceremonial plastic Kukri, and on a secret mission to buy some revolutionary new underwear.

While the stout yeomen of England clung valiantly to their white string underpants and vests, a new space age material was being tested on unsuspecting minors like me.

Every Sunday afternoon, somewhere between *The Big Match* and *The Golden Shot*, Radio 1 DJ Alan 'Fluff' Freeman topped up his BBC salary by filming outside a shop called Brentford Nylons, promising busy mums that nylon underwear could not only shrug off irritating skid marks, but also resist any attempt at incineration.

Fluff Freeman's floppy hair and lopsided grin proved irresistible and I was put on trials in a pair of pale-blue underpants with matching bedsheets. One problem: Fluff never mentioned the resulting static build up, so for five years a generation of children went down for breakfast crackling like a bowl of Rice Crispies! A real (drum roll) ... *hair-raising experience!* (*Hooray!*)

Nylon underpants took over the world. They were everywhere, from swimming pool changing rooms to bus shelter roofs. Yellow and blue; striped and paisley. Personally I always fancied the bright orange ones, and would've got them too if not for an article in *The Stratford Express* where a boy scout spontaneously combusted while reading a Girl Guide Annual inside his nylon sleeping bag. Apparently his Young Scientist Proficiency Badge had to be awarded posthumously at a ceremony hosted by The Crazy World of Arthur Brown.

The experiment was over and a disgraced Alan 'Fluff' Freeman moved on to flogging OMO soap powder. I never got my orange underpants but it was still work-in-progress for those boffins at Brentford Nylons, and their hard work eventually paid off when they utilised the boy scout's right-hand friction action to produce the wind-up torch we know today.

Boy Scouts, Hovering Buttocks and Baloo the Bear

Apart from making knee-length khaki shorts more popular than Jesus, Lord Baden-Powell had a business plan called the 'Powell Movement', involving a worldwide chain of shops selling uniforms, knives, tin plates, Girl Guide attractant, dirty old man repellent, woggles, scarves, books and badges.

Ours was in Woodgrange Road, Forest Gate, opposite a Methodist church where a bronze preacher loomed over the church entrance clutching a bronze bible in his long bony fingers. The preacher must have been twelve foot tall and looked like he was about to step down and clunk off towards Forest Gate station like that bronze giant in *Jason and the Argonauts*. God works in mysterious ways but I know plenty of little cubs and brownies who had to steel themselves and hurry past that bronze motherfucker if they wanted to get anywhere near a bar of Kendall Mint cake.

The 11th Newham met at Park Primary school, so after a long day scaring girls, I went home a young man about town and returned three hours later dressed as a Jolly Green Herbert. Every week, we proved our allegiance to the queen by collecting jumble, and in return they taught us how to make fire using kindling, matches, and a thermos of petrol. We performed CPR on a track-suited dummy before using it as a goalkeeper during five-a-side, and learnt how to hover over a chemical toilet full to the brim with other people's faeces. Good stuff.

In the summer, we were released like spring lambs to gambol around the Brecon Beacons using only a compass and a bottle of Cherryade to navigate by. We canoed down the River Wye, threw stones at the bloated corpses of giant salmon, and abseiled down the Black Mountains which, I admit, left a hefty deposit in my Action Man underpants, and later transferred to the inside of my sleeping bag.

Once a year we raised money for Lord Powell's luxury yacht by offering ourselves to complete strangers with a chirpy '*Bob-a-Job, mister?*' Most people entered into the spirit, but it was always the old ladies who had us cut their grass, redecorate their kitchen and give them a cut and blow dry, before gleefully handing over one bob (a shilling, or 5p, or 0.0001 Euro).

Our spiritual leaders were a bus driver called Akela and his beautiful wife Baloo, a big-bosomed lady who wore a tight green shirt, a khaki skirt, and a beret perched upon her long brunette hair. All the boys took her knot tying lessons very seriously and she became the first woman I ever saluted to with two fingers up.

But Baloo wasn't the only thing simmering gently in our own scouting juices.

Every year an International Scouting Jamboree was held in Gillwell Park, Chigwell, and the moment we stepped from the coach, we sensed something in the air … and I'm not talking about dense wood smoke and the smell of burnt Walls pork sausages.

Because standing under their national flags were long-legged, bilingual, Swedish and American Girl Guides who made our heads spin like little cockney weather vanes, and left a group of Sea Scouts from Germany quaking like the wreck of the Graf Spee.

Just a few hours earlier, we were brothers-in-arms, sitting around the camp fire singing *Ging Gang Goolie*. Add two Girl Guides and an Oxo cube, and suddenly we're warring tribes of competitive little bastards, fighting for the right to stand under a Russian girl climbing a rope ladder with a Bowie knife between her teeth and a beaver skin hanging from her belt.

The Boy Scout motto is 'Be Prepared', and I was now in a constant state of preparation for any girl or woman in uniform (See Susannah York, Helen Mirren, Wonder Woman, and a Russian girl called Helga.)

Secondary School Looms or Bobbing and Weaving with Wendy

As John Lennon wobbled precariously on Yoko's white stepladder in the Indica Gallery, I was in my last year at Park School under the guidance of a kindly gentleman who happened to be the perfect body-double of Field Marshall Bernard Montgomery.

He ran his classroom like a microcosm of British society, with his pupils spread before him in an orderly line of decreasing ability starting at base camp with the brightest, and finishing top right with me ... the lonely goat herder. No troublemaker. Just a content young Herbert happily cleaning shin pads and sorting his Batman cards.

That all changed the day Monty showed a new pupil to a desk six upwardly mobile points above mine. Wendy was her name. Legs up to her knees, dress up to her chin, hair down to her eyes. She blew my top hat right off and that morning's boiled egg and soldiers immediately began doing the fandango with a swarm of agitated butterflies. I stopped fingering the Caped Crusader and retreated slowly back into my bat-cave. Exactly one hour later, I gave Robin one last playful tap on the bottom, came out, and fell head over shin pads in love.

My courting technique was, and remains, based upon the US Military's Shock and Awe tactic: basically, showering a young lady with a barrage of Tommy Cooper and Harry Worth impressions. It must have worked on Wendy because two days later I received my first-ever love token while standing at the front demonstrating the inflatable life vest strapped under each chair. She handed me a handwritten note in green felt tip: *I luv you.* Okay, so she couldn't spell, but neither could I and this was a flashing green felt-tip that even Joe 90 couldn't miss.

In an effort to move up the league table and be nearer Wendy, I began copying from text books before handing my work in, ready for the weekly change of positions. It was a success and on Monday, General Montgomery gave a rueful smile before relegating Colin Zamboozu to the back seat. Yay! I was on my way. One seat nearer to Wendy and copying so feverishly, I had to be careful not to overshoot and end up in the middle classes.

Dear reader, I'd love to say that I drew alongside Wendy and looked lovingly into her one good eye as we country danced out of the classroom and into the adult world, but that frantic whirr of recycled knowledge being stored in colour-coordinated files soon reverted to the slow chug of half empty bags being dumped by the bins. Considered thoughts about Saxon life and the Open Field Farming System was replaced by ladies hanging from Nimble hot-air balloons, and a Scottish folk duo singing *Football Crazy*.

But at least I'd had me some reciprocated love, and proved once and for all that the British education system was ripe for abuse by anyone prepared to work hard at it.

Magpie and Sue Stranks

Beatles or Stones? Osmonds or Bay City Rollers? Trumpton or Sooty? I know winkles who would die on them hills. A similar question could be asked about 1960s female children's TV presenters.

Many will share fond memories of *Blue Peter* and the expert way Val Singleton slid her hands up and down a phallic shaped squeezy bottle. But in 1968, Val faced some stiff competition from a young pretender who caught everyone off-guard with her hot pants, pigtails, and posh accent. She presented a show called *Magpie,* and, on those days when she didn't bother wearing a bra, well, let's just say a boy could lose an entire tube of Smarties down the back of his old man's armchair.

Val realised she was being usurped and those hemlines began travelling north but she knew the game was up when her opponent stripped down to some Victorian underwear for an hilarious piece with Tony Bastable. Yep. That was the day when Susan Stranks reached through our television to ruffle my hair and leave my heart akimbo.

In those days if a young person wanted a *Blue Peter* badge, they had to set aside six months to scale Mount Everest on the back of a guide dog. *Magpie* badges were way easier to get. For 'Six for Gold' all you needed to do was write a tall story! I sent mine to Thames Television hoping that Sue Stranks would fish it from the waste bin and send me the badge along with a signed photo of herself in a wet T-shirt. With luck, we might become pen-pals, culminating in her helping me out of my Boy Scout jumper. A week later, the 'Six for Gold' badge arrived, along with the rubber-stamped signatures of all three presenters. It was two inches in diameter and carried the image of a sweltering sun in sunglasses. A rare and precious thing.

I knew that wearing it outside would only serve as a target for the boy with the crossbow, so it was kept inside its very own Fort Knox – a Quality Street tin, guarded day and night by a pair of size seven tartan house slippers.

I never did get my signed photo but I'm happy to say that Suzie baby stayed in my dreams for many years, and even now occasionally pops around to borrow some sugar.

I Saw Elizabeth Taylor near the Carpet Shop in Green Street

In the 1960s, apart from a Chad Valley Give a Show projector, there were few opportunities for a young film buff to nurture and polish his little fascination. No streaming, no DVDs, and no Betamax. And the closest we got to watching anything 'on demand' was when Uncle Gordon loaded his projector with a reel marked *101 Dalmatians*, only to share ten blistering seconds of a lady disrobing before he pulled the plug and dashed upstairs for a mild heart attack. Nope, it was either waiting for the big television premieres at Christmas or Easter, or going to the cinema (formerly known as the picture house).

I've never liked the taste of brown ale, and you won't catch my old man squeezing into a cowboy outfit, but we did share a similar taste in movies. Whether it was British and American actors serving up a steaming bowl of badly injured Germans or Charles Hawtrey lifting his kilt in *Carry on Up the Kyber*, we were there, brothers in arms, chortling away. Yep. Life with Papa was simple. Be it the FA Cup Final or *Where Eagles Dare*, it was always ninety minutes of action, house lights up, and home in time for *The Magic Roundabout*.

Going to the cinema with my mum was an altogether different carton of popcorn. Musical blockbusters were very popular in those days, and she loved them. But whenever a new one was released, it always seemed to coincide with her husband doing secret stuff with MI5, so it became my job to act as her cinematic security blanket.

The day began with a brief game of hide-and-seek, and usually ended with me being dragged from behind the deckchairs and getting strapped to her shopping trolley like Hannibal Lecter. Then it was a brisk push through the streets of Plashet Grove, and straight onto the crimson carpet and polished brass accoutrements that will always be the entrance lobby of the ABC Cinema in Green Street.

Obviously, there's not much action in romantic musicals so before she could pluck her first Kleenex I was usually counting the cigarette burns on the seat in front. Week after week, she wheeled me back for the next musical torture. *Sound of Music, Fiddler on the Roof, West Side Fucking Story*, and the epic *Oliver,* after which for some reason I developed an overwhelming desire to eat sausages. And no, I haven't forgotten Richard Harris warbling his way through *Camelot,* which was so fucking slow, I lost the use of both legs and slid under the seat in front.

She was also partial to a historical blockbuster and, admittedly, Elizabeth Taylor in *Cleopatra* kept me going with its sword-on-sword action. However, I sat through three hours and twenty minutes of *Doctor Zhivago,* and never once saw Omar Sharif fill out a prescription.

In the lobby afterwards, while brushing stray popcorn from her cardigan, she pointed to a poster advertising another forthcoming musical torture, *My Fair Lady,* and while adjusting my ropes for the long push home she said:

"Ooh, I love Audrey Hepburn! Do you fancy it?"

Actually, what I fancied was a Raleigh Chopper so, as she fastened my hockey mask, I gave this muffled response:

"Quith pro quo a Chopper bike Clarith."

She stared at me. A minute passed. Then another. Then, shrugging her shoulders, she began pushing me along Green Street while singing to bemused Pakistani shop keepers:

"Who will buy my sweet red roses? Two blooms for a penny?"

End of School Report: 'He couldn't have done much better if he had tried.'

In 1969, while John and Yoko tied the knot in a set of hotel bedsheets in Amsterdam, I was following the exploits of a cartoon clown in a French text book. And thanks to that little clown I can now shout *'Zut Alors!'* whenever France gets knocked out of the World Cup.

Summer term took its toll on Mr Perryman. It began with him being a virile doppelgänger of General Montgomery, and finished with him slumped over a desk like Captain Mainwaring. And as this was his last gig before retirement, it was agreed he should spend a week in France with thirty of his noisiest pupils at a hotel called *Les Enfants Anglais ne sont pas les Bienvenus.*

The hotel was typically French, with continental breakfasts, complimentary berets, strings of onions, and every bathroom having a mysterious knee-high basin. Janet Freshwater told us they were for cleaning our bums, but, to be honest, we just stood in ours and pissed across the bathroom into a Tizer bottle.

It was great being on tour. We visited a monastery in Normandy called Mont St Michel, where I bought three, coloured glass balls in a rope net to help my nan during the annual herring harvest in Forest Gate. The rest of the week we played football, curling lightweight beach balls like Pelé and Jairzinho, and generally showing off to the girls.

We couldn't put our fingers on it. Girls who were once mortal enemies now looked completely different! Whatever it was, it spurred us on to do ever more fancy football trickery like no-hands throw-ins, three-legged penalties, and keepy-uppies with a greased piglet.

You know that old saying, 'What goes on tour – stays on tour'?

Well, nothing went on … except I still can't join a queue in a Post Office without remembering that holiday in France when one of those little cockney buttercups made such a big impression on this particular bilingual-overhead-scissor-kicker,

Me and the Phantom were standing behind her in the Bureau de Poste, waiting to send postcards home to our parents who were busy throwing wild extravagant parties. She had her hair in pigtails and with her short starched dress and ankle-high trainers, she looked like Florence from the *Magic Roundabout*. Her name was Kim and she approached the counter and with great confidence, spoke in perfect Franglais:

Kim: *Bonjour, mademoiselle. May I have quatro stumps seafood plate?*

The Phantom: *Fuck Moi.*

The Postmistress: *Zut alors!* (falling backwards onto a pile of parcels)

Turns out Kim was a linguistic genius who went on to have a distinguished career at the Foreign Office, and now lives in Norwich with a man called Dylan and a Skye Terrier with no legs who glides silently across the carpet.

Back home in Stratford, there was one final hurdle to climb before boarding the last train to secondary school. The 11 Plus (known by Margaret Thatcher and the Department of Education as 'dead heading').

Ours was at the same time as George Harrison released *All Things Must Pass:* a hauntingly poignant song about the transient nature of human existence ... but absolutely no fucking use helping me pass the 11 Plus.

I might've stood a chance if the questions were on Season 1 of *Flipper.* But no. Instead, they asked unfathomable things like how many apples Mr Green sold to Mr White after he'd shot Mr Pink in the buffet car on a train travelling backwards at 30mph.

Results were in. Instead of going to Stratford Grammar, I was off to Rokeby Apprehensive School for Boys. Whatever the fuck that was.

In 1969, a prom was a leisurely stroll along Margate sea-front, not the chance for an emotional smooch to *Lilly the Pink.* Consequently, our last day was a low-key affair involving chasing down slices of Battenberg with beakers of diluted squash while playing boardgames like Mousetrap or Frustration (surely a metaphor for life even with its revolutionary Pop-O-Matic action).

And that was that. Nil-nil at half time. Teachers had done their best, and if it wasn't for Jimmy Greaves, Adam West and Freddie Frinton, I might now be the Prime Minister of England or the King of Italy. Instead, I'm skint and typing this in a snug pair of counterfeit Calvin Klein underpants.

Excuse me for a moment ... ah, that's better.

East Ham Boys and West End Shops

First day of the summer holidays and I woke up with tingling toes and an overwhelming desire to squeeze into a sequinned leotard. What a dream I had. Tap dancing around Brown's Fishing Tackle shop with Sue Stranks looking on approvingly from behind a rack of Barbour coats.

Only one snag. I've seen enough family parties to know that men will only step on a dance floor when dragged there by a team of brewers' Drays. But wasn't it Elvis who got the girls shook up with his Little Shimmy Osmond? And what would I give to pirouette down Tennyson Road leaving a trail of glittering stardust before scissor kicking Bobby the Bastard in the nuts when he jumps out from behind a parked car? Man, if I learned to dance, I could do ten minutes behind Nana Mouskouri, and earn enough money for an ABU zoom all-England 13-foot match rod with screw-in quiver tip.

However, a quick check in my Pears' Encyclopaedia confirmed that professional dancers follow a strict diet, which meant NOT going out with my old mate 'Spotted Dick and his Merry Band of Bread Puddings'. Sod that. A career considered and discarded without leaving my Geoff Hurst pyjamas.

So, with nothing on telly until *Paint Along with Nancy*, I decided to catch the bus to East Ham and spend the day loafing about with Cousin Jeff. You know, simple stuff: playing football, shooting air rifles, or spending an hour ironing the wrinkles from his Subbuteo pitch.

I found him sitting on the pavement, weeping over his post office savings book.

'I need more money, Smudge,' he said sadly.

Dear reader, today my little cousin is a multi-millionaire businessman whose international products carry the royal seal of approval but in 1970 he was just another light-fingered little cockney. So, it was his idea to top up those savings by catching a Red Bus Rover to a place where American tourists were handing over five pounds for a strawberry Mivvi. London. The greatest city in the world, twinned with the 1959 British Heavyweight Champion, Mr Brian London.

By tea time, the two of us were back in East Ham with pockets full of plunder from West End department stores. Key rings, diaries and floaty pens, ready to sell at knock-down prices. It was a thrilling and well-paid little racket which continued throughout that summer. Each visit we lifted ever more expensive items until we convened one day in Carnaby Street with a cheesecloth T-shirt with diamanté peace symbol, and a pair of gold Wellingtons from Biba. Top quality stuff but very difficult to offload over a playground in East Ham.

We were also taking a massive risk of getting caught in possession by Uncle Charlie, so we gave up the wholesale thieving and Butch Cassidy had to find another way to top up his dwindling supply of silver coins.

In the meantime, *(opens car boot and looks both ways)* how you off for a 1969 Liberty desk diary?

My Dad's Knob or Kirsty Young and the Yellow Tennis Ball

Lido is Italian for beach. The English translation is a freezing expanse of clear liquid; chemical composition: 60% water, 30% chlorine, 9% urine and 1% Robinson's Barley Water.

It became apparent during the First World War that many of England's finest were badly undernourished and in need of some healthy exercise. So, the government dug a series of large holes around the country and filled them with water before cordially inviting local dignitaries to relieve themselves in the shallow end. After a quick thumbs up from the Lady Mayor, another Lido was born.

But there was a problem. Taking a dip in one of those vast areas of unheated water was responsible for more intakes of breath than an entire box set of *Debbie Does Scott of the Antarctic* DVDs. Basic training was definitely recommended.

I did mine at Clacton-on-Sea. Watched by my cheering family, I leant into a cold, north easterly in a pair of knitted woollen trunks, gusset full of wet sand, and edged out into the freezing seawater until it lapped at my preschool winkle. Then, and only then, could I take a wee into the North Sea like that little bronze boy in Brussels. By the tender age of four, the Junior Sea Cadet badge was mine, thank you very much, thank you very, very, very much.

Lessons continued on Sunday mornings at the world-famous West Ham swimming baths where a plaque in the lobby confirmed that Captain Matthew Webb had trained before becoming the first man to cover himself in lard and swim the English Channel. It was here I received my first introduction to a gentleman's changing room: a curious mixture of Old Holborn, chlorine and legionella.

After getting undressed together in a small cupboard, my father handed our belongings to a man trapped inside a wire cage, along with this friendly warning:

"Here you go mate … and I know exactly how much is in the fucking wallet."

Then it was into the shallow end where the old man stood like the Rock of Gibraltar while I paddled around him like a little royal yacht.

Occasionally, terrible screams would reverberate around the tiled walls and Victorian roof lights as grown men launched themselves from the top diving board like Johnny Weissmuller, only to enter the water horizontally with loud stinging belly flops.

"Never be a flash bastard, boy," the old man warned helpfully.

It would've been around 1964, in one of those musty old changing rooms, that I saw my old man's knob for the first and, thank goodness, last time. Dear reader. Never has a traumatised young Herbert been more deserving of a hot Bovril and a pack of Chipmunk crisps.

By 1969, I was a full-blown junior Herbert, 2nd class, showing my licks over Whipps Cross Lido, a mere bus ride from Stratford Broadway, and a small trek along a sandy path through Epping Forest until we reached a white rendered wall and copped the first big waft of chlorine. It was the biggest Lido in the country and to the exciting sounds of splashing and laughter, we went straight into a ritual called The Dance of the Wet Changing Room Floor which involved hopping from foot to foot while removing nylon underpants over freshly polished, oxblood monkey boots. Then, your brand new Ben Sherman shirt (£7) and a pair of bleached Levis (£19), were swapped for a small brass fob and a safety pin (3d). Happy days.

On the day in question, it was me, Colin, and Sprouty heading towards the scorching sun and the white noise of a thousand people splashing in a pool the size of three football pitches, and for some unexplained reason, we decided to link arms and make a grand swaggering entrance in case our future wives were waiting poolside. Sadly, the paving slabs were so hot, we ended up skipping across them like a troupe of Irish dancers.

Undeterred, we laid down our towels by the tiered fountain, and I took my hairless body and two matching testicles to the edge of this vast arena of freezing water. After a quick knee bend, like Captain Webb, I dived in with only the remnants of a beef dripping sandwich as protection.

SFX: SPLOOSH! Followed by high-pitched underwater scream: BLAAAAHHHHHHH!

Was this how my life ended? Hanging limply in mid-water, my testicles already tucked up drinking Malibu and orange, while the sonar beep of my heart slowed to a stop?

It was touch and go, but thirty seconds later my lifeless body floated slowly to the surface where Colin was leaning over the pool.

"Is it cold?" he enquired.

And that's when I spotted her. There was no mistaking those grubby knees and the straggly blonde hair. It was The Girl from the Prefabs with those big blue eyes! Bloody hell. King Neptune had thrown me a lifeline and, this time, I was determined not to let her slip through my little webbed fingers.

On went my yellow rubber flippers and after shuffling to the edge of the pool with a yellow ping-pong ball snorkel clenched between my teeth, I jumped back in and set off like a yellow submarine with a pair of blue meanies hanging lifeless from my undercarriage. The cold never bothered me anyway.

What happened next was one of those life changing experiences.

There, trapped under a grille at the bottom of the pool, was a yellow tennis ball, and for a tennis ball it sure looked mighty sad. I tried pulling at the grille but it wouldn't budge. How did it get there? It should have been thundering around centre court or at the very least being stuffed down Anne Jones' frilly knickers, but instead the yellow furry captive was at the bottom of Whipps Cross Lido, trapped in its own silent underwater dungeon. It was a mystery alright, and would've made a great episode on *The Undersea World of Jacques Cousteau*.

For a few precious minutes I had forgotten about The Girl from the Prefabs, and by the time I up-periscoped, she was gone. What did half-boy, half-submarine do? He did what Jacques Cousteau did when that giant octopus wrapped itself around the propeller of *The Calypso*. He blubbed his bleedin' eyes out … in French:

"Merde, merde, merditty, merde."

On the bus home, we shared a triangular iced Jubbly, and its orange food colouring left us looking like sad little Oompa Loompas.

It was a big day in my underwater courting development but why did God waste a perfectly good Slazenger tennis ball, just to stop me meeting The Girl from the Prefabs?

Fifty years later, a world-weary Herbert would appear on BBC Radio 4's Desert Island Discs.

Herbert: *... and as I watched those white horses gallop across the English sky, I realised a veil was being drawn over my Swallows and Amazons summer and that the yellow tennis ball was a prophecy of what lay ahead in my search for The Girl from the Prefabs.*

Kirsty Young: *Oh what beautiful story! And may I say, (wipes away a tear) very moving. Can we have your last record?*

Herbert: *Certainly. It's that 1979 choral masterpiece I'm Only a Poor Little Sparrow by The Ramblers.*

Kirsty Young: *Hmm, nice ... let's hear it.*

The Tale of the Golden Hind

Alice was Mum's eldest sister and she produced three daughters while I was still an unwrapped cross-head screwdriver in my old man's tool box. Alice's husband did his best but everyone could tell from the unopened boxes of Meccano that he wanted someone to take fishing rather than have pretend tea parties with a selection of soft toys. So, when Cousin Jeff finally arrived, Uncle Charlie immediately rushed outside and started digging for worms. Those three sisters, Maureen, Kath and Pamela, sensed that the pack had been reshuffled but to their credit, they knuckled down and lived happily together in a little crooked house, across the road from the little crooked academy of football, known by American sport pundits as the Anne Boleyn Association Soccer Ground.

But big trouble lay ahead for my little cousin. There's an old American Indian proverb:

'Elderly Buffalo, watch out for young Eagle, and young Eagle, watch out for disgruntled elder sisters.'

Early one morning … just as the sun was rising … I heard three maidens moaning as they frog-marched me and Jeff through Stratford railway station towards Platform 8, before bundling us into the heavy smoker's carriage of the 9:15am Inter City to Southend Victoria.

Forty minutes later, Pam and Kath were filling our pockets with pebbles as Maureen suggested we paddle in the choppy waters of the Thames estuary. Then, with one last instruction to speak to as many strangers as possible, Jeff's three sisters disappeared into the Kursaal in a puff of green smoke.

Alone at last. Two intrepid explorers ready to investigate one of the world's most notorious honeypots. Las Vegas? Coney Island? Forget about it. Southend was doing that stuff before the Yanks discovered slot machines. Yesterday, Sprouty had told us that the streets of Southend were paved with gold, so when a tenner floated by … we let it go. What's the rush? We had all day. Hooray!

First up was a mid-morning brunch in a café alongside the Dolphinarium, where we tucked into some candy dummies and a plate of chocolate honeycomb, hand-crafted by local artisans. We listened to the dolphins' desperate chattering, and having watched over fifty episodes of *Flipper*, I was pretty sure they weren't enquiring about my delicious marzipan fruit.

After that, we continued along the sea wall towards the boating lake where gigantic fibreglass swans were re-enacting the Battle of Trafalgar, powered by competitive dads pedalling faster than Kevin Keegan in *Superstars*. All in all, a typical and magnificent day at Southend.

What happened next would shape our young cockney lives for at least two weeks. It was a visit to one of Southend's most iconic attractions and, ladies and gentlemen, I'm not talking about Madam Zelda's Clairvoyant Whelk Stall.

I refer, of course, to the *Golden Hind*.

When Sir Francis Drake moored up alongside Southend's famous mile-long pier, I don't suppose for one moment he expected his ship to be commandeered by an enterprising Southend council, have the guts ripped out of it, and a hand-painted painted sign with no punctuation hung from the masthead:

WAXWORK CHILDREN WELCOME

To show punters what to expect, there was a Perspex window showing a scene from *The Pit and the Pendulum* with a poor wretch with bulbous eyes, stretched out with a mechanical axe swinging above his chest, all overseen by a Cromwellian soldier, a crushed packet of Bensons and a discarded tin of 3-IN-ONE. This light-hearted tableau worked perfectly to entice families to skip through the turnstiles ... only to run screaming out the other side with damp shorts and wet knickers.

Not even that episode of *This is Your Life* when Eamonn Andrews dressed in a ball gown to surprise Lionel Blair had prepared us for the barbaric medieval tortures on display. Guillotines, thumb screws and branding irons, all made worse by the faces on the models bearing a distinct resemblance to popular celebrities. For example, the hooded monk with the branding iron most definitely had the beaming face of Tommy Steele, and three members of the Spanish Inquisition looked suspiciously like the Beverly Sisters.

Dear reader, Jeff and I were world-weary young cock-a-leekies, but even we needed a whole bottle of Sexton Blake's Stiff Upper Lip just to look at the floor and hurry past each exhibit. And we would've got away with it too if not for the grinning face of Bob Monkhouse inside a diving helmet being filled with bubbling water. I'm not kidding, we ran straight into Peter Pan's Playground and didn't calm down running until we were holed up safely inside The Crooked House.

That night was spent in Aunt Alice's spare bedroom, where we sat up in our pyjamas like Morecombe and Wise, discussing man's inhumanity to man. The bed was made from three double mattresses piled on top of each other, and was supremely comfortable as long as you didn't turn too quickly and propel your partner out the other side onto the Scalextric track.

Up to Our Necks in Hookers and Sausages

Old fishing tackle shops are magical places. Like the smell of cinnamon that's pumped into Disney stores at Christmas, each tackle shop had its own distinctive aroma from the sweet vanilla, maggot sawdust and water repellent from nets and wax jackets. It was a working man's opium den. A place you could forget your troubles, have a cuppa, and toy with freshly varnished rods or coyly brush your fingers over brightly coloured floats.

Jeff got a job in Robertson's in Prince Regent's Lane which involved standing under a 40-watt bulb skinning hundreds of frozen chipolatas before mixing them with flour into balls the size of a grapefruit, and left ready for the addition of a secret ingredient. The secret ingredient was bullshit, supplied by a man who looked like

Max Wall's Professor Wallofski. His name was Mick and his job was to re-enact the capture of giant carp using his own sound effects of line zinging from a reel, as mighty fish swam off with mouthfuls of special sausage meat.

Thanks mostly to my cousin's frostbitten digits, local anglers and meat suppliers were soon queuing for one of Mick's performances. He even did a Saturday matinee, with indoor fireworks and split-cane ear-trumpets for the hard-of-hearing.

After our exploits on Sandown Pier, we were both fully committed to the adrenalin-fuelled hobby of sitting by a pond eating cheese, and we didn't have a care in the world apart from possibly drowning in a deep-sea diver's helmet. Instead of petty thieving, our days were spent retrieving tackle from trees, untangling line from cheap reels, and accumulating ever more tackle.

Dad came home one day and tossed me a canvas holdall about five-foot long. Inside was a fibreglass rod, a cheap reel, and assorted hooks and floats. Tied to the zip was an address label:

Master Wilbert Trumpington,

Some Hope,

Little Hampton,

Sussex

I suspect young Master Wilbert may still be waiting for his special delivery from those magnificent men at the British Road Service.

Life was good but it was no box of chocolates (Forest Gump), or a bowl of All-Bran (The Small Faces).

On a golden pond in Manor Park, two boys from the genus Yobbo Yobbo Nauti Nauti Arseholus helped my new fishing rod arc gracefully through the air before splashing far out into the pea-green pond. Unlike Excalibur, it didn't rise again, so I began the long walk home wondering how to tell my old man. You'll never guess what happened. Outside West Ham swimming baths, I found a five-pound note fluttering on the pavement. It was a sign! A sign that I shouldn't tell the old man and instead go straight to a hardware shop in West Ham Lane which sold fishing tackle as well as mousetraps, paraffin and galvanised buckets. With the fiver I was able to buy a new fibreglass rod and an Intrepid reel formerly known as the Prince.

From being an *Aladdin Sane* and feeling *Low*, everything was now *Hunky Dory*, and the old man never found out that his only son couldn't punch his way out of Major Tom's handbag.

A Night on Bare Mountain

Thanks to the continuing generosity of BRS customers, I soon had enough tackle for a three-month expedition up the Zamboozu, and every Saturday afternoon, I set off with a team of donkeys for base camp (Jeff's house), within earshot of the despairing groans from Upton Park. Once there, Aunt Alice laid out a delicious roast dinner while Uncle Charlie watched Les Kellet and Jackie Pallo wrestle themselves to the floor at the Poplar Baths.

When the roads were clear of men bent double from carrying the heavy burden that comes from supporting London's finest team, Uncle Charlie climbed behind the wheel of his blue Ford Anglia and gunned its powerful 997cc engine while me and Jeff filled its generous boot with cheese sandwiches. A quick trot down the A13 and by 7pm we were at a gravel pit in Aveley, hunkered down between gigantic aggregate mountains and watching orange-tipped peacock quills ride along on the crest of the wave. And by 9pm, as the sun cast its own lines across the deep gravel pit, I offered upwards this simple ditty to the tune of Arthur Askey's Bee song:

"Oh, what a glorious thing to be, fishing a pond owned by the Blue Circle Cement Company."

It was usually around sun-set that Uncle Charlie began waving his arms madly.

"These ... fuckin'... poxy ... fuckin' ... midges!"

There were clouds of the little blighters, loitering with intent, tag-teaming with Kamikaze mosquitoes to dive bomb the shit out of him until dark, when low flying bats finished the job under a bomber's moon.

Meanwhile I sat twenty yards away under Wilbert Trumpington's fishing umbrella, shivering my nuts off and vowing never to go night fishing again, wearing only a jungle hat and a 1971 West Ham away shirt.

It's All Swings and Roundabouts, or, The Tale of the Chopper

West Ham Recreation Ground. Once a monastery, then a brewery, now a place for The Children of the Revolution to hang around eating Quavers. It had all the usual playground equipment including a six-seater rocking horse with flared nostrils which rocked so viciously my cousin flew right off and landed in a rhododendron bush. She still carries the scar and for some reason blames me. Sorry, Theresa.

But it was The Slide which stood head and shoulders above the rest. Tall as a double-decker, its enclosed upper platform provided the perfect place for a young man to smoke a cigarette or read a newspaper before making his descent. Depending on atmospheric conditions, this meant flying down so fast you shot straight into the paddling pool, or else getting stuck halfway down and having to complete the journey like a giant crab. Those old slides were so high, an orderly procession of climbers and sliders was absolutely imperative because any backlog around the upper platform meant bundles of gaily coloured rags plummeting twenty feet to the tarmac.

I was up there one morning, reading an interesting article in an *Eagle* annual, when below me a young man jumped onto my bike and sped away as fast as his little thieving toe-rag legs could fucking carry him. By the time I got down to ground zero, my bike had disappeared. A sad day. Brightened only by the opportunity to replace it with the sexiest bike of all time!

My father's response was similar to Brigette Bardot's after Peter Glaze invited her to the Crackerjack Pantomime, so I bought some Turkish Delight and set up my Chad Valley Projector to give my mother a Power Point presentation about the pros and cons of The Raleigh Chopper, its importance in our consumer society and the joy it brings to any boy looking for the meaning of life. It was a compelling case, especially when I played my joker and sang *Mother of Mine* in the style of 11-year-old 1971 Opportunity Knocks winner Neil Reid:

"Mother of mine, you gave to me all of my life to do as I please ... I owe everything I have to yooooooou ... mother ... sweet mother of mine."

Clambering down from the dining table, I turned with tears in my eyes.

Herbert: *Well, what do you reckon?*

Mum: (looking out of the window) *What about, love?*

Thanks a fucking lot, mother, sweet mother of mine.

Undeterred, I roped myself to her ankles and for the next two weeks relinquished every ounce of self respect until she agreed to fund a new bike.

Can you guess what she chose for a replacement?

Was it a) the super spunky Raleigh *Chopper*, including fantasticola handlebars, wing mirrors, twin chrome cow horns, long padded high-back seat and a T-shaped gear stick? Or b) the effeminate Moulton *Shopper*, a small-wheeled bike for the busy London commuter favoured by female go-getters like Tara King, finished in a powder blue with a high-pitched tinkling bell and handy grocery basket?

Did you guess? Well, here's another clue for you all.

Picture my father in a phone box outside Eddy Grimstead's bike shop on the Barking Road, finger in one ear trying to hear his wife over the busy rush hour traffic.

Dad: *Jean is that you? Are you sure the boy asked for a Shopper?*

I never had my bike stolen again, even when it was left unattended with a sign reading 'PLEASE HELP YOURSELF'.

Cricket Balls and the Tonka Toy Ambulance

Throughout those crazy hazy Dave Dee Dozy days of summer, it seemed that every football in Newham had fucked off over the horizon like the final scene from Albert Lamorisse's film *The Red Balloon*. To fill the sporting vacuum, cricket bats were retrieved from under the stairs and used to smash cheap wooden stumps into the rock-hard pitches of West Ham Recreation Ground, opposite the bingo hall.

Goodbye Gary Sprake and Colin (ding dong) Bell. Hello Gary

Sober and Colin (tinkerty tonk) Cowdrey.

Like most twelve-year-old boys, I was fluent in stupidity with fearlessness as a second language, and it took a few times before I realised the damage a cricket ball hurtling at 30mph could do to the body of a finely tuned young athlete.

The first was when Freddy Gillard sent one hopping onto my top lip, leaving me teetering in circles like a mighty Scots pine, before flopping limply to the ground like a pole-axed Brontë sister. With a mouthful of loose teeth, I wandered home, lips like Mick Jagger after a session on a Zoom ice lolly.

Next week, I was back and seriously overestimating the protection offered by a pair of pale-blue nylon underpants. Inevitably, I copped one six inches below my elasticated snake belt and while Buster and Little Jocky were rushed to hospital in a white Tonka Toy ambulance, Fred's younger brother delivered one of the biggest sporting travesties of 1969: out KBW (Knob Before Wicket).

Once again, I wobbled home and watched *Playschool* with a pack of frozen prawns on my throbbing testicles as Brian Cant bounced around on a bright orange Space Hopper, with Humpty and Jemima looking on, totally nonplussed.

With Buster and Little Jocky fully recovered, I ventured to the crease one last time. However, even after stuffing a Tupperware box down my underpants, I still felt strangely exposed. Turns out Buster and Little Jocky were still behind the boundary line, relaxing in two tiny deckchairs, and sipping Pina Coladas. Traitors!

So be it! I didn't graduate from The Sherpa Tensing School of Cricket for nothing. As Fred wiped his Doctor Marten's in the dust like a raging bull, I thumped the bat onto the crease and squinted towards the figure now hurtling towards me, preparing to release one of his 50mph heat-seeking googlies.

Ladies and gentlemen, I'm afraid I was out second ball.

Mr Plumb in the Bathroom, having a Barclays behind the Lead Piping

Father's mission that Sunday morning was to replace the draughty sashes in our front room with some trendy space-age aluminium louvres. Dear reader, if Barry Bucknell had seen my Papa doing his stretching exercises with a tool belt waving around under his belly, I reckon Britain's first celebrity DIY expert would've ridden his Black & Decker work-horse to the top of the Post Office Tower, and very publicly tossed himself off.

DIY wasn't my old man's favourite hobby. In fact, he didn't have a hobby unless you count clearing a room using his home-made mustard gas. He knew his way around a paint brush alright, but fixing a shelf usually involved plenty of slapdash, some haphazard, and a smidgeon of brute-force. For this window job his tool kit was simple: a crowbar and a Mario Lanza LP.

It was bleak midwinter and the perfect time for a young man to sit in a freezing front room watching Jack Hargreaves wrestle a cod from the blustery North Sea while his father ran through his entire repertoire of blood-curdling blasphemies. Three hours later, the front room smelt of linseed oil, Jack had landed a 20lb cod, and I was sitting in a duffel coat with a dew drop dangling perilously from my little frozen hooter. Mum came in to inspect the trendy new window.

Dad: (proudly) *Well … what do you think?*

Mum: *Oh, Charlie they're lovely. Actually, I'm not sure …what do you think?*

Dad: *Oh, for fuck's sake, Jean!*

I loved our old front room. It was safe and cosy. Everyone needs a laughing place and that was mine. It mattered not one jot that the pavement was so close that you could hear passers-by complaining about 'the fucking council'. During the 1970's power cuts, we sat there, snuggled together by candlelight, sharing a tin of sardines and singing *We Shall Overcome* while our resident mouse strolled casually across the carpet making Mum scream hysterically.

At the far end of the room was a door leading to a blast furnace called The Kitchen. Inside, it was an oven with four gas rings and a high-level grill going full blast. Beside it was the outline of a woman in a snowstorm of flour, cracking eggs and whisking away like Mr Kipling's demented lover. At the rear of the kitchen was a sliding door leading into a small room with a bath and handbasin. From there was another door, like a set of Russian dolls, which led into a cramped toilet. Inside the cramped toilet was another door hiding a hot water cylinder. And behind the hot water cylinder was a 1968 mint copy of Swedish erotica obtained by swapping a Webley air pistol.

And it was here that I sat, trousers around ankles, studying those black and white pictures and trying to work out why any plumber worth his salt would stand before the lady of the house wearing only a cravat and a pair of sunglasses? From inside that little room I would dream about The Girl from the Prefabs. Did she remember our brief encounter? Was she brushing her hair at a dressing table and humming that old Kodak classic *Someday My Prints Will Come*?

Do you want to know a secret? Do you promise not to tell? When it all got too much, that little philosophical Herbert would adjust his GI helmet and help himself to a well-earned Sherman.

Tell Me Why I Don't Like Sundays

Outside the kitchen, covered in a light dusting of self-raising flour, was a small wooden coffin on legs. It was called a radiogram, and every Saturday morning a man inside it called Stewpot read music requests and birthday messages to children around the country, including their age and full address for anyone taking notes. *Junior Choice* had a regular audience of over *eleven* million which allowed the BBC to brainwash an entire generation of young citizens with comedy, pop and classical records. Ten years later, those children would become anarchic Punk Rockers and burn brightly for a few years before handing the baton to the New Romantics who cocked the whole thing up.

Ed Stewart: *I've a request here for John Lydon of Benwell Road, Holloway. He is 10 today and his mum has asked for anything by Andy Stewart. Well, John, we hope you have a lovely day and here's Andy Stewart singing Donald Where's your Trousers?*

On Sunday mornings, the coffin opened for business around 9am with Al Martino circling in a holding pattern while Tom Jones serenaded his biggest fan singing *With These Hands*. At 11am, her husband came inside after spending two hours cleaning his brushes, ready to paint the new window while Cliff Michelmore and Billy Cotton wrestled in figure-hugging briefs for the right to become the UK's family favourite. At 12:30pm, that hilarious northern bastard Jimmy Clitheroe began pedalling his awful jokes around the front room, which was my cue to run up the off-licence for two bottles of Newcastle Brown and a bottle of Tizer.

At 1pm sharp, the entire country sat down for a roast beef dinner (*phew*).

Ten minutes later, Mum set up a large pasting table with a selection of homemade desserts including lemon meringue, apple pie, rice pudding, spotted dick, bread and butter pudding, treacle pudding and apple crumble. Disappearing back into the kitchen, she then returned with a sweet trolley loaded with rhubarb tart, more rice pudding, baked apple and ice cream, tinned orange flan with Carnation milk and treacle tart and custard.

How I maintained the body of a finely tuned Harry Secombe I shall never know.

After dinner, while Mum stalked the kitchen with her Ronco Mouse-Chop-O-Matic, my father gallantly began washing up. He did this by tossing me the tea towel and sitting down to watch *The Big Match*. Then we all watched a war film involving a German POW camp which was father's cue to send flatulent Morse code messages to the French Resistance. Around 4pm, with both sentries asleep, I touched base with John Steed and Tara King (if she wasn't tied up) until 5pm when Papa lifted his backside and let one go.

Off went the telly.

On went the radiogram, and Charlie Chester floated into the front room, closely followed by the smell of a Heinz Toast Topper.

That, my friends, is what you call a Sunday afternoon.

World Cups 1966 and 1970, and Peter 'The Cat' Bonetti

As The Beatles put the finishing touches to *Paperback Writer,* the uniformed butlers at the Football Association moved between wing-backed chairs, lifting newspapers from upturned faces and whispering: *'Wake up, sir. It's time'*. Yep, those red-eyed, white-haired, blue-blazered Rip Van Winkles of the FA were taking a well-earned breather after shagging their way through lines of beautiful hookers for the right to host the 1966 FIFA World Cup. Now it was time for them to head off to Luton Airport and welcome some of the greatest football teams in the world ... and the Argentinians.

Before the tournament began, the Football Association sprang into action by losing the priceless Jules Rimet trophy from inside a partially nailed unguarded hardboard display cabinet. Detective

'Nipper' Branston was asked to stop planting drugs on members of The Beatles and look for a lead. He found one. It was on a dog called Pickles, who led him to the trophy hidden under a bush. As a reward, Pickles got a new collar, and 'Nipper' went back to planting Mars Bars on or about Marianne Faithfull.

The tournament ran like a well-lubricated Tory minister. Boy Scouts fulfilled all ball-boy duties, and only six police officers were required to control a good-natured and only slightly racist crowd. The tournament ended with Queen Elizabeth knighting the Russian linesman and flashing Bobby Moore one of her dazzling smiles as I joined a twenty-a-side down Whalebone Lane until it was time for tea and *Meet the Wife*.

England winning the World Cup? No big deal. We won everything.

For the next four years, I studied the Little Indoctrinated Citizen Exam (*LICE*), convinced England would win again at the 1970 World Cup in Mexico, with the finest team in a generation. The squad were so good they even released a record that would knock *Paperback Writer* from No.1, and include a B side with twenty of England's finest footballers singing about a stick of cinnamon.

It was Sunday in England and midday in Mexico. England had strolled through to the quarter-finals and we settled down to watch the satellite broadcast. Dad took on extra fluids and I wore a Chad Valley oxygen mask for the altitude, both confident that Bobby Moore's trumped-up charge for stealing a bracelet and Gordon Banks' upset stomach wouldn't stop Alf Ramsey getting his second knighthood and World Cup Willie winning a weekend away with the Esso tiger. Twenty minutes to go and England were comfortably beating the Germans 2-0. Then, after some poor handling from Peter Bonetti, England's replacement goalie, the Germans went on to win.

I looked at Dad. He looked at me. No words were spoken. In Mexico, David Coleman went into one. In Stratford, Dad went into the kitchen where I overheard the following muffled conversation:

Mum: *Well, how did they get on?*

Dad: *How did they get on? I'll tell you how they* (undecipherable) *got on! That useless* (sounded like 'plucking') *Peter Bonetti. Calls himself 'The Cat'? I'll tell you what. He's a useless* (undecipherable but sounded like ponce).

Mum: *Oh dear. Do you fancy a sandwich?*

Dad: *Yeah, alright … got any tinned salmon?*

The kitchen door opened and the cat rushed upstairs to hide under the bed.

A Journey to Chronic Chest Problems

As raggedy arsed children of Great Britain hurried between social engagements, a selection of tobacco-related confectionery was provided to ease their journey towards a hacking cough and two brown fingers. Very popular was the industry standard, white candy cigarette with red tip. Also available were liquorice pipes and chewing tobacco (coconut strands), and for boys who could appreciate a nice cardigan there was a chocolate pipe and lighter gift box. Me? I favoured a plastic cigarette whose tip glowed and issued a puff of white smoke like the announcement of the new Pope.

This pubescent smoking paraphernalia was all fine and dandy but a glowing red tip was never going to be enough to impress the classy young broad doing handstands against the off-licence wall. Even upside down she exuded sophistication, and I was especially drawn by the way she tucked her dress into her knickers. Yup, the only way to grab her attention was to get some of those chocolate cigarettes which came in replica soft packs like American Airforce pilots on board a Flying Fortress. I got a pack and headed off with my co-pilot, Flight Lieutenant C. Zamboozu. Ten yards from the target I shook the pack and with a cool flick of the wrist sent one upwards to my mouth like Robert Mitchum in *To Catch a Snout in a Dead Man's Mouth*. Dear reader, have you ever tried controlling a bucking Flying Fortress with a chocolate cigarette lodged up your right nostril? Thought not. Colin and I aborted the mission, turned for home and spent the rest of the day sitting on a kerb gobbing down a drain.

The dangers of passive smoking were still a well-kept secret so family elders puffed away merrily while we played Mousey Mousey in a haze of Kensitas. Some nights it was like a scene from *A Foggy Day in London Town* and I remember Uncle Charlie doing his best to put us off smoking by saying it would 'stunt your growth' which was pretty rich coming from a sixty-a-day man built like Giant Haystacks.

The closest I came to packing it in was during a football match over Temple Mills where, instead of a half time slice of orange, we shared a solitary Benson. This was a regular practice and quite acceptable as long as everyone adhered to the strict social etiquettes:

1. Always take a brief *lug* rather than a leisurely *drag*.
2. Never put too much filter into your mouth and *bum* it.

Any minor transgression could result in a group kicking, so, in retrospect, I got away lightly.

On the day in question, a cigarette was being passed around and I decided not to use my Adidas ivory cigarette holder, and instead took a huge lungful – held it for a few seconds – before blowing the residue smoke out of my nose like a cool-as-fuck Bernie Winters. Team mates looked on as Colin broke the stunned silence:

"Give it back, you cunt ... you look like a fucking dragon."

The Colour TV and All That Sail in Her or The Bombing of Poole Harbour

Unlike Meadowlark Lemon, Ferguson Colour Star never played for the Harlem Globetrotters, mainly because Ferguson was a 22-inch colour television. The day he arrived, I took the day off school, poured myself a tumbler of 10-year-old ginger wine, and watched the Test Card in glorious colour.

There wasn't much else in the way of daytime viewing, just the occasional school programme and a bearded man discussing degree-level calculus. Things perked up briefly for a *Playschool* lady in a pink dress, but after a particularly dour episode of *Crown Court,* the dairy, as my old mum would say, was definitely wearing off.

Fortunately, the day was saved by a steady stream of public information films.

These little films taught us everything from Keeping Britain Tidy to how to survive a nuclear blast by climbing inside a school desk. And thanks to Kevin Keegan and Alvin Stardust, a generation of scatterbrained children are now able to skip safely across the M25 and take tea in the central reservation. But of all those public-spirited five-minute masterpieces there was one so thrilling that when it came on, Buster and Little Jocky would rush downstairs and settle alongside me to watch.

It was to deter young smokers by suggesting a prospective boy or girlfriend would be repulsed by your stinky tobacco breath. To prove the point, a husky-voiced London girl took a moment from her Capstan Full Strength to snog a boy who then pulled a face and staggered backwards before falling theatrically into a canal. Only one problem: they had seriously underestimated their target audience because there wasn't a boy in Greater London who wouldn't wait patiently in line for a kiss from that young actress/chimney. Personally, I would've ripped out my lungs and laid them at her feet with an ounce of Old Holborn.

From then on, every girl smoker looked especially flighty, ready to drag me to the nearest tobacconist for a good seeing-to. I believe the actress was a young Linda Robson and I continued fantasising about that smoky-voiced cockney harlot throughout most of 1969, the early part of 1970, and a particularly slow Christmas Eve in 1976.

Of course, there were easier ways to overcome this smelly breath conundrum, and that's to spend a weekend with the 11th Newham Scout Group, because a beret and rucksack pretty much guaranteed there wouldn't be a girl for fucking miles. However, those camping weekends did give us free rein to develop double bronchitis with complications as we puffed away like laboratory Beagles.

Dear reader, there now follows a dark tale that would have likely earned the public information people a BAFTA for most compelling children's drama involving twenty Benson & Hedges.

Picture the scene. A group of uniformed boys (collective noun: a pack. Singular noun: a knob) waiting at Poole Harbour to catch a boat to Brownsea Island (owned by the National Trust and used by the Scout Association). To kill time, a few Boy Scouts were attempting their Shoplifting Proficiency Badge in the harbour gift shops. The choice that summer for light-fingered little cunts was glass stink bombs, and groups of clean-cut Boy Scouts stamping on them inside the shops provided good cover for those of us more experienced in casual thievery.

I'm ashamed to say that I stole a small leather dictionary for my old man and a barometer in the shape of a lifebelt for Mum. The tacky sea-side lifebelt quickly found its way into my mother's priceless artefact bin, but the old man used that little dictionary for many years. When I told him forty years later that it had been stolen, it went straight in the bin. Not kidding.

Anyway. Fully stocked with stink bombs, Jelly Tots and a packet of Benson & Hedges, we caught the ferry to Brownsea Island and pitched camp. Then, after emptying two gallons of disinfectant into a bucket with a toilet seat on it, we set off to explore and found a deserted pebble beach where I could stare out to sea like Jack Hawkins in *The Cruel Sea,* puffing merrily through those Bensons.

Until then my lungs had been accustomed to a gentle drip of ¾ inch dog ends. Now, with that tidal surge of nicotine, the Compass Rose began listing badly and ended with me depositing a large portion of sausage and baked beans over the smooth cool pebbles while simultaneously crapping my regulation grey shorts.

And that, dear children, is how Brownsea Island got its name.

Pool Balls, Spermatozoa, and the Olympic Park

Bad news from the front. According to a boy we met at the top of the slide, our new secondary school was like *The Clockwork Orange,* full of sadistic ultra-violence. So, to take our minds off the imminent threat of a punctured lung, me and my droogs joined a youth club offering low price floodlit football.

Our journey took us across the central island on Stratford Broadway where a granite obelisk commemorated that old philanthropist and stretcher bearer, Samuel Gurney. There was also an old drinking trough for horses, and some subterranean toilets for anyone caught short galloping across six lanes of busy London traffic. There was an attendant down there who oversaw proceedings from a room big enough for a man to boil a kettle and lay his head upon a *Daily Mirror*, and the unwritten code amongst local yobbos was to venture down a few steps and rouse the poor soul with a chorus of '*WAKE UP, YOU LAZY CUNT!*'

Happy days ... unless you were a toilet attendant.

Carpenters Road Youth Club. The perfect place for a youngster to enjoy a cup of tea and lose their change on a Jokers Wild fruit machine. Before handing over my two-shilling subs, I watched two boys clump the fuck out of each other with pool balls. I had two choices. No.1: wet myself. No.2: join a large group playing football under the lights. I chose No.2, with a hint of No.1, and played into the night. I did alright and went back a few times before calling it a day when Lynda Crystal and Julian Orchard made an offer I couldn't refuse on BBC2, with a double header of *The High Chapparal* and Milligan's *Beachcomber*.

It turned out that one of those boys tearing the other a new arse would be in my new class and later show everyone his penis, on which he had drawn, in blue biro no less, a tiny facsimile of a solitary long-tailed sperm, insisting it been stranded there since his last bout of lovemaking. His name was Victor and the boy was a genius.

What happened to that old pool table? Well, forty years later it was heaved onto a skip to make way for a nine-billion-pound Olympic Park which David Cameron promised would make Stratford E.15 the most desirable postcode in East London. Oh well, that's okay, then.

Tom Brown's School Days without the Top Hats and White Breeches

And so it came to pass that only a few months after The Beatles' Apple Roof Top Concert, I headed off for my first day at secondary school, dressed not in my favoured field marshall uniform, but in an over-size black blazer and grey trousers, finishing two inches shy of a brand new pair of black clodhoppers. I was sailing very close to Charlie Cairoli territory and to top it all I was carrying a black plastic briefcase from Rathbone Market, which contained top-secret military plans and a woodworking apron. That briefcase turned out to be the perfect aerodynamic shape for my new chums at the rough 'n' tough Rokeby High School for Highly Strung Delinquent Boys with Antisocial Tendencies.

By lunchtime I had watched two fist fights and another 1st Year being lowered into a cauldron of boiling piss. None-the-less, after swapping the briefcase for a Gola sports bag, Rokeby became the perfect place to have a laugh while learning SAS survival techniques from some of Stratford's finest.

The main building was architecturally inspiring if you like flat roofs, aluminium windows and hard-wearing concrete, and the daily routine was one of casual violence peppered with long periods of standing in the rain while teachers bellowed.

"Right. We're gonna stand here all day until someone tells me who pushed the bloody fire alarm!"

The four Houses were Forest (*Gate*), Upton (*Park*), Abbey (*Mills*), and Manor (*Park*). The headteacher was Mr Scott or, as we called him, *'Yes, sir, sorry, sir'*. He wore black tinted glasses and stalked the corridors with a black cape billowing behind him like Ozzy Osbourne. The story was that he had been blinded during a gas attack, and was now seeking revenge on society by scaring the daylights (shit) out of hard-nosed skinheads, or, as we called them, *'Yes, sir, sorry, sir'*. I only crossed him once, and as a result spent three days standing in a stress position outside his office. The stress was whether he would call my old man.

Teaching qualifications must have been less formal in the 1970s because it seemed many teachers were employed on a first-come, first-served basis. For example, the music teacher never came out from behind his *Daily Express* while his pupils memorised Newton's 3rd Law of Music (never listen to Donny Osmond).

126

The PE teacher was a former sergeant in the army. We knew this because his name, rank and serial number were stencilled onto a kit bag hung proudly from the climbing frame. He was a short-arsed bully who delighted in smashing boys across the buttocks with our own plimsolls. He also showered with us and enjoyed parading naked through the changing room, obviously proud of his very small winkle. He got his comeuppance when a fifth-former knocked seven bells and one set of wind chimes out of him after spearing his kit bag with a javelin. I'm afraid that PE teacher and his little knob was never seen again. His replacement was a round-shouldered man with ginger sideburns and a rugby shirt who introduced himself by walking up and down the sports hall bouncing a basketball, and recounting in no uncertain terms why twelve-year-old boys shouldn't fuck with him. To make his point, he fired the basketball towards the hooped net, only for it to fall short and hit the brickwork.

I reckon Jungle Jim did his teacher training overseeing the construction of the Burma Railway because any minor infringement left him fumbling excitedly for his stash of bamboo canes. He was a cruel man, but fair, and ensured everyone got at least one whack across the fingers. This man had no sense of humour, and in acts of heroism worthy of a Victoria Cross, the same few boys would regularly feign stupidity just to receive one of Jim's bamboo reprisals. And for readers who have never been smashed across the fingers with a length of bamboo, be assured that afterwards it's almost impossible to hold a pen let alone write anything. And that is why I don't have a fucking clue what Mr Jungle was supposed to be teaching.

We called the woodwork teacher Chippy because, just like the Bush Kangaroo, he was always rummaging around the front pouch of his brown overalls. His main job was to smoke roll-ups and hand out bandages to blood-stained boys. Posters around his classroom explained the production of iron *Slag* and the versatility of the *Bastard* file, which kept us amused as we hacked at lumps of wood before gluing ourselves to the finished project. The autumn term saw the wood replaced by a lump of iron, and the process repeated with the addition of a tub of bright green Swarfega.

Miss Lovejoy was an art teacher who cruised serenely around the corridors leaving a wake of teenage boys and teachers crashing into concrete columns. Even serial truants hurried back from the chip shop for one of her lessons, where she liked to drive boys crazy by walking across the desks like stepping stones, displaying her latest pair of skimpy knickers. I'm sure that when we trooped out afterwards, bent double like a troupe of hunchbacks, she opened her lunch box with a satisfied smile and tucked into a nice piece of German sausage.

PE in the Showers

Our first ever PE lesson was a cross-country run around the back streets of Stratford: a straggly line of stick-thin boys ambling along beside heavy traffic and talking jive, before putting on a heroic spurt near the finish line like a low-budget *Chariots of Fire*.

Usual rules applied. Anyone forgetting their kit hoping this would somehow preclude them from being thrown to the floor by the Judo teacher had to choose from a dustbin full of mouldy soiled strip. I clearly remember watching a football sock climb from that dustbin and inch across the wet floor before throwing itself into an overflowing urinal.

We never touched a rugby ball but tried just about everything else, from football to fencing and judo to javelin. We even dived headfirst into a long jump pit and held a robust session of five-a-side country dancing. Whatever the lesson, after forty minutes we were shepherded through the communal showers like a sheep dip. Six shower heads, thirty-five boys, and not one of us thought to bring a bar of soap!

Dear reader. Earlier in this book I referred to the smell of a gentleman's cloakroom at West Ham swimming baths. Let me tell you, it was NOTHING compared to the eye-watering atmosphere of the boys' changing rooms at Rokeby. How to put it? It was like out-of-date Cheesy Niblets in the sleeping quarters of an abandoned pig farm, and when the exit doors were eventually flung open, a musty stench set off like an invisible dirty bomb towards Stratford Broadway where lady shoppers would mysteriously collapse over the fish stall. On the plus side, we did get a healthy resistance to legionella and were shrugging off most tropical diseases by the second year.

To avoid bronchial and impotency problems later in life, every boy had to learn three stages of changing room survival.

No.1: getting dressed before the PE teacher could finish his own shower and strut around displaying his tiny knob and large pair of complimentary knackers.

No.2: getting dressed while protecting one's own bare arse from being whipped by a wet towel.

No.3: undertake the study of knobs to evaluate where one stood in the Great Winkle Stakes Handicap of Life.

On display were specimens of varying lengths, widths and colours. Some were bent and curved. Some were skinny and crooked like their owners. There were notable exceptions, and a boy from Ghana would've definitely given Mary Millington a run for her money. Suffice to say, it was like a butcher's shop window with glum-looking turkeys dangling between strings of pork and apple chipolatas. Me? I had some way to go, but after a towel down and a Wagon Wheel, I consoled myself by humming that old English folk song *Green Grows the Rushes O:*

I'll give you one O, oh no, you won't, you know …
What is your one O, mighty oaks from little acorns grow.'

Or something like that. To be honest, it was all a bit disheartening.

My Huckleberry Friend, Moon River, Donny Osmond and Me

After a long week practising the Eton Boating Song, and one last double period of Blow Football, I used to grab my fishing tackle and catch the 241 to Canning Town where Lynda's flat overlooked The Royal Victoria Docks. It was 1971 so fog still rolled in off the Thames and hung around the huge tankers tethered like dogs with huge rusty chains. What with the fog, the creaking chains and the ships mournful foghorns, it was like a dockyard version of *The Hounds of the Baskervilles.*

Even though the booming sound of a tanker's foghorn could dislodge a roof slate or rattle your jewellery, it was never loud enough to drown out Donny Osmond murdering his puppy on *Lift Off with Ayshea.* Don't ask why but at 13 years old, I could quite happily spend thirty minutes with *The Partridge Family*, but never saw the fascination with The Osmonds and their collection of brilliant white choppers. I mean, what good are they? I needed their cheesy wholesomeness out of my life. *Won't somebody help me, help me … help me, please?*

SFX: Outside the theatre, we hear the faint sound of my cousin Theresa and her mates singing:

We luv you, Donny, oh yes we do.
We luv you, Donny … we do.
We luv you, Donny … we dooooo.
Oh Donny, we luv you … (repeat 100 times)

Lynda's flat was three doors down from the Seamen's Mission (*to remain in a perpetual state of intoxication*), and above the offices of a building firm. At 5pm a gold Ford Granada would pull up outside to transport me along the A13 towards Romford, and another weekend fishing the little rivers and magical ponds of Essex.

The chauffeur was my uncle John, a joiner by trade who now managed the building company called Bowden & Willis (established in 1850). He was a small wiry man with a great sense of humour, who listened to Radio 4, and unlike my dad, used the full complement of screws in an MFI wardrobe. He was married to aunt Eileen and lived with their daughter Denise in a bungalow in Collier Row. After a plate of egg and chips I then spent the remainder of Friday evening reading his Bernard Venables fishing books, before going to sleep on the settee ready for an early start Saturday. The time John gave to his fishing mad nephew is something I'll always appreciate and by answering my incessant questions he became my very own Mr Crabtree. Most importantly, he taught me not to never tear around a lake screaming my fucking head off.

So, Huckleberry Finn had Uncle Tom and his cabin, and I had Uncle John and his bungalow. And while Huck lazed by the Mississippi catching Br'er Catfish, I lazed by the canal in Carpenters Road, catching Sticklebacks and luxuriating in the pong of rendered animal fat from the Knights' soap factory. The only difference was that Huckleberry Finn was a fictional character, and I was a real boy, like Pinocchio ... and real boys want to be tucked into bed by Shirley Jones.

Yesiree, Bob. Like Group Captain Douglas Bader, my pubic hair was now reaching for the sky, and as I sat beside that oily water, lazily dipping my fingers into tubs of maggots, I dreamt of Shirley Jones in her Partridge Family costume, fussing around while I caught enough Sticklebricks to build a fire station. That's right, folks. David Cassidy's step-mum was one of my favourite things. Like raindrops on roses, whiskers on kittens, and German girls dressed in

Lederhosen slapping each other's thighs as their breasts jiggled underneath pretty embroidered shirts ...

Imagine, if you will, a gentleman's outfitters in South America. In the background, we hear Bobby Crush playing *Edelweiss* and watch a portly gentleman in a Luftwaffe uniform poke his head between some changing room curtains ...

Herman Goering: *Mein Führer, we are receiving reports that someone called ze Herbert is taking ze piss out of your favourite things!"*

Adolf Hitler: (looks up in a rage) *Vhaaat? Meine kittens with ze varm voolen mittens?*

Herman Goering: *Ja, mein Führer and vhat's more ... he has a pair of ze talking testicles!*

Adolf Hitler: (shaking his head sadly) *Ah ... if only Mutter hadn't donated meine to ze Albert Hall. Herman! Get meine fishing tackle, I'm going over ze club lake.*

Herman Goering: *Shall I make you a flask of coffee?*

Adolf Hitler: *Ja, please, and could you throw in a few Jammy Dodgers?*

A 1970's Halloween Night

As a young Jamie Lee Curtis went trick or treatin' on a warm Californian evening, I was in Stratford E.15 watching Bernard Cribbins read *The Devil Rides Out* on *Jackanory*. Outside, there was a complete absence of hollowed-out pumpkins, and the only Slasher movie was an 8mm Golden Rain production from a mail order company in Upton Lane. And as far as the Bogeyman was concerned, well, let's just say he was sitting beside me in the guise of Colin Zamboozu, whose forefinger was doing regular nine-hour shifts rooting around his upper lip.

At 13 years old nothing could scare me apart from any girl over eleven, that German dwarf in *The Singing Ringing Tree*, the circus clown with a white cone hat and knickerbockers, and Jimmy Clitheroe when I eventually saw him on telly and realised he was a 60-year-old man dressed as a schoolboy. So, Halloween? Meh. It might have got a mention on *Blue Peter* but, quite honestly, for most kids in the UK the 31st October was just another step towards fireworks night.

This situation worked perfectly until 1978 when John Carpenter made *Halloween,* Jamie Lee grew a long pair of legs, and Britain went completely and utterly pumpkin-shaped.

A 1970's Firework Night, or, Some Guys Have All the Luck

A few weeks before Bonfire Night, there was a noticeable increase in abandoned toddlers crawling among the autumn leaves, as their push-chairs were commandeered so elder siblings could take part in the age-old British custom of begging for money.

Its new occupant always looked slightly crestfallen, slumped forward in a roll-necked jumper and a pair of jeans that finished with two footless stumps. Its head was a Tesco bag full of crumpled paper and its cardboard face displayed a perfectly trimmed goatee. To add a dash of realism, it sometimes wore a Boy Scout cap. With this abomination, and thanks to the generosity of most working-class people, a young racketeer could chisel enough money to buy a tin of Tom Thumb cigars and a pack of size 14 hooks.

Our route was along Vicarage Lane, stopping outside the butcher, the baker, the candlestick maker, a haberdashery shop with orange film over the window, a greengrocer, and approximately one hundred and fifty tobacconists. It was a punishing rota but (*drum roll*) it kept us off the streets!

SFX: An old lady whispers to her husband: *"What did he say?"*

But like those dodgy two-bar electric fires dangling precariously over every bath in Newham, there was always an (*drum roll*) 'element of danger'!

SFX: Same old lady says: *"Right, fuck this. Come on, Ronny, we're off."*

Rather than making a guy, there were rumours about gangs saving precious time by plonking their youngest member in the pram with a mask on. Unfortunately, this industry was rewarded by a drunk wobbling out from a pub and stabbing little 'guy' straight through the heart. I'm not kidding. That really put the wind up the whole Guy Fawkes industry and from that day me and Colin never left home without a stab-proof vest made from Bacofoil and cardboard.

By 1st November, pyres as tall as *The Wicker Man* were on every area of waste ground, and guarded day and night by five-year-old sentries and a junk yard dog. These communal pyres prompted telly presenters like Sue Stranks (in her flimsy blouse), and Val Singleton (with her enigmatic Mona Lisa smile) to begin issuing warnings about the baby hedgehogs who fling themselves onto the bonfires in protest against America's role in the Vietnam War and that *The Ballad of John and Yoko* was slipping down the charts.

Fireworks were big business. Full page adverts were carried in the National press as well as peak time telly. Even children's comic characters like Lord Snooty succumbed to the easy money of product placement and began carrying armfuls of brightly coloured sponsored squibs. And I seem to remember Biffo the Bear doing a rousing rendition of *Light up the Sky with Standard Fireworks*.

As far as the Moffatts were concerned, Firework Night was a good excuse to get hold of a catering pack of Walls pork sausages and convene around one of the larger gardens in Romford. We always knew when it was aunt Christine's turn because Mum began searching for four-leaf clovers to stitch into her Davey Crockett hat made from a dozen rabbit paws! Reason? Well, Christine did a lovely jacket potato but when uncle Gordon took charge of the firelighters, let's just say there was a little trepidation. I was there when his Roman candle destroyed a crop of tomatoes like a dose of Agent Orange, and his Catherine Wheel careered off the fence and nearly stopped Lynda's husband from devouring an entire tray of chicken legs!

Public information films warned of the dangers to life and limb, but manufacturers continued producing fabulously nutty fireworks like the head severing Helicopter, or Nigel Farage's favourite, the Jumping Jackboot. And I will never forget my aunt Pat praying to the Lord God of Baked Potatoes when Gordon gave her three young children hand-held flares, which sent sheets of molten fury spewing from its flimsy cardboard handle. The instructions read:

'HOLD FLARE AT ARM'S LENGTH. LIGHT ON A GAS RING. NOW POINT IT AT YOUR FRIENDS LIKE A FLAME THROWER AND WATCH THOSE FELLOWS RUN.'

Even the humble sparkler had a dark side in the hands of cousin Jeff and Billy Boy, who produced an ingenious synchronised display by writing *B O L L O C K S* in the cold November air.

But the firework consistently voted No.1 by readers of *Little Bastard Weekly* was the Brocks Banger. Small, easily hidden, and perfect for breaking open to make genies. They could also be tied to a girl's satchel, exploded inside a milk bottle, or smuggled into the school toilets where a loud volley would disrupt the caretaker's afternoon siesta:

"OI, YOU LITTLE BASTARDS! You'll give me a fuckin' heart attack!"

Ah, the wit of the cockney caretaker.

Some shop keepers felt it their civic duty to restrict the sale of bangers so, to get a pack 'no questions asked' meant having to walk over a mile to an inconvenience store next to Bobby Moore's sports shop in Green Street, where the shopkeeper was more relaxed about selling weapons grade explosive to 13-year-old schoolboys. I rehearsed my lines carefully:

Nonchalant Herbert: *Morning, can I have a Mint Aero and a pack of Golden Wonder, oh, and while you're at it, give us a box of those Brocks Bangers.*

Conscientious Pakistani proprietor: *Certainly, young man, that'll be ninety-five new pence, please.*

Satisfied Herbert: *Thank you kindly.*

After splitting the box we carried them home in our pockets, unaware that, behind a bank of CCTV monitors at BBC Television Centre, Val Singleton was watching us and shaking her head sadly. Meanwhile, over at Thames Television, Sue Stranks was pulling on a thin cotton T-shirt, ready for her weekly appointment with an army of boy fans already waiting in front of their tellies with smoke-blackened faces and singed eyebrows.

Charlie Smith or Having a Snifter with the Boys from the Hood

According to my mum, when I was a pint-sized Caligula, Dad was happy to push me around West Ham Park in a Paddy Hopkirk, fully-sprung, white-wheeled pram. No big deal, you might say, but in the late 1950s most men would have rather sawn off their own fucking arms. Luckily, Charles Smith was not most men. His adage was always a healthy *'Fuck 'em'* and it was this attitude which led him to the Crown Court in 1953 to collect his first criminal record. Don't get me wrong; he was no Cat in the Hat McVitie, but he would've definitely given Little Miss Naughty a run for her money.

Six foot tall, lean and handsome. Men enjoyed his company and ladies adored him. But he never strayed and only took orders from one woman. Sadly, he disobeyed them. Like when he was supposed to meet my mum in Forest Gate to choose a new settee, but instead chose to discuss Greek mythology with the landlord of The Pigeons while his wife stormed home to lightly dust her 12oz rolling pin.

Yes, folks, he liked a drink, and was called to the bar more regularly than Rumpole of the Bailey. Every Friday he arrived home, happily pissed, ready to stand under a bare light bulb while my mum gave him a good pounding. He did this with a benign smile, never raising his voice, let alone a finger. It was a fair cop. He'd done the house-keeping, now he was doing the time.

Mum: *Charlie, do you know* (lighting a Molotov cocktail) *how long I've been standing here, worrying myself bloody sick?*

Dad: *Jean … JEAN … I'm telling you* (ducking a frying pan) – *it was JUMBO'S* BIRTHDAY!*

*Jumbo – a nice man. Small, squat, and the exact replica of Charlie Drake.

After running out of clean pots and pans, she usually went to bed and left him downstairs sleeping it off. I lost count of how many ginger nuts I got through watching these weekly interrogations, but I always consoled myself with the following thought:

'Oh well … at least it's not Christmas Eve.'

It was Christmas Eve in the Doghouse

The night before Christmas was the perfect opportunity for Dad to take stock of life and celebrate the birth of our Lord Jesus Christ. He did this by having a good drink with his chums, while his wife dusted off her Bruce Lee moves in preparation for a Battle Royale with Cheese.

And that's why, on Christmas Eve 1971, while other families were enjoying *The Andy Williams Christmas Show* (*BBC1 2:50pm*), my mother was hoovering the same bit of carpet while simultaneously checking the window for any sign of her wayward husband.

He had form for these midwinter misdemeanours. Eight years earlier, with my father still not home, I had gone to bed dreaming of sleigh bells and glow-in-the-dark putty. *Where was he?* Turns out he wasn't in the Co-op buying a train set, instead he was in Queen Mary's Hospital nursing a broken nose after holding a vigorous debate with four other fellows also celebrating the season of goodwill. That time he was with a mate, a bit of a scoundrel called Charlie Brown, and when uncle John went to the pick him up, he found the two of them calling to each other from behind hospital curtains like a pair of love-struck yodellers:

Charlie 1: *Charlie, is that yooooou?*

Charlie 2: *Yes, Charlie, I'm over heeeere!*

So, there was I, sprawled across the carpet, memorising the Christmas TV Times while Mum smashed her Hoover Junior Deluxe into my ribs.

The big question was what to watch on Christmas morning? *Laurel & Hardy* (BBC1 9:00am) or *Billy Smart's Circus* (ITV 9:05am). This was serious business. Not only did children in the sixties live under the constant threat of nuclear annihilation, but, without the invention of video, we only got one chance to see a telly programme which meant making more heartbreaking decisions than Meryl Streep in *Sophie's Choice.*

However, my televisual problems were of no concern to the lady with her arm deep inside a 30lb turkey, and at 5pm she ordered me out onto the snowy streets:

"Go find your bloody father."

Never one to disobey orders, especially on Christmas Eve, I pulled on my Russian snow patrol mittens and headed along a snowy Tennyson Road, whistling the melancholy motif to Roger Whittaker's *I'm Gonna Leave Old Durham Town.*

I saw Sprouty tucked up inside his fireproof prefab enjoying *Carry On Christmas* (ITV 5pm). Would he care to join me? His response was a two fingered yuletide version of the Boy Scout salute, especially charming as I had spent most of Bonfire Night helping him perfect his 'split variation' pole dancing routine. Using Boy Scout semaphore, I wished him a Merry fucking Christmas before continuing down Whalebone Lane where the street lights cast an orange tint on the snow stretching before me like the magical world of Narnia. There was even a gentleman in a fawn coat relieving himself against one of the ornate lamp posts. Dear reader; that snowy scene could've been anywhere in the world – Switzerland, Bavaria. St Moritz. But it wasn't. It was Christmas Eve in Newham and it was blooming beautiful.

I tried all the old man's usual haunts, and each time – like that boy wearing blue knickerbockers in William Frederick Yeames' famous painting – I asked the landlord:

"When was the last time you saw my father?"

It was a Christmas mystery, and something told me it wasn't going to end with everyone singing carols around a roaring bowl of figgy pudding.

I met Jumbo who suggested I try a club on the Romford Road which was ten minutes on a sleigh pulled by huskies … but thirty minutes sliding along in a pair of size 8 slush puppies. I checked my Timex Young Explorer. Hmm? Twenty minutes before the *Blue Peter Pantomime* (BBC2 5:45pm). If I was to have any chance of seeing Val Singleton in thigh high leather boots, I needed to put on a spurt. So I did and if do say so myself, I looked rather dashing.

At home, the credits were rolling on *The Dustbin Men Christmas Special* (ITV 5:30pm) and mum was running her fingers over an improvised trench warfare tool (now on display at The Imperial War Museum).

I found the club and stamped my feet on the 'Watneys Welcome' mat before stepping into a wall of sound. Not *Phil Spector's Christmas Album,* but a room packed with laughing men and glamorous women holding glasses of Cherry B. The familiar smell of cigars and beer closed around me like a Yuletide Yankee Candle. Marvellous.

I spoke to a bald man feeding sixpences into a Joker's Wild Fruit machine.

"Excuse me, Mister. Do you know Charlie Smith?"

Without taking his eyes from the three melons in front of him, the man nodded towards the bar where a lady with two melons led me through the crowd until we came upon 'Charlie, Champion of the World' holding court with his mates. He bent down as I shouted into his ear.

Herbert: *Mum says it's time to come home.*

Dad: *Alright boy, I'll just finish this.*

Two hours, one bottle of lemonade and a bag of cheese and onions later, we gave ourselves up.

Did he get what for? Yep. Old Charlie, Champion of the World, got well done up like a yuletide cockney kipper as his wife employed her entire set of Christmas Kung Fu powers. Did he return fire? Nah. Instead, this giant of a man teetered like Rooster Cockburn and wished his beautiful wife a Merry Christmas before slumping into his armchair to watch *Carols from Kings* (BBC1 7:30pm).

A 1970's Christmas: a Time for Contemplation, Stockings and Other Hosiery

For my uncle Derek, Advent began with the first television appearance of the K-tel Veg-O-Matic, or quasi-religious Buttoneer. Derek loved all that stuff. One year he delighted Aunt Jean with a full set of whisky tumblers made using a Ronco Bottle and Jar Cutter. A thoughtful gift, which would eventually leave an entire lodge of freemasons with smiles like the Joker.

For the rest of us, Advent began with the arrival of the Littlewoods

Autumn Catalogue which my aunts fussed over like it was baby Jesus himself. Eileen ran 'The Club' with a ruthless efficiency and could have a pair of hard-wearing boys' trousers on top of your wardrobe before you could say, *'Sorry, Ei', can I pay you next week?'*

It was like Amazon Prime except the cost could be spread, with a little interest being charged. My own interest was a little charged by the pictures of ladies modelling stockings and suspenders which shed some much needed light on the mysteries of ladies' undergarments but didn't help in my long battle against short-sightedness.

I also admit to checking out the toys and games. I know, I know. For a 13-year-old working-class rebel, I should've known better, but don't tell me John Lydon would've turned down a set of Subbuteo Floodlights or a Peter Pan Chocolate Dispenser.

But apart from a blonde lady in a pink baby doll nightie, and a Young Scientist Chemistry Set, there was one other thing in that glossy dream factory which always made my heart go boom-boom-boom.

Christmas 1972 was my last chance to get a Raleigh Chopper with its low-slung, easy rider padded seat and Virgil Tracy gear stick positioned perfectly for catching my testes which were coming along nicely, thanks for asking. So, I marked the page with a giant fluorescent arrow and left it by the bread bin under the glare of an angle-poise lamp for mum to find. Oh boy. Colin reckoned that with a bright red Chopper between my legs, the lady in the baker's would definitely sort me out a nice piece of warm bread pudding.

The big day arrived and the family met in a through lounge in Collier Row, where the gift exchange rattled on longer than two *Gone with the Winds* and a *Postman Pat Christmas Special*. All afternoon I leant against the patio doors accepting a steady stream of Avon novelty soaps including an Andy Capp talc dispenser. (Andy was a character from a *Daily Mirror* strip cartoon, famous for drinking, smoking, and beating the crap out if his wife. The perfect gift for an impressionable young talc user.) When Jeff and Billy Boy got one too, I sensed that

Andy Capp may well have been on special offer. Anyway, by the time aunt Dolly crashed into the front room with a hostess trolley full of cold meats, it was obvious that another year had passed without a Chopper-shaped present being wheeled in by my cheering family.

I slipped outside and under a cold wintery moon, swore upon the power of my oxblood monkey boots that I would one day be the owner of my very own Raleigh testicle tickler.

I kept those home fires burning for a few months but, quite honestly, life was already busy trying to control a full set of raging hormones. My voice had dropped one octave and Buster and Little Jocky were now hanging so low that they banged together like dinner gongs whenever I stepped into the bath.

Please, Sir, I Want to Become a Beatle and Have Sex

Between August 1964 and August 1966, The Beatles toured the USA four times and SCOTUS (Street Cleaners of the United States) collected nearly three thousand pairs of damp knickers and over one million tons of crumpled concert tickets. From Candlestick Park to West Ham Park, everyone wanted a slice of the greatest musical phenomenon since Fred Flintstone rocked up against Frank Sinatra.

Me? I was getting onboard with the *Double Decker*s.

Inside the radiogram, between the Tom Joneses and the Mario Lanzas, were some of Lynda's old records. There was *Great Balls of Fire* by Jerry Lee, and *Idle on Parade* by Anthony Newley. I'm telling you, music never sounded better than it did belting out from that old radiogram.

Lynda also left *Beatles For Sale,* with her preference for each Beatle scribbled onto the cover, and leaving no doubt that George Harrison would've taken one hell of a beating. To squeeze every ounce of fun from my rapidly shortening childhood, I used to play that album at

45 rpm, so The Beatles sounded like Pinky and Perky. And even at that breakneck speed, *Mr Moonlight* sounded rather tasty.

A series began on Radio 1: *The Beatles Story*. It was introduced by Brian Matthews and ran for twelve consecutive Sundays. For those few months, nothing could tempt me out of my room apart from a bowl of bread and butter pudding. It was THE GREATEST STORY EVER TOLD.

I spent most of my 13th birthday in the Co-op deciding between *Let It Be* or *Sgt Pepper*, and I was just sticking *Sgt Pepper* up my jumper when the assistant asked if I was okay? Anyway, I paid for *Let it Be* and the two of us were on our way home.

The Beatles were now bigger than Jesus Christ and Susan Stranks. Even my old *Mary Poppins* EP had to move downstairs with Dad's bloody awful Honky-Tonk piano records. Then a large portion of the The Beatles back catalogue was parachuted straight into my bedroom from Denise: *Strawberry Fields, Dizzy Miss Lizzy, Magical Mystery Tour*. One gloriously haphazard bowl of Beatle music with a loving spoonful of Beatle sugar.

Then an acorn landed in the form of Lennon's Plastic Ono Band, and I became a political Herbert. Then the glorious melodies on McCartney's *Ram* arrived. Then I became a spiritual Herbert with George Harrison and spent my evenings pulling thoughtfully on a chocolate pipe while getting to grips with models in the Littlewood's catalogue.

By age fourteen, I had finally caught up with the rest of the world.

Five years earlier, on a Sunday in February 1967, The Beatles were in Stratford filming a promo film for *Penny Lane* – riding white horses and drinking in The Salway Arms. It would've taken me five minutes to jump aboard my tartan house slippers and become part of Beatles' folklore by strolling alongside Dr Winston O'Boogie.

Pub Quiz Question: *Which 1967 Beatle's video is the only time John*

Lennon and Joe 90 appeared together in public?

An opportunity of a lifetime – lost because I was round my nan's house in Forest Gate, holding a press conference with Topo Gigio and a half a pint of winkles.

Watching Meg and Sandy With a Peg on My Nose

I don't care what people say, it's pretty stressful negotiating a school corridor with your back to the wall while wielding a broken chair leg. So, it was nice to get home, sprinkle sugar on a slice of bread, and then slide across the front room carpet before coming to rest in front of my 22-inch rectangular brother. From there I fell in love with Samantha, the beautiful witch, got *Lost in Space* with Zachary Smith, and voyaged to the bottom of the *Land of the Giants*.

Man, those American imports. How cool must it be to wear cut-down jeans in a Florida National Park, and speak to your father via walkie-talkie? Especially on the days when he was letting those sprouts out the back door.

Sun-kissed Herbert: *Come in, Dad. Are you receiving me? Over.*

Ranger 'Chas' Smith: (holding a walkie talkie upside down) *Phruuhhhp. Go ahead, boy. Over.*

Freckle-nosed Herbert: (now sitting on a speeding dolphin) *Mum says come home straight away, there's an emergency! Over.*

Ranger Smith: (stepping inside the Park Tavern) *Phruurhhpp. Sorry, son … you're breaking up. Over and out.*

It was around tea-time when Ferguson began throwing a wobbly usually as Amy Turtle was about to remember her lines. His blank stare triggered a well-practised drill involving Mum diving towards a large red button marked 'Panic Stations' which sent a distress flare to a man called Uncle Reg.

He wasn't really my uncle and he wasn't really a TV repair man, but he was the best chance we had of watching *Ask the Family* instead of spending the evening singing Kumbaya. I liked *Ask the Family*, especially the way Robert Robinson gave middle-class families a gentle ribbing when they couldn't recognise Beethoven's *Ode to a Beverly Sister*.

Uncle Reg arrived with his meters and gadgets, and while mum made tea, he squeezed behind Ferguson, removed the perforated hardboard cover, and, like an Olympic fencer, thrust a screwdriver deep amongst the multi-coloured resistors. Miraculously, and in the exact time it took him to consume two chocolate digestives, Sue Lawley's legs would reappear and mum would thank him like he had just performed open-heart surgery on her favourite son. Meanwhile, Dad handed over £8 knowing he had been well and truly tucked up.

Some nights, when it seemed like the entire cast of *Crossroads* was trapped in a sand storm and Shughie McFee was screaming like a Scottish banshee, Papa would have me stand on the window sill and hold the TV aerial aloft like a little Post Office Tower. If that didn't work, he then whacked Ferguson on the head while repeating this mysterious Aztec incantation:

"*You* (thump) *bastard!* (thump) *Fucking* (thump) *thing* (hard thump)."

A Brief Encounter of the Third Kind

There was a pattern developing.

Barbara Eden (*I Dream of Jeanie*), Elizabeth Montgomery

(*Bewitched*), Carol Hawkins (*Please Sir*), Goldie Hawn (*Rowan and Martin's Laugh In*), Ami Macdonald (*The Avengers, Man about The House, The Saint, Man at the Top, Rent-a-Ghost, The Morecombe and Wise Show, etc.*), and Patrick Cargill's two on-screen daughters (*Father, Dear Father*). Yep. I was placing all my love eggs into one blonde basket, thereby limiting my chances of finding a girl who shared my fascination with German Panzer tanks.

Luckily, my world was about to be turned onto its little bald head.

Eagle Ponds. On one side, the manicured lawns of Snaresbrook Crown Court. On the far bank, a private school, and on the other, the sandy shoreline of Epping Forest. Which left a long strip of concrete separating the busy London traffic from the dark green water and the heady smell of diesel and rotting weed.

The pavement was long and featureless apart from a few benches and the bleached white trunk of an ancient oak. On this particular day, the pavement was also home to half a dozen round-shouldered young anglers sitting on tackle boxes, puffing merrily away like a row of factory chimneys.

The oak tree was half in the pond and half on the pavement. It had no branches but the trunk was as thick as a dozen Bonnie Langford's all roped together. I've seen a Victorian postcard of a woman standing alongside it holding a parasol, and it looked exactly the same as it did in 1972. Carvings on the trunk were testament to its age and attraction to courting couples: *Albert loves Myrtle, Maureen Loves Trevor,* and the slightly more abstract: *Spurs Can Go Fuck Off.*

Its thick, knotted roots reached down into the pond like tentacles, providing the perfect place for a young angler to hunker down, eat a Cornish pasty, and watch his little red tip bob about on the oily green water.

And it was from there that I caught the six inch perch now staring up at me from inside a keep-net, with a look suggesting that, given the chance, it would rip my fucking arms off.

Three girls from the private school came along and stopped behind the old oak, racking up the pressure on me to disavow Jack Hargreaves and become a working-class version of Leslie Phillips. One of the girls had long red hair and emerald eyes, and in a well-spoken Celia Johnson voice she spoke to me.

"Caught anything?"

Of course, the little stripy fish, which I placed in the girl's hands, captivated them for a few seconds before it leapt from her slender fingers back into the pond. Screaming with laughter, her well-bred mince-pies looked into mine and we both acknowledged exactly what she was thinking:

"You'll be fucking lucky, matey!"

Then, without a backward glance, they continued on their way.

Bloody hell. Now I know how Trevor Howard felt in *Brief Encounter*, when Celia Johnson fucked off down the steps towards Snaresbrook Underground.

Dear reader, Robert Newton's Third Law of Emotion states: *Sticks and stones can break your bones, but only love can break a young man's fixation with blonde actresses*, and thanks to that brief encounter with some red hair and a la-di-da accent, I was now free to fall in love with any girl too old for those dressing up clothes in a Bunty's Cut-Out Wardrobe.

Yep. A real red-letter day.

That night, after reaching down to say goodnight to Celia Johnson, I fell asleep dreaming about Robert Newton, one of Britain's finest actors, whose portrayal of Long John Silver in *Treasure Island* must surely rank alongside Gregory Peck's one-legged sea captain in *Moby Dick*.

In the dream, Long John was about to fasten an elastic band around the beak of Captain Flint, his parrot, when a gentle knock came from the cabin door. It was Jill Richardson from *Crossroads,* and Patrick Cargill's two daughters from *Father, Dear Father.*

"Can we borrow some sugar?" asked Jill.

"Ha ha, come inside, me golden-haired hearties," said Long John Silver.

"Pieces of eight, pieces of eight," said Captain Flint.

A Bone Runs Through It

Whalebone Lane was half a mile long and fifteen paces wide. I walked that alley every day for ten years and never once saw Gregory Peck dressed as a one-legged sea captain.

But in 1964 on my way to primary school, I did see two Teddy boys go at it with bicycle chains, culminating in one vanquished quiff being repeatedly smacked onto a bloodstained pavement. Six years later, I joined a large group of Rokebians watching two boys kick the shit out of each other, before I continued home for my 4:40pm televisual rub down with *Ace of Wands* on ITV about a crime-busting stage magician and his pretty sidekick who, if I remember correctly, often went without a bra.

Don't get me wrong. Whalebone Lane wasn't some desperate no-go area used for settling disagreements. On the contrary, it was the closest my band of close-knit yobbos would ever come to a Disney theme park.

On one side were park railings set into a dwarf brick wall, and on the other was a hotch-potch of old doors and corrugated sheeting, enclosing hundreds of back gardens. In between was an all-weather football pitch cleverly disguised as a pavement. Ornamental lamp posts ran down the middle, offering themselves as goal posts, cricket stumps, and somewhere to hang upside from like red-faced cockney vampires. Football matches played there continuously, only stopping for old ladies who insisted on pushing their trolleys right through the fucking penalty area. If the ball went into a garden, the kicker had to quickly scale the fence and trespass against those that would trespass against us. It wasn't the dogs that scared us, it was those same old ladies now scampering from their back doors shouting obscenities that no young footballer should ever hear.

A pedestrian gate into the park sat between two cast iron columns each with a large iron ball on top with spears sticking out like Kaiser Wilhelm's helmet. More athletic boys would clamber up and sit astride the Kaiser's helmet, while the rest of us stretched our arms hanging from the lamp posts.

Running across the alley was a row of ornate iron bollards which Colin said were cannons captured from French warships during the Napoleonic wars. If this was true, then Emperor Napoleon got his own back on the jolly jack tars of Stratford because whenever I tried leaping over one, Buster and Little Jocky would scream like a pair of air-raid sirens. Come to think of it – leap frog? French?

At the end of Whalebone Lane, opposite the pie and mash shop, was a small red-brick building with a clay tile roof nestling in its own copse of lime trees. A handsome little building which could've sat nicely in the grounds of Buckingham Palace if not for the GENTLEMEN sign and the great smell of Zammo.

It was the cleanest public toilet in Newham. Brilliant white porcelain urinals served by highly polished copper pipes running down from high-level china cisterns. Brass locks on the cubicle doors sparkled like new pennies, and a bright red weighing machine gleamed like a fire engine. It was a clean machine. Even handwritten messages in the cubicles were neatly spaced and grammatically correct. Yep, those toilets were definitely a nice place for a slash but interestingly, you never saw anyone pushing a mop around or drilling those circular holes in the cubicles to pass secret messages through.

The Nonce and the Brand New Telephone

There were regular stories in the local paper about knickers being stolen from washing lines, often accompanied by a blurred image of a figure disappearing over a fence like Bigfoot. Newham also had its fair share of flashers (collective noun: a gordon), locked and loaded, ready to share their winkles with the world.

So, with this information to hand, Colin and I were fully prepared for that day when a gentleman dressed as Lord Baden Powell and clutching a copy of *Scouting for Boys* offered us one of his dodgy-looking toffees. Declining his offer, we retired to a safe distance before shouting:

"OI, FUCK OFF, YOU DIRTY OLD BASTARD!"

Ah, the wit of twelve-year-old cockney jail-bait.

My old man, showing little understanding of the sociological pressures that some middle-aged men have thrust upon them, set off with the Burgermeister and a group of villagers to *"kill the nonce"*. Fortunately, Lord Baden Powell had already changed his name to Cozy and was now busy reinventing himself as a rock drummer.

Another popular pastime was for gentlemen to phone random ladies and offer their impression of an athlete running a half marathon with trousers at half-mast. This was never a problem for us until 1972 when the GPO pulled some wire through our wall and delivered a dozen directories carrying every phone number in Greater London.

Our first phone was a thing of beauty. Bruce Wayne may have had his racy-red bat phone and Tara King her sensuous cream handset, but ours was two-tone green which perfectly matched the Zamboozu jungle setting of the hall wallpaper. The first number I ever dialled was TIM (846) to listen to the lady on the speaking clock:

'At the third stroke, you will become punctual and slightly aroused, you naughty boy!'

The only drawback was having to share a party line and hear our neighbour complain about her husband's piles, which were apparently hanging from his arse like a bunch of grapes.

Having our own phone meant Mum now didn't have to stand in a public phone box that reeked of piss while catching up with the latest Moffatt gossip. Nope. Now she was Grace Kelly in *Dial M for Murder,* swanning around with the handset under her chin and the receiver hanging loosely by her side.

When she placed a call it was like the Chinese Tea Ceremony. First, a cuppa was prepared. Then, after drying her hands with a tea towel, she made her way to the hall to perch a spring-loaded, brushed aluminium pop-up phone-book on her knee. Then she lit a cigarette, dialled the number, and waited a few seconds before saying:

Mum: *Hello,* (insert name of sister) *it's Jeanie.*

There followed a forty-minute catch-up without any hesitation, deviation or repetition.

When it was our phone's turn to dance noisily off its cradle, she answered it by recounting our number in a well-spoken melodic rhythm before dropping her voice one aitch, once she was absolutely certain the caller wasn't Princess Margaret:

Mum: *Ooh, hello* (insert name of sister).

Then, and only then, could the gossip continue in earnest. **

It was a few months later when the heavy breathing calls started.

At first, Mum politely asked the caller to desist. When that didn't work, she resorted to blowing a high-pitched whistle down the phone which left the caller clutching his ear and her husband scrambling awake from his evening slumber.

"Bloody hell, Jean! Can't you put the poxy phone down like everyone else?"

* nonce – a sex offender, not to be confused with the 1968 Sandie Shaw hit *Monsieur De Nonce.*

** earnest – a female, working-class dialect comprising theatrical high-pitched phrases like: 'Noooooooooooooo', or the ever popular '*Ooooowhargh*' (a shortened version of 'Oh, I never!'). Examples can be found in Ealing classics such as *Hue and Cry, The Mouse That Roared,* and the 1980 cult classic *Bulldog Drummond Meets Mary Millington.*

Getting the Raging Horn for Goldie Hawn

One Sunday morning, I'm in bed doing *The Sparky* crossword, next minute I'm clomping across the sticky carpet of a public bar, carrying crates of light ale, Double Diamond, brown ale, barley wine, Mackeson Stout, Guinness, Worthington E, and bloody Watney's Red Barrel. I didn't even ask for the job, but suspiciously the landlord called me 'Charlie's Boy'.

The crates were kept out the back, protected day and night by the stench from the men's toilet. I never complained about the working conditions because, to paraphrase Al Pacino in *The Godfather,* this was the life my father had chosen. Anyway, after a few months I was the proud owner of a single hair on my chest and two extra on my testicles.

I liked the money (50p) but the joy of rising early on a Sunday morning to hold your breath outside a gentleman's toilet soon waned, and I rewrote my CV.

They say that an Opal Fruit never falls far from the Rowntree, and my next job was stacking beer and wine in the off-licence in Tennyson Road. Same gig. No ammonia. It was owned by the Bass Brewery and had a shop floor big enough to hold a small disco. Nowadays it would be crammed with enough produce to fill a small Co-op, but in 1970, it was empty apart from an ice cream cabinet and three girls dancing around their handbags.

Everything was stored behind fifty feet of polished oak counter which still had the original beer pumps from when punters brought in their own jugs to fill with beer before heading home to lather up the old genitals in a tin bath while listening to Dick Barton.

The landlord introduced me to a large German Shepherd to ensure I kept my thieving little hands to myself, and the only place away from Hans and those bloody sheep was down a damp cellar where ciders, fortified wines and soft drinks waited to be dragged up the iron steps and stacked behind the counter. Down there, away from prying eyes, I would take big swigs from the Tizer and Corona lemonade before re-screwing the tops. Up yours, Hans!

Before long, I was working the till and given unlimited access to sweets, crisps, cigarettes and spirits. And in case you're wondering, no, I didn't swipe anything … apart from a few bars of Old Jamaica and the occasional packet of Henry Winterman cigars.

Tobacco was kept upstairs where the owner's daughter liked to bend over and show me her knickers. She was in her twenties, very pretty, with messed up blonde hair like Goldie Hawn. She was also engaged to a cravat-wearing pillock who didn't deserve those mini-skirts and long shapely legs. However, this didn't stop me falling madly in love, and every Saturday morning Buster and Jocky would run through a series of physical jerks in preparation for our weekly encounter.

Though Goldie very kindly continued showing me her knickers, she never did find room in her heart for a 13-year-old love-struck lemonade guzzler. Consequently, my Saturday afternoons were spent in a cold bath with a pair of steaming testicles, seeking a quantum of solace from the poetry of William Wordsworth as I wandered lonely as a cloudy lemonade towards sexual maturity.

It's a Kind of Magic

There was a little shop opposite the off-licence. Built on the squint, which tempted many entrepreneurs to try making a go of its prime location in the middle of fucking nowhere. At one stage it was a ladies' hairdresser, next it was a grocers. But in 1971 a man resembling the shopkeeper in *Mr Benn* was using it to sell top quality bric-a-brac. His window was always worth a look and one day I noticed two books with dust jackets especially designed to attract teenage boys. And as I was in training to become one, I handed over 20p and rushed home to hang a 'Do Not Disturb' sign on my bedroom door. Yep. I had a new hobby, and this one didn't involve red maggots or masturbating.

They were *magic* books. The first celebrated famous magicians like Harry Houdini and Chung Ling Soo, who died catching a speeding bullet between his teeth. It was very interesting and I used some of Houdini's techniques to curl up in the airing cupboard whenever the old man was having trouble with those Sunday sprouts.

The second was *The Illustrated Book of Magic* by Will Dexter. Brilliantly nutty, it showed young wizards slicing up their father's playing cards, or making smoke appear from their mum's best wine glasses. Some of the tricks used highly corrosive chemicals, and the accompanying illustrations showed delighted mothers clapping excitedly as sons bowed to the audience with blistering skin and tears streaming from bloodshot eyes.

As you can probably guess, my ambition to manage an off-licence with Goldie Hawn was now replaced with sharing a dressing room with a beautiful assistant in a glittery swimsuit. I got more books from West Ham Library, and was soon hanging around a magic shop in Tottenham Court Road where giant dice hung from the ceiling and ventriloquist dummies looked down from the shelves. Professional stuff, all very pricey. My price range was more whoopee cushions and itching powder. Nevertheless, I was soon impressing the ass off my little cousins by leaving pretend dog turds on their *Noddy* annuals.

Card tricks, The Indian Rope trick – you name it, I half understood it, and it wasn't long before I signed up to perform a magic show at a school fete, hoping this would help me become the youngest President of the Magic Circle and swap secrets with Ali Bongo while drinking tea from a chocolate teapot.

To be rich and have lots of fans! Lots of girls to prove that I'm a man! Yes, I think I would like that.

The day of the fete arrived and the sun was shining as I peeked from behind the stage curtains, hoping to see a row of pretty girls preparing to throw me their knickers. Instead, sitting in the front row, was Bobby the Bastard loading his Johnny Seven with rubber bullets. Kids, I'm afraid the old bottle went, carrying with it my dreams of sharing a changing room with Anita Harris.

And that's when Colin found me behind the Tombola stand.

'What's wrong, Mr Magico? And why is there a mouse squeaking in your back pocket?'

Colin was a true friend. We both knew it was my April*.

Dear reader. It's one thing to capture the imagination of a boisterous bank holiday crowd, but it's another thing to catch a speeding rubber bullet in the chops, so I stashed away my suitcase of tricks and helped Baloo find the culprit who had goosed her while she was demonstrating map reading to a group of rough looking boys.

All these years later, I'm still waiting to do ten minutes sandwiched between Mike Yarwood and Petula Clark. However, I did manage to climb inside a coffin with a woman in a sparkly costume when the opportunity arose during a Goth weekend in Whitby. More from Elvira later.

* April = rhyming slang from the Doris Day film 'April in Paris' = Aris = Aristotle = Bottle = Bottle and Glass = Arse = Arsehole = Donny Osmond.

Clint Eastwood Says Goodbye to the 11th Newham Boy Scouts

After a long weekend doing unspeakable things in an Epping Forest youth hostel, a line of industrious pipsqueaks were bicycling home, each wearing a yellow plastic poncho against the driving rain. Only the Scout caps distinguished them from a giant yellow caterpillar. At the back, glasses blurry and peddling furiously on his small-wheeled bike for the busy commuter, was the Man With No Name, whistling the motif from a *Fistful of Dollars* in time to his pumping knees.

Home safely in Tennyson Road, and after giving my bike some fresh straw and a pat on the crossbars, I headed inside like a saddle-sore Milky Bar Kid where Mum was rustling up some chow. Around the camp fire we sat, eating her world beating scrambled eggs on toast with Heinz ketchup. *Home Sweet Home.*

You know what it's like – being pumped up after a boisterous weekend with the chaps – so I decided to share a joke with the old man which had the rib-tickling punchline *'Tintin and the Crab with the Golden Prick'*. I expected at least a nod of approval as he extended a warm welcome into the adult community. Instead, I was given a heart-warming whack on the arse for swearing in front of my mum. No matter that on many occasions his language was more colourful than Zippy and Bungle's notorious X-rated 1980 *Christmas Rainbow Special*, I still spent the next hour sitting in a bowl of ice cool water watching Napoleon Solo get tied to a chair by a glamorous spy with T.H.R.U.S.H.

That was a proper stag weekend, that was. There's nothing more exciting than learning the Batman theme using three keys on a piano, and waving your willy towards a group of girl hikers from Woodford County High. Yep. A memorable weekend. So why spoil it by going back to school?

So, while Napoleon Solo struggled with his bonds, I began weighing up my chances of getting Monday off. I worked out the odds to be 50:50 if I invoked the overly harsh whack on the arse.

With freezing rain smashing against my bedroom window, I collapsed onto the bed. Outside, coyotes were calling. A real three-dog night. Milky Bar Clint pulled his Scout cap down over his face as Buster and Little Jocky settled alongside him, exhausted after a long day riding side-saddle and clinging valiantly together like a pair of Gaucho's leather water bottles.

Fashion Part 1: 'I'm Only a Poor Little Herbert, My Feather's all Stubby and Brown.'

After reading one of those Richard Allen paperbacks about London youth gangs, I decided that becoming a teenage desperado might be a good way to find a girl, settle down and, if I wanted, even marry.

Skinheads were still roaming the streets in their braces and Doctor Marten's, ready to answer any theological question that may arise. According to Richard Allen, they were also getting regularly laid by accommodating skinhead girls, often without any need for a pre coital drink at Bobby Moore's wine bar. Yep, becoming a bovver-boy was an option, but for someone who collects two cauliflower ears sparring with a Freddy Mills punch bag, it was a big hill to climb. And if my old man had caught me in ox blood officer boots, he would've clipped my ears with his special 'stop-being-a-twat' clippers. Anyway. It was 1972 and like a cheese sandwich left out in the sun, the skinhead cult was already on the turn.

There was however, the much less confrontational Suedehead, with their uniform of sta-press trousers, black loafers, dog tooth spectacles, off-the-shoulder Crombies, and metal heel-protectors to scour goodwill messages into the school hall floor. Yep. That'll do nicely.

First, I had to shed my Herbert cocoon by leaving a bag of military uniforms by the canal in Victoria Park and handing my scout cap to cousin Mark. Then it was time to go shopping in preparation for my new job as head doorman outside the girls' changing room at Deanery High School. To help in this quest and to prove I was a right little hard-nut, I was accompanied by my mum and her purse.

We went to Granditers, a youth outfitters in East Ham, where she forked out for some two-tone Tonic trousers before her X-ray specs saw through the overpriced Fred Perrys and she dragged me outside in search of cheaper alternatives. So instead of an authentic Ben Sherman I got a red and white check shirt from the Co-op. And instead of polished black brogues spitting sparks on the pavement, she got me a pair of hard-wearing, chisel-toed corduroy shoes with thick brown moulded rubber soles which looked suspiciously like dog poop. Friends called them my 'Pa Rugs' after the *Hillbilly Bears*. How we laughed.

Even I knew that this new get-up wasn't enough to entice a

beautiful skinhead girl to join me for a steamy session of Battling Tops. There was nothing else for it but to forgo my carefully coiffured *Catweazle* haircut, and try something a little meaner. Perhaps a Bobby Moore with a touch of Les Kellet?

Like most barber shop windows, the one in West Ham Lane displayed black and white photos showing Italian-looking men with heavily lidded eyes and dark wavy hair. Inside, hanging from the barber's chair, was a leather strop to sharpen cut-throat razors, and on the walls glass shelves were packed with clear blue tonics, steel combs, shaving soaps, and a specialist shuttlecock called Dunlop Fetherlite.

I went with a mate of mine called Ivan the Greek, a self-assured young man, who plonked himself into the empty barber's chair.

Ivan: *A number one please, Mr Luigi.*

And while Luigi fired up his clippers, I picked up a copy of Reveille and helped myself to a mild heart attack thanks to an airbrushed lady from Swindon.

Five minutes later, Luigi whipped off the cape like a matador, and Ivan stepped from the chair. With his olive skin and closely cropped hair, he looked cooler that Steve McQueen stepping from a chest freezer in Bejam's. Bloody hell. This was the final piece of my fashion jigsaw! Move over Ben Sherman. Jog on Fred Perry. Adios Abercrombie.

I jumped into the still-warm barber's chair.

Herbert: *Same again please, Mr Luigi.*

Mr Luigi: *Are you sure, Little Herbert?*

Herbert: *You bet your sweet ass, Mr Luigi!*

Off came the Joe 90s, and I squinted into the mirror at my blurred reflection. With skilled efficiency, Luigi's clippers moved across my scalp like a Ferrarri Flymossio, and while my blonde hair joined Ivan's on the cutting room floor, I imagined some sweet skinhead girl sweeping me into her tattooed arms as my cheering classmates carried me across the playground like a conquering hero.

The clippers came to a screaming halt.

Mr Luigi: *All done Little Herbert.*

(I put on my Joe 90's.)

Herbert: (in a strangled voice) *Oh, my Christ!*

Staring back from the mirror was the poor wretch who cleaned the petri dishes in Marie Curie's radiation laboratory. To be precise, a four-eyed bald boy with corduroy shoes and a red-checked shirt.

When I got home mum took one look, swooned, and fell to the kitchen floor. And at school, my mates carried me across the playground chanting: '*Pa Rug … Pa Rug.*' How we laughed.

Richard Allen must have shifted thousands of those little pulp novels, and always on the look-out for the next BIG thing. I liked to imagine him wandering down West Ham Lane and stopping outside the barbers to peruse those 10 x 12" photos. There it was! Between The Crew Cut and The Page Boy. A photo of a white bowling ball wearing black NHS glasses – The Herbert.

Richard smiled. He knew a cult when he saw one

Football Hooligans, Men in Helmets, and The Battle of Agincourt

Our science teacher played non-league football, and one afternoon a coach-load of his pupils agreed to miss the chance of watching a cover teacher set himself ablaze with a Bunsen burner, and instead follow Mr Limeburner through the Blackwall Tunnel for a midweek cup game.

'*Welcome to Plumstead FC*' read the sign on the rusty grandstand. Quite honestly it looked more like a communal toilet in East Berlin. Something was missing. There were no glossy programmes, no hot-dog stands, just people sloping forlornly along like hillbillies in *Deliverance*. I'm not saying Newham hasn't seen some cousin-on-cousin action, but south of the river … even the dogs had club feet. *Hooray!*

After disinfecting our Category A seats, we started endearing ourselves to the locals with some good old-fashioned foul-mouthed bonhomie. And it was during a medley of English folk songs about White Hart Lane that half a dozen hairy bikers walked past us in black leathers and non league facial hair.

Dear reader. Why, why, why would forty boisterous 14-year-olds (collective noun: a strop) want to rile a collection of hairy bikers from South London (collective noun: a throttle)? Two reasons: winkles, knobs and pricks (okay, three reasons).

"Greasers, greasers, greasers, greasers!" we called.

I'm not kidding. If heavy metal looks could kill …

The game had it all: muddy balls, toe punts, and sliding tackles. Mr Limeburner hit the winner with a gravity-defying pile driver, and afterwards, while he shared a bottle of Matey with his victorious teammates, we made our way back to the coach across some wasteland when it went dark. The groundskeeper must've removed the AA batteries from the floodlights. The lack of light signalled an ambush from those hairy greasers. It was hair-raising stuff as they charged towards us while we clambered aboard the coach as bricks and bits of concrete rained onto it like arrows at Agincourt. As we pulled away in a cloud of dust, Howard Woolly stood at the rear window giving tremendous V signs while shouting inspirational quotes from Henry V.

"And those gentlemen in Stratford now a-bed
Shall think themselves accursed they were not here,
And hold their winkles cheap whiles any speaks
That fought with us upon Saint Crisp n' Dry."

For ten minutes, my little pooper was going full pelt. Safely through the Blackwall Tunnel, I realised I wasn't frightened after all and reverted to being a cocky little bastard.

At 11pm, we were dropped off outside the school gates and I walked down a foggy Whalebone Lane with a sore throat and that feeling of invincibility you get from surviving a near death experience.

In the early seventies the Sunday papers were full of rival punch-ups and train wrecking football fans. West Ham had their own crew and without getting too philosophical, you did feel a little pride when your side charged at the opposition waving stolen policemen's helmets.

But talk is cheap and I was never mental enough for the troublesome ICF (Inter City Firm). I suppose with a bit of effort I could've managed the STD (Stratford to Debden under 14s), but it's effort, though … that's the problem. That night with my hands down my Geoff Hurst underpants, I weighed up my options. By morning I knew it wasn't the life for me. Sod that. Grabbing my teddy bear, I went downstairs for a nice bowl of Frosties.

Lunch with Bobby Moore or Last Summer Term at St Clares

Last day of term they collected us up like shrimps in a giant triangular fishing net before releasing us into the main hall for an end-of-term movie. It was the same every year. *The Hill,* featuring Sean Connery running up a sand hill in a gas mask. I've got no idea who kept choosing it, but the PE teacher with the small winkle was always standing behind the projector whooping support for the sadistic army police officer played by Ian Hendry.

And when the East London weather wasn't being its usual inclement self, we were herded inside for another celluloid visitor called *Goal!,* the official film of the 1966 FIFA World Cup. Close-ups of any German player brought rumbles of theatrical boos but any England shirt brought a ripple of approval, apart from Jack Charlton who for some reason was unkindly compared to '*a fucking giraffe*'. But the biggest cheer was always saved for the England captain. He was a local boy, you see. In fact, he was so local you could see him most lunchtimes going into the pub opposite the school playground.

The Bakers Arms was a back street haunt favoured by footballing greats such as Greavesie and Hursty, who tried to remain incognito while boys called Smithy and Sprouty completely blew their cover. It was only when the blonde gentleman stepped from his gleaming white Scimitar Sports that those teenage testicles began bouncing around like Tigger at Pooh Corner. Yep. Bobby Moore. International footballing great, loved and respected around the world, having a crafty one with Ronnie Boyce before driving home to Chigwell to decorate the spare room.

But as entertaining as it was to watch international footballers hide behind parked cars, a young man still had to eat. Unfortunately, the school dinner token system had been hijacked by unruly Flashman types, so many of us followed a strict diet of chips and bread pudding from the local health food shops. On one occasion, instead of getting my arm broken defending a boiled plimsoll in parsley sauce, I visited a new sweetshop where boys in black jackets and crisp white shirts were already trousering confectionery quicker than a flock of thieving magpies. Quite frankly I was appalled, especially when I later found a Galaxy Ripple in my blazer pocket. The sweetshop closed for a few days before re-opening with revolving knives, steel shutters and razor wire spread across the counter. This helped … but only slightly.

There is no doubt that being naughty in the company of a large group of like-minded boys is a wondrous thing. School trips were the perfect opportunity for this activity, and as this was my farewell tour before moving to Romford, I decided to jot down a few reminders.

First you have to learn seat allocation on the coach. Starting at the back with The Psychopath, The Hard Nut, The Troublemaker, The Stroppy, The Nutcase, The Naughty, The High Pitched Squeaky, The High Pitched Excitable, The Slippery, The Geezer, The Twat, The Ponce, The Nonce, The Waster, The Tealeaf, The Herbert, The Screamer, The Big Wanker, The Little Wanker, The Chancer, The Sleeper, The Dozy, The Berk, The Dustbin, The Twerp, The Schnide, The Swot, The Goody Two Shoes, and, of course, The Puker, who was allowed to sit anywhere and propel his fizzy drink and egg sandwich into the nearest duffel bag.

I also learned how to remain upright in a force 5 gale on the beach at Hastings while my classmates, dressed like marauding Scottish football fans, chased a party of private school girls along the pebbles as if the Bayeux Tapestry itself had come to life.

On a trip to France I admired the craft of The Tealeaf going about his business, swiping souvenirs to order while we queued at the bureaux de change to see a young woman who had large tufts of underarm hair poking from under her blouse. On the ferry home, I watched flick knives being hidden inside Dr Marten's, and boys tip-toeing through customs in case they sprung open and sliced off their toes.

On a geography field trip to Harlow I learned how chatting up young mothers in a shopping precinct was a good way to make your testicles glow like two bowls of Ready Brek, but left the pros and cons of living in a new town totally inconclusive.

And finally, in a barge on the Thames estuary, I learned about salty mud flats from a Polish science teacher, and about Reggae and Dub music courtesy of an enterprising boy called Ossie, who had somehow smuggled aboard his entire record collection. I can confirm there's nothing better after a long day analysing the saline composition of sea water than a bit of heavy bass and a thoughtful drag on an Embassy No 6. In fact, thanks to Ossie, I still associate the Trojan record label and the *Skinhead Moonstomp* with the flora, fauna and salt marshes off the east coast of Britain.

Choosing A Career or A Day at the Races

We looked like the 1973 all-England Scarecrow Convention. A straggly chain of battered school blazers, queuing to see a careers officer who was wearing his own battered blazer and a long face, suggesting he would rather be on the home straight at Ascot Racecourse.

The event was being held in the school library so while queuing I took the opportunity to flick through a 1970 *Charles Buchan Football Annual*, where someone had inked-in Rodney Marsh's teeth and added a speech bubble suggesting an inappropriate relationship with Tottenham striker Alan Gilzean. What monster would deface a world-class showboater like Rodney Marsh? Snotty Jenkins? Wanker Watson? My guess was the senior librarian who had been making it increasingly clear that the sparkle had gone from tracking down stolen books in an inner London boys' school. Sure enough, through the frosted glass of his office, I saw a figure throwing some rope over a rafter.

Finally, the careers officer pressed his stopwatch and began my allotted 45 seconds. Skipping any foreplay, he handed me a leaflet about becoming a dental technician. To save time, I agreed, mostly because the girl on the front looked like the blonde one from the Pepsi advert. That was it! Career sorted.

But wasn't this all a bit rushed? Should I not consider following my father into the services?

Author's Children: *What! Granddad was in the SECRET SERVICE? The man who smoked Rothmans while handing out presents dressed as Father Christmas, trusted with secrets which could've compromised a succession of Tory governments and brought down those grandees of the Romford Conservative Party?*

Nope, I'm talking about The British Road Service: a nationwide parcel delivery company whose drivers were wearing leather jerkins and black leather caps while the biker from The Village People was still playing with his Evel Knievel stunt cycle.

Dad was a foreman at the Stratford depot and his role was to bring harmony wherever there was discord. He did this by inviting disgruntled individuals to join him clocking-out on the punching-in machine, before holding a vigorous discussion where they clocked and punched each other before clocking back in on the punching-in machine. Or something like that. It was all very confusing.

Dad's brother Bill worked there too, and in the school holidays I was Bill's co-pilot, delivering parcels to James Bond's relatives in Basildon, and to Bob Hope's brother in Stanford Lee. I liked Bill, he was always chuckling. Especially after scaring the life out of his nephew. You see, Bill's lorry had sliding passenger doors which he liked to pin open as we thundered down the A13 at 50 mph. Bill was an ex-commando so, for him, falling from a moving vehicle presented no fucking problem whatsoever. However, for a Boy Scout yet to pass his Clinging onto a Shiny Leather Seat Using a Pair of Clenched Buttocks proficiency badge, it served only to provide a valuable insight into the life of a rodeo cowboy.

After a hard day's screaming, I spent the last half hour wandering the loading bays, copping half crowns from Dad's friends, and watching men huddle around damaged boxes. According to Bill, those damaged boxes had fallen from the lorries and the contents were now being distributed to worthy causes. I know the suspension on those old lorries couldn't have been great but the scale of this industry suggested the streets of East London had more pot-holes than Cheech and Chong.

Even with soiled underpants and a pocket full of silver, I knew those shenanigans were fishier than Michael Fish eating a fish finger sandwich and more blind eyes were being turned than a Russian optician.

But there's an old Apache saying: '*Never look um gift horse in um mouth.*' Especially when that gift horse comes home with a Goblin Teasmade for his wife and a carrier bag full of records for his only son. Come to think of it, there can't be many boys in the early 1970s who were introduced to Lou Reed, The Who, and Hawkwind, by their charity-loving fathers.

Apart from my father being overly dismissive of Shaw Taylor on *Police 5,* I never questioned these activities until 6am one morning when Inspector Barlow and the *Softly, Softly* task force began searching our house from top to bottom. To be honest, their search was a bit half-hearted and I remember one copper asking to borrow a step ladder so he could check the loft. Dad shook his head politely.

They left empty-handed apart from my father, who they kept at West Ham Police station for ten hours until, like a run-down battery, he was released without charge. I thank you.

He came home for his tea like nothing had happened but I did catch him later, coming down from the loft carrying two Prestige pressure cookers and four boxes of disposable lighters. Not wishing to rock the boat, I put on my brand new Phillip's headphones, turned up the volume, and listened to Hawkwind's *Sonic Attack.*

On May Bank holidays a convoy of green lorries left the Stratford depot and headed east for some inter-depot fun and games. It was a big day in the BRS social calendar, and even the guard dogs joined the wives and children, rolling around dangerously in the back of the lorries.

The destination was a field in Ongar, which had already been transformed into a M.A.S.H army storage depot with olive-green lorries around the perimeter, areas marked off with rope, and orders being barked from a Tannoy. Trestle tables buckled under the weight of sandwiches, cakes and the expectations of three hundred working-class souls. Let the games begin!

Imagine, if you will, a Highland Games. Plenty of big old beer bellies, but very few ginger beards and only one sporran. Dad and his mates did a tug-of-war against the Tottenham depot, and dragged them across the finish line … and then another fifty yards towards the beer tent. Inspired by his victory, I entered the egg and spoon race and finished a very valiant fourth. At the end of the day, proper medals were distributed and a good time was had by all.

The old man tucked away his tug-of-war medals in the sideboard along with a few dart tankards and a cribbage board. The fact that he even kept them meant something. Perhaps they were the working man's equivalent of a Bachelor of Arts, bestowed upon him by his peers?

Anyway. Before moving to Romford, my mum chucked the lot out, along with a shoebox full of my old West Ham programmes. Apparently, we were making a fresh start and there was to be no room for any heirlooms or sentimentality. Fair enough, but she found room for her brass ashtrays in the shape of diamonds, hearts, spades and clubs. Oh yeh, she managed that alright.

The Saucy Birds are Spooky Spooky

Before William Peter Blatty dotted the 'i's and crossed the crucifixes on his international bestseller, most people thought an exorcist was some kind of acne embrocation. And that's how I came to be so totally unprepared for a possessed 15-year-old girl to give ME the willies … the exact opposite of what nature intended.

Like all ghost stories, this one begins with a boy called Budgie.

Budgie had an overlarge head and Marty Feldman eyes, and he kept a collection of bird's eggs in a suitcase under his bed, each labelled alphabetically and hunkered down safely in its own cotton wool nest. In those day, collecting birds' eggs was terrifically popular, especially by boys whose fathers didn't own a car and had no access to Esso football coins.

Budgie also had a collection of *Razzle* magazines which were also filed alphabetically – starting and ending with the letter R.

One day, while lounging around Budgie's flat perusing a blackbird egg and two ladies from Epping, he suggested we stop swigging his dad's Bristol Cream and instead visit his big sister and her friend, who could make that girl from *The Exorcist* look like an Avon lady demonstrating a cucumber face mask.

We found them in a deserted school playground near Plaistow Station. They were a few years older than us and sitting on some stone steps. We couldn't help but notice that Budgie's sister was carrying some pretty large bosoms, which put us on the back-foot straight away. Her name was Deb and, thanks mostly to those bosoms, we handed over 20p in return for the promise of a scary story about a fighter pilot trapped in a burning plane.

Until then her friend had remained silent. Now she began swaying her head in time with Deb's graphic account of a pilot desperately trying to escape from a burning cockpit as it plummeted to the ground. Debbie was a natural and as her voice rose to a crescendo, the other girl began thrashing around and screaming so loudly that our well-developed narrator had to slap her face to break the possession!

What the fuck? Our jaws dropped, our bowels opened, and together we shivered our collective timbers. I'm not kidding. I hadn't been that frightened since Kenneth Williams read *The Fall of the House of Usher* on *Jackanory*.

Traumatised, especially by Debbie's large Bristols, we trooped back to Budgie's flat to take a more circumspect look at those *Razzle* magazines, and in particular a lady standing in front of a gas-effect fire like the Lone Ranger with black electrical tape across her eyes and a pair of six shooters pointing dead ahead. Colin reckoned it was our lady art teacher, and on close inspection in a mirror above the fire place, we saw Mr Limeburner holding a Polaroid Instant.

Budgie's sister definitely had a gift for the theatrical, and if those bosoms had been given the right support, Debbie may well have given old Bernard Delfont a run for his money. Instead, she chose to stay in Stratford and keep her husband warm in The Two Puddings.

What about the girl with the fly-away hair? Was she really possessed by the demon Pazuzu or did she simply have designs on our small change? The jury is still out but we found out later that her name was Paula Winkle.

Harris's Corner Shop or Knickers Ahoy!

This little shop was like a mirage, hidden between a thousand yards of replica terraced housing. If not for the smell of fresh ham and cola cubes, you could've missed it all together.

Harris's was our go-to shop for a last-minute pack of Hula Hoops, and my half-way house as I trudged back from the paraffin vending machine lugging two gallons of Esso Blue. Rain, snow or icy blow, its little 'OPEN' sign always faced outwards. Even when his wife went into hospital to have twins, Mr Harris only closed up for half a day because he couldn't wait to get back onto the bacon slicer, even though she had made it perfectly clear she was going back to her previous job (see *Amityville Road Horror*).

In 1971, to spite every grocer in the United Kingdom, Prime Minister Ted Heath decided the country should start counting in tens. To make his decimal point, boys in my class were given a blue plastic presentation wallet containing some freshly minted coins. Shiny and mysterious, they kept us fascinated for the exact time it took to exchange the lot with Mr Harris for a quarter of Dairy Maids, a Funny Feet ice cream, a pack of Cola Spangles and some Colgate toothpaste for a ring of confidence … like Simon Templar's, only slightly lower.

Actually, I needed a confident ring. Morale was low. Sex was rearing its ugly head and my dreams were getting darker than Glyn Poole and Bonnie Langford going at it on *Junior Showtime*.

One day, we were in the waiting room at the top of the slide having a discussion about VD. Apparently, it lived in the toilets under Stratford Broadway and the only way to avoid it was by wearing a pair of Pat Jennings goalkeeping gloves. We also had it on good authority that overdoing the old Shermans (formerly known as the Barclays) could leave you with a rupture which meant having to wear a contraption endorsed by Truss Conway. I'd seen an advert for one in *The News of the World* and I certainly didn't fancy wearing one of those blighters on the beach at Broadstairs.

If that wasn't enough, boys also had to keep a look-out for any packets of OMO washing powder being displayed in a kitchen window. Apparently, this, along with a solitary pair of red knickers on the washing line, were internationally recognised signs that the lady of the house was happy to wrestle away your virginity. This idea may have been left over from WWI, where French women did a similar thing, offering to wash British soldiers' uniforms while their husbands were away hunting frogs.

Yep, confusing times for a hard-drinking bachelor in Joe 90 glasses.

I Love the Smell of Pie and Mash in the Morning

Once upon a time, you couldn't move for cauldrons of bubbling green liquor and hour-glass vinegar bottles. Even today, people will crawl across a broken marble table-top to defend the honour of their favourite pie and mash shop. There were some big contenders, too. Cookes of East Ham, Manzes of Walthamstow, and Top-Hats!, a short-lived venture near Harrods in Kensington.

But only one pie mash shop carried with it the hopes and dreams of a four-eyed winkle wearing a camouflaged jungle hat.

Lediards had been dishing up to the local community since 1912. Like a tardis, its narrow shop front disguised the fact that there was enough room inside to squeeze twelve angry men, twenty hungry children, and a dozen old ladies including tartan shopping trolleys. Boarded walls were painted a racing green, and dusty Victorian lighting hung from the ceiling on chains. It certainly warranted its place in the 1970 *Michelin Guide*, and proudly displayed its two Michelin Stars above the live eels and a triangular display of orange Fanta cans.

Its secret pie recipe wasn't one for the vegetarians. When Mahatma Ghandi visited East London in 1931, a Pathé news team captured him leaving Lediards and wheeling theatrically across the pavement before passing out in the middle of West Ham Lane.

Punters queued patiently outside before winding their way around an internal etched glass partition which offered a little privacy to the customers already eating. The dining area looked like those old Victorian workhouse pictures where a series of long communal tables had punters crammed together, everyone looking terrified in case any newcomer plonked themselves down to share the latest on their haemorrhoids (farmers). After collecting a plate of food, customers slid silently away like Olympic skaters through the sawdust strewn across the floorboards.

There was no conversation, just the scraping of spoons on china.

What was the secret of their success? Well, it wasn't the Lediard men, chained downstairs in the basement covering themselves in flour. No, it was the beaming faces of the Lediard ladies who made this such a thriving business. A relay of calm efficiency, with one particular young lady who left an indelible stain down the shirts of a thousand working class winkles.

Apart from her dazzling smile and blue eye shadow, it was blindingly obvious that she stripped down to her underwear before stepping into a semi-transparent, two sizes too small, buttons-straining-ready-to-pop house-coat. She looked like Brigitte Bardot, and men travelled miles for a two-minute interaction with Stratford's very own Lady of the Purée de Pommes de Terre.

On those special days when Brigitte was serving, Buster and Little Jocky got very agitated and made a big fuss about fastening their tiny bicycle helmets. You see, they knew the ride was about to get very bumpy.

Brigette Bardot: *Hello, sweetheart, how can I help?*

Flashing my Timex Young Explorer, I spread out some coins and delivered my best Steve McQueen impression:

Twelve-year-old Herbert: *Two pies and two mash, please … lady.*

In an act of kindness shown by vivacious East London women towards young men with glow-in-the-dark watches, she retained eye-contact while slapping on the mash and wiping the wooden spoon expertly across the plate. Then, with a playful smile, she slipped two pies onto it before pouring the delicious pale green liquid seductively across the lot. Dear reader; something was stirring, and I'm not referring to the delicately flavoured parsley liquor.

But the Lediard's pie and mash empire had a dark secret hanging over it like a dirty old tea towel. Rumours circulated about horse meat being used in their pies! Scotland Yard investigated, but apart from finding two horseshoes, a jockey's helmet, and an envelope stuffed with cash ... nothing was proven which allowed Sweeny Todd's naughty young brother to continue reigning supreme and leave the young men of Stratford dreaming about Miss Lediard laying them across the pie trays and whispering the secret of her delicious pie filling.

Frankie Dettori: *Well? Was it horse meat?*

Frankie Howerd: *Neigh, neigh and thrice neigh.*

Bringing Part One to a Climax

During the 1970s, if a young man wanted to understand the complex love-hate relationship between Zachary Smith and Robbie the Robot, then he had to look outside the confines of an Airfix box. I wasn't totally innocent, and knew never to discuss biology with a Scout leader naked from the waist down, but as far as the old 'in-outs' were concerned, me and my droogs had more questions than Russian donors to the Conservative Party.

For example. What could I offer the gorgeous Adrienne Posta apart from a quick Tommy Cooper impression and a Knickerbocker Glory down the Wimpy? And if, by some miracle, I managed to scale the perfectly proportioned legs of Aimi Macdonald, then what was I supposed to do when I got up there?

Luckily the Sex Education Fairy left something where I was sure to find it … alongside my old man's chrome ashtray.

It was a sex education book about a cartoon dog with a 'pop up' penis and 'pop out' testicles, who seemed more than happy sharing his genitals with the world. It was a real page turner and I noticed that when the dog lolled its tongue from the corner of his mouth, it yielded some excellent results with a lady poodle. I stood at our front room window and tried something similar with some passing schoolgirls, but met with only modest success.

Going to a single-sex school meant there were few opportunities to meet young ladies, and this was compounded by spending Saturday nights on frosty river banks. Yep, Herbert the Unready was still Nun the Wiser when it came to knowing what women want. That's why me and my band of sexual warriors had no option but to follow the clues hidden in British society.

Like studying the courting rituals on ITV sit-coms such as *Doctor in the House* before moving up to *Confessions of a Taxi Driver,* where the same actors went on location with a suitcase of frilly knickers, a dash of pubic hair, and more knob jokes than an episode of *Bagpuss*. We soon recognised that women fall into two camps: vampish man-eaters like Fenella Fielding or ferocious battle axes like Rita Webb.

Strangely, there was never any mention of contraception, and frantic love scenes were rarely interrupted by Robin Nedwell fitting one of those Dunkirks we had heard so much about. However, we did gain an appreciation of the tensile strength of stockings and suspenders, and learned that most girls would allow one blouse button to be undone … per one fish and chip supper consumed. So, to see a young lady in her matching bra and knickers would cost the equivalent of a well-stocked Mac Fisheries.

The night before my family joined the Great Cockney Exodus to Romford, me, Colin, Sprouty and John Pitt went to the Forest Gate Odeon to see an animated X-rated film called *Fritz the Cat*. It was like *Tom and Jerry* but with shagging and drug taking. It was absolute crap and I started to think my last night out in one of Forest Gate's top attraction had been wasted. Then the support film started. It was about a young Swedish woman's endeavour to achieve satisfaction without the aid of a box of Milk Tray. It made a big impression on that collection of bowler hats and false moustaches as she did stuff that no self-respecting *Playschool* lady would ever get up to ... or, in one case, lower herself down to. On the way home, we all agreed that Swedish women would make good and faithful wives, yet none of us could work out why the film had been called *Climax*.

And that was that. Fourteen glorious years charging around Newham, doing fuck-all. The next day, my tour of North Romford off-licences would begin.

Back home, stretched out between the tea chests, I thought back to that Swedish film, and in particular a scene where the heroine got strip searched by a brunette policewoman. Man, oh man, what I would give to have a girlfriend with pubic hair so dark, thick and plentiful that it looked like she was giving birth to Kevin Keegan!

Ladies and gentlemen, I thank you.

(Stage curtains close, house lights up, and everyone wishes they had pre-ordered their hot dogs and Kia-Ora.)

END OF ACT 1

INTERMISSION

The following has been certified and passed with a U certificate by the British Board of Film Censors.

A Brief History of The Herbert

They have walked among us since the dawn of time. In Wookey Hole, Somerset, there are roughly drawn cave paintings depicting early humans hunting and fishing. Look closely and you will see one figure sitting apart from the others, cataloguing different sized rocks. This is the earliest known evidence of the genus Homo Flacido. Otherwise known as Herberto Semi Erectus.

There are many examples throughout history. The Bayeux Tapestry is thought to show numerous embroidered Herberts, dawdling along looking at their feet during the famous battle scene, and many of Chaucer's characters exhibit recognisable Herbert traits such as stubbornness, non-compliance, and always quietly subversive towards authority.

Military records from Waterloo describe how a young infantryman found himself behind enemy lines and inside Napoleons private quarters. After pocketing a solid gold inkwell, the young private deposited something on the emperor's gilt-edged writing desk that was not only ungallant, but also indicative of the poor diet of the British infantry at the time. During World War II, Pathé News liked to show ordinary soldiers happily deferring to the officer class. In reality, when the troop ships returned home, many working-class Herberts were last off, and pushing prams full of European antiques down the gangplanks ready to be off-loaded to their close cousins, the entrepreneurial Geezers. During the 1960s, a Spotty Herbert became a term of ridicule, forcing many to withdraw from society. However, thanks to the efforts of HFP, they were introduced back into the wild and we are proud to say that the Herbert population is now flourishing once again.

So, if it's peace and quiet you're after, then pick up your inflatable tube in the foyer and join us as we float along the lazy river looking up at cloud formations.

Remember to collect all your belongings and we hope you enjoy the rest of your stay in Herbertland.

Advertisement sponsored by Herberts For Peace.

AND NOW, BACK TO THE STORY ...

Mum in West Ham Park before flying to Hollywood

Private Charles Smith taking a well earned break from playing cribbage with his pal Sherpa Tenzing

Herbert of the Yard

Joe 90

Me, Colin and Sprouty

MI5 Headquarters

Whipps Cross Lido showing
Colin doing his 'dying swan'

Fred Mills demonstrating
the old one-two

The old oak tree from Brief Encounter

Man holding Kendall Mint Cake

Mr Crabtree being cool. Pete being a knob

Filming Penny Lane in Stratford

Council approved Hogwarts

The only man to sing Mr Moonlight
faster than Pinky and Perky

1 Rita Smith	5 George Smith	9 Flo Smith	13 Aunt Queenie	17 Charlie Vaughn	21 Bill Moffatt
2 Polly's sister Flo	6 Bill Smith	10 Harry Smith	14 John Adlam	18 Eileen Moffatt
3 Pat Moffatt	7 Ralph Feinnes	11 Bertha Smith	15 Dolly Moffatt	19 Brian Jupp
4 Jim Smith	8 Kath Smith	12 Bill Godfrey	16 Derek Moffatt	20 Uncle Jack

22 Maureen Vaughn   26 Barry Smith   28 Polly Moffatt   31 Pamela Vaughn
23 Denise Adlam   27 Peter Jackson   29 Christine Moffatt   32 June Moffatt
24 Kath Vaughn   30 Lynda Moffatt
25 Susan Godfrey

Charles and Jean Smith   September 1956

Jean Dolly Bill Christine   Lyn   Derek Pat Alice Eileen

The Magnificent Seven (plus two)   August 1969

ACT 2

ROMFORD (1973 TO 1980)

'We all have Hitler in us, but we also have love and peace … so why not give peace a chance?' John Lennon

Collier Row, Fields of Waving Corn, and the Chop Suey Centre

Like the Huguenot thief (Pierre the Burglar), the Jewish baker (Jacob the Bageler) and the Roman percussionist (Isoceles the Triangle), residents of London inevitably move out to the sticks. And in May 1973 it was our turn to wait for the removal van. John Pitt stopped on his way to school and wished me luck. A touching moment, only spoilt when he asked for his binoculars back.

A man called Horace arrived with a BRS lorry and we loaded it with stuff gleaned from over sixteen years of marriage including four brass ashtrays, a print of a bluebell wood, and a fourteen-year-old scarecrow clutching a fishing rod. The only thing missing was the woman still removing any forensic evidence of our nine-year stay. My deeply religious father looked at his watch.

"Christ all bleedin' mighty, boy… go in and tell her to hurry up."

So, I did, and exactly one hour later she came out carrying with her the cat, and the great smell of Domestos.

All set, Horace began wrestling with a long gear stick protruding

184

from the cab floor. It was touch and go but they finally got engaged and we set sail for the most easterly of London boroughs – Havering (twinned with New York, Paris and Stalingrad).

Heading down the Romford Road, I looked back with two ounces of trepidation, three fluid ounces of excitement and one teaspoon of sadness. Did The Girl in the Prefabs even know I was leaving? Was she crying unconsolably while her best friend tried to console her?

"Don't worry, love, they're all the fucking same."

Most importantly, how had a Polish goalkeeper called Tomaszewski single-handedly knocked England out of the 1974 World Cup qualifiers?

With me in the back was a tea chest crammed with my most prized possessions: Beatles LPs, a 1971 Pears' encyclopaedia, a David Nixon Magic Annual, assorted fishing tackle, half a dozen *Creepy Tales* comics, a Polaroid instant camera (including spare flash cube), an Aurora glow-in-the-dark Hunchback of Notre Dame, a pair of bleached Levi's, a well-thumbed copy of Swedish Erotica, and the Subbuteo Angling board game. Not much to show really, for fourteen years doing sod all.

Anyway, forty minutes later we turned left at Romford Dogs towards Collier Row where the Bairstow Eves Choir were lined up to welcome us with a medley of WWII songs: *There'll Always be an England, Any Old Iron*, and Dame Judy Dench's favourite, *Knees up Mrs Brown*.

Three hours later, Horace was on his way back to Stratford with a twenty-pound note and a bottle of Scotch, and I stood at my new bedroom window staring out towards a back alley and some garages. The lady next door was in her garden and threw me a friendly wave. How to respond? I did what any sexually immature teenager would … and hid behind the curtains. Seven years later, that lady would play a major role in one of the happiest days of my life! Importantly, for the lady concerned, it wouldn't involve having to stand before me in her bra and knickers.

Apart from thousands of identical semi-detached houses and a severe lack of bomb sites, Collier Row felt nice and familiar. No. 82 Collier Row Road was a three-bedroomed terrace with a tiny kitchen and a box room big enough to accommodate one Jimmy Krankie and two Diddy men. It also had a front garden where my old man could park his Ferrari Testarossa when he eventually got around to passing his fucking test.

Up the hill was a parade of shops set in a 1930's facade of red brick and Crittall windows. There was a small camera shop the size of a Box brownie and a chemist where my mum's sister Dolly worked. There was a butcher for your mince, a dry cleaner for your chintz, and a baker offering French sticks, Belgian buns, and Captain Scott's favourite … iced fingers. If a romantic evening was in order, then you had the Chop Suey Centre or the Community Centre to practise short mat bowling. There was also a supermarket crammed inside a former cinema which was so big that during her first visit, Mum had to leave a trail of breadcrumbs back to the trolley park.

But one shop stood legs astride as the undisputed champion of the Collier Row retail experience. It was, of course, F. W. Woolworth, offering everything this freelance Catweazle impersonator could wish for, including fishing tackle, pop records, geometry sets, disposable underpants and a woman with a fondness for sixteen-year-old schoolboys (more from the lead singer of the Shangri-Las later).

The Moffatt exodus was now precisely 89% complete. Pat near Romford dogs; Derek in Gidea Park; Lynda and Bill in Harold Hill; and Dolly, Eileen and Christine with us in Collier Row. Aunt Alice was staying in East Ham so Jeff could finish his education and continue lifting pocket watches from elderly gentlemen distracted by the excellent value crockery in Green Street Market.

My parents, on the other hand, had concluded they had nothing to lose from me moving school in the middle of my O' levels, and, quite honestly, I wasn't bothered either. I was more excited by the possibility of having new classmates who wore deodorant and lipstick for PE. Come to think of it, my biggest concern was finding somewhere that sold red maggots!

Here Come the Girls or What the Fuck Happened There?

The first weekend, a coach-load of brother-in-laws arrived (collective noun: a shuffle) to form a through-lounge with complimentary serving hatch. By Sunday evening the smell of fresh plaster toyed playfully with the smell of boiled fish as Mum dropped pieces of cod under the floor boards in an effort to recapture the cat. Me? I was having my usual pre-school anxiety and so, because Steve Zodiac was in Los Angeles auditioning for a part in *Captain Scarlet*, I spent the evening hyperventilating in a deckchair watching Jane Fonda in *Cat Ballou*.

Next morning and, after throwing up in the sink, I waved farewell to my mother who was already up a ladder furiously bleaching the front gutters. The route to my new school passed a newsagent's where the owner kept a small monkey in a cage in the back garden. As I walked past I sensed a little hostility from that little captive primate watching me intently. I smiled, hoping we might become friends, but every day for the next eighteen months that fucking monkey would scream and bare its arse at me as I hurried past like Damien from *The Omen*. Apart from that, everything was fine and dandy.

North Romford Comprehensive. Modern. Concrete. Straight out of an episode of *Thunderbirds*. Like my old one, this headteacher also wore a billowing black gown. But instead of making skinheads melt into concrete columns, this one blew kisses to everyone as he skipped along the corridors. He looked like an effeminate Vladimir Lenin, and a week later he (Lenin), decided the new boy (Joe 90), should introduce himself to the school by speaking upon the subject of road safety during morning assembly. This was to be done with another new boy called Richard, but when the big day arrived, Richard the Lionheart was too busy vomiting into his sports bag so it was down to me. Alone in poop creek, somewhere between a rock and a cleft stick.

Doing five minutes about road safety under the glare of three hundred teenagers was a tough gig, especially as there's not much that hasn't already been said, and more eloquently, by both Tufty and Alvin Stardust. Anyway, I sat there like a condemned man with a dry throat swallowing jagged pieces of his last hamburger. A few days earlier, aunt Eileen had returned from the Costa del Sol and brought me back a Spanish leather key fob, so I sat behind Lenin (the cunt), twiddling it between my trembling fingers and thanking Our Lady of Spanish Souvenirs that Eileen hadn't brought me a pair of wooden castanets.

I began my talk in a low falsetto as one hundred and fifty nubile girls mentally de-bagged me, and one hundred and fifty boys thought *'What a Fucking Twat'*. When, and only when, everyone understood the perils of wearing flared loons while negotiating a busy A12, I sat down to a round of deafening silence. *'Oh well, better luck next time ...'* as a five-foot tall Diego Maradona said to a six-foot tall Peter Shilton.

I had no problems integrating. In fact, I joined the basketball team and was soon squeaking around the court slam-dunking like a Harlem Gobstopper. I think I also impressed my new classmates in the school swimming pool by completing 25 metres in a blur of foam before standing poolside while the girls contemplated this long-haired lover in blue-tinted glasses. Was he truly the son of God, or an imposter like those German soldiers in *Went the Day Well?*

Like I've said, for a young man dressed as a Captain of the Household Cavalry, Stratford had been a lean place to meet girls. Apart from fifteen female cousins, the closest I got to a pair of knickers was when I found some outside a launderette and pulled them over my head to amuse Sprouty. Now I was literally surrounded by them. Gorgeous in grey uniforms, white shirts, white tights and long legs. Pretty sisters, dark-haired ravers, plump girls, tall girls and blue-eyed blondes all smiling at me and whispering behind geography books covered in *Smash Hits* posters of Marc Bolan.

Like beautiful sharks, they circled in a feeding frenzy while I hung grimly to the side of a dinghy like an insecure bag of chopped fish guts. I believe this song by David Bowie sums up exactly how I felt:

'I'm only a poor little Sparrow,
No colourful feathers have I,
I can't even sing,
When I'm nesting in spring
The turnips don't grow very high.'

Come to think of it … that may have not have been David Bowie.

For three weeks I lived the life of Donny Osmond and came home each day like a chimney sweep covered in black mascara from all the fluttering eyelashes. Crumpled love letters and scribbled CVs were pushed into my sweaty palms as candidates waved across the crowded room. Like a four-eyed Caligua, all I had to do was give the thumbs up and wait for next day delivery.

Dear reader. If only those girls had formed an orderly queue, I might have developed some courting techniques and become a content young Herbert. Instead, like double decker buses, they came along every hour, normally in threes, and waited with their engines running while I rattled through my Frank Ifield impression. I went for a dozen interviews but never came close to climbing aboard one of those double deckers and losing myself in their delicately perfumed tartan upholstery.

Thankfully, especially for any of my grandchildren who might actually read this, that's where comparing 15-year-old schoolgirls to double decker buses must come to an end.

Unsurprisingly, I lost my way on simultaneous equations, got muddled about the formation of oxbow lakes, and slid down the education charts quicker than Jimmy Osmond's version of *Voodo Child*. Within two months I was waving goodbye to the O' level stream and doggy-paddling across to the CSE stream, where the girls were equally pretty but the rest of us were resigned to working in the cut-throat world of flipping hamburgers.

Vlad and the senior leadership at North Romford Soviet Federative Socialist Republic Teachers Union (N.O.S.F.E.R.A.T.U) did their best, but controlling boys in platform shoes sliding around in puddles of testosterone was too much to ask. My report card read:

'A nice boy but easily distracted. All in all, a disappointing start.'

One thing was sure. The Girl from the Prefabs needed to show up pretty soon because I was in a perpetual state of arousal with Buster and Jocky staging hourly uprisings and making me walk stiff-legged like Kenneth Moore in *Reach for the Sky*.

Andy Warhol, Winning Hearts and Minds

There it was, on the front door mat. A Valentine's card. A chance for me to begin the long journey of finding a mate, and for my mother to start the even longer journey of renting out my room. Following the clues, I found out that my Valentine would accept any reasonable offer and was available for interview in the newsagent's with the monkey where she worked on Saturdays.

A good first impression was required so after some consideration, I settled upon the scene from *Gone with the Wind* where Rhett Butler asks Scarlett O'Hara for a Melody Maker and a pack of Juicy Fruit. The big day arrived and after waving a damp flannel under my armpits, I pulled on my favourite tank top, puffed up my favourite chest, took a big breath and walked past the newsagent's three times before venturing inside. Would my secret Valentine make me and my testicles the chirpiest threesome this side of the Beverly Sisters?

There she was. Standing behind a horizontal sea of newspapers wearing a light-grey cashmere jumper and her long brown hair curling over those slender shoulders. She looked at me with those dancing brown eyes and breathed a soft:

"Hello."

Dear reader. My bottle was going faster than a speeding bullet as I mentally translated what she really meant:

"Hurry up, big boy, I haven't got all bleeding day. There's a box of Golden Wonder to price up and I've still got those Woman's Weekly's to put out."

My courting technique was, and remains, based solely upon information gathered from *Bunty* comics and *Hai Karate* adverts, so my response sounded like I was using Norman Collier's faulty microphone:

"Hello … me … you … Romford … fancy … Saturday … on bus … next perhaps … pictures?"

She said yes! Good old Norman … ollier.

I couldn't believe it. A beautiful girl was going to accompany me to the Romford Odeon without any need for duct tape or rope! And according to my calculations, she should be rooting around my

Sherbert Lemons by next Saturday tea-time.

Film choice was important. Nothing light and fluffy. She needed to understand what the fuck she was dealing with. I had heard about Andy Warhol from David Bowie and if it was good enough for *The Man who Sold the World* then it was good enough for a twat wearing an olive-green jungle hat. So instead of the wildly successful *Love Story* starring Ali 'Quick Draw' MacGraw, I decided to show my young concubine around the radical New York underground scene with a Warhol film called *Trash*, which included heroin abuse, impotence, some gay action, and a side order of transvestitism. Importantly, this was going to happen somewhere between Romford Station and the North Street Bus Garage.

We watched the film in open-mouthed horror, me, my Valentine, and my untouched Sherbert Lemons. Afterwards we walked down South Street in traumatized silence as the Romford Brewery discharged a cloud of processed yeast to lay a protective cloak of John Bull across our young trembling shoulders. To this day, whenever I smell warm milk and Weetabix, I get terrible flashbacks to Warhol's impotent lead actor, and dread some kind of retrospective brewer's droop. Thanks a lot, David (so called) Bowie.

Despite Andy Warhol's best efforts, I was still in touching distance of my Valentine's affection. Perhaps some sparkling repartee? I weighed in with a solid five minutes on the different types of maggots available from Edko's Tackle shop, and followed that with a detailed explanation of the rules to Round the Clock on a dart board. By the time we got to The Bell and Gate, the silence was classified as stony, and a kiss on the cheek was as close as this Joker got to depositing his crown jewels in the Gotham City Sperm Bank.

"How did it go?" Mum asked.

Honestly, I didn't have a bleeding clue.

I had tried on more disguises than Secret Squirrel. From the gum-chewing Yank, to the courteous Walter Raleigh. I even sprinted alongside a bus full of girls with my knees pumping like Billy Whizz. So far, not one of them had stepped away from their mates to peel me an Opal Fruit.

I thought my problems were solved when I found a paperback called *The Happy Hooker* behind the sandpaper sandpaper in Dad's shed, but apart from an eye-popping chapter on ping-pong balls, even some fresh insight from a high-class call-girl couldn't stop *that* convoy of buses from pulling away in a cloud of dust.

Inevitably, word spread around the knitting circles of North Romford that I wasn't David Cassidy's long-lost brother after all.

So, I joined the queue of long-haired wastrels peering through the gates of Eden towards those nubile creatures who were dancing in translucent nighties around a giant effigy of the Bay City Rollers and singing the ancient Celtic incantation:

'*Shang-a-Lang ... Shang-a-lang ... Shang-a-Lang ... Shang-a-lang ... Shang-a lang.*'

Ah ... they don't invoke the devil like that anymore.

The Phillips Cassette Player

On the first day of Christmas (a partridge in a pear tree), Romford Debenhams was transformed into a Winter Wonderland thanks mostly to an electrician from Canvey Island. Excited children could now follow a trail of imitation snow and twinkling lights through Gentlemen's Gabardine Raincoats towards Santa's Grotto which nestled between Ladies Knickers and Lava Lamps, (a winning combination).

On the third day of Christmas (drummers drumming), my papa wandered the loading bays of the British Road Service looking for a birthday present for his aspiring bootlegger son. He negotiated a deal on a Phillips EL 3302 cassette recorder, and by Sunday evening (Lords-a leaping), I was denying some well-earned royalties from the likes of Marc Bolan, Cilla Black, Labie Sifre, and all four of The New Seekers.

And on Christmas Day (twelve bells-a-ringing), after a full turkey dinner and one brandy snap chaser, I loaded that cassette recorder with a Memorex C120 to capture the joy and excitement of a festive afternoon in a through-lounge in Romford.

Picture the scene.

Uncle Derek had commandeered the Jump Jockey and was now trying to juggle a Scalextric controller and a large Bristol Cream. Little cousins were sprawled on the floor with identical Barbie make-up sets. On the mantlepiece a bubbling green lava lamp cast an eerie glow over a Cape Demonti Tramp, making it look like Grandpa Munster in his basement laboratory. Aunt Christine woke from her nap singing 'Ernie' (the Christmas No.1) while Father Christmas gave his wife her Christmas goose. Bill Godfrey was surreptitiously opening a tin of Tom Thumb cigars so he wouldn't have to share one with my father, who was busy emptying a roll of Kodak taking pictures of the skirting. Uncle Charlie was sipping tea from a delicate bone china cup, while Alice and Dolly buttered their third loaf with aunt Jean feverishly opening more tins of salmon. Mum's new Estée Lauder was battling the smell of Aunt Pat's new house slippers, while Lynda and Denise swanned around wearing inflated bonnets connected to a pair of Pifco portable hair dryers. By the patio doors aunt June was blessing her husband with a large glittery wand as he stood ram-rod straight by the drinks trolley like a key holder to the nuclear code, ensuring Lynda's husband didn't take liberties with the Johnny Walker.

Yep, it was business as usual as my family recreated the orgy scene from Frederico Fellini's fantasy masterpiece *Satyricon*.

And all the while, that Phillips cassette recorder captured the lot on its magnetic tape. An irreplaceable social documentary of a family at war with the festivities, ready to be handed down through generations as a priceless heirloom.

Well, it would've been if I hadn't recorded over it on Boxing Day (thirteen sprouts a trumping) with the television premiere of *A Hard Day's Night,* including audio of the old man's post-Christmas flatulence drowning out Lennon's witty one-liners;

Dad: *Paaaarp.*

Herbert: *Daaaad ... I'm recording this!*

Dad: *Phruuuup ... sorry, boy.*

I saw Linda McCartney in Collier Row Woolworth's

By some miracle, a boy in our class managed to get himself inducted into the non-virgin fraternity with help from a lady in Woolworth. His daily updates about continuing a sexual relationship behind a busy Pick & Mix aisle definitely livened up a few biology lessons, especially when she took him out to the back alley and revealed the secret of the Black Magic Box.

I had a bit of a cold after dragging a pair of 3" platforms around a soggy sports field in the pouring rain, so I popped home and took a quick squirt of Sinex before legging it up to Woolworth to check out the check-out lady with a soft spot for 16-year-old schoolboys. With luck she might take ME around the back!

I hung around the record department, warming myself up with those two oiled-up models on the Roxy Music *Country Life* cover, and taking a crafty peek at that minx Linda McCartney on *Wings Wildlife* who was showing way more thigh than was absolutely necessary.

Suddenly, a lady fitting the description appeared, and I almost fell into the revolving cassette display.

'I saw her by the candy aisle
She turned and smiled at me, you get the picture? (Yes, we see).
And that's when I fell for the Lady Round the Back.'

She looked a right handful. Dyed red hair, stunning green eyes finished off with a dusting of sparkly green eye shadow. Oh, Lordy, she's coming my way!

Herbert: *Excuse me … have you got Solid Gold Easy Action by T.REX?*

Lady Round the Back: *Hang on love, I'll have a look.*

Her voice was so full of east-end promise that, to use the jargon of the American military, she took me to DEFCON 1.

Lady Round the Back: *Here we are … that's 99 pence, please.*

Herbert: *Do you take American Express?*

Lady Round the Back: (head to one side) *Don't sod about, darling …*
there's people waiting.

We definitely shared a moment, but this wasn't the time to discuss

Mickey Finn's bongo playing. The question was: how did I get those armour-piercing eyes to lock onto mine and take ME around the back?

'I felt so helpless, what could I do?
Imagining all the things she would doooo.'

I decided to go with the sympathy gambit used by Eamonn Andrews against Bobby Fischer in the 1974 World Chess Championship. I would shamelessly use her maternal instinct.

It was still hammering down outside so I lifted the lapels of my blazer and waited in the rain until she finished her shift. According to the Sinex advert, I could be out there for up to eight hours.

'Look out, look out, look Out!'

The whole thing was a bit of a car crash. The bit where you smack your face on the steering wheel leaving your hooter throbbing like a little Belisha beacon. She came out, looked towards the heavens, put up her brolly and gave not one fucking glance at the boy with the glowing red hooter and a fully loaded Smith & Wesson in his trouser pocket.

'She didn't stop and ask me why… all I could do was cry.
I'm sorry I fell for The Lady Round the Back.
(Lady Round the Back … and now she's gone)
(Lady Round the Back … and now she's gone)
(Lady Round the Back … and now she's gone.)'

The Scottish Play at North Romford

First period after lunch and one hundred and fifty pupils trooped into the dining room where an invisible layer of Mulligatawny still hung somewhere midway between floor and ceiling. Under our table was a skid mark of custard which had skilfully avoided the cook's mop by disguising itself as an HB pencil. The lesson was English literature and the sun pouring through a large expanse of aluminium windows was already braising this collection of sweaty, long-haired, jock-strap wearing sixteen-year-olds. And that was just the girls!

For reasons known only to the Head of English, the entire 5th form were about to simultaneously study Macbeth from a man limbering up like it was opening night at The Globe Theatre. Mr Falstaff was his name, and this was his annual opportunity to reproduce one of the finest Laurence Olivier impressions since Freddy 'Parrot Face' Davies' acclaimed Hamlet at the Queen's Theatre Hornchurch, and within minutes he was sweating profusely while single-handedly re-enacting the entire castle battlement scene. What a prize was bestowed upon this country when Anne Hathaway refused to dig any more worms and William Shakespeare had to swap his fishing rod for a goose quill and a bottle of Quink.

But to fully appreciate the great man's work you have to hear it, and from over by the fire exit we only caught snippets of dialogue when Lady Macbeth got put up the Macduff by three kitchens in a cauldron … or something like that.

Minds wandered. Some to the damage they could do to David Essex. Some to that evening's fish fingers. In my case, it was to a flaxen-haired beauty on the next table, absent-mindedly toying with her ringlets like a Shakespearian Harmony Hairspray advert. A boy called Duncan was drawing a penis in his text book, and opposite were three girls going to a lot of toil and trouble to titillate us by leaning back on their chairs and flashing their industrial knickers and ripped tights.

Didn't they know that leaning back on chairs was dangerous, and that they could hurt themselves … or even others?

Anyway. That was that. Like a discarded Elizabethan ruff thrown upon the fast-flowing waters of the River Avon, my chance of getting an English O'level floated away downstream, and the sweat stains on Mr Falstaff's mustard-coloured roll-neck jumper were all in vain.

A New Girl in Town or All in All, It's Just Another Kick in the Balls

In 1974, audiences queued for hours to see *The Exorcist,* and take the opportunity to throw up in a cinema ashtray. I wouldn't get to see it for another few years but I did buy the book and it sat on my bookcase waiting for me to pluck up some courage.

Meanwhile it was time to knuckle down, focus on exams, and definitely NOT fall in love with a girl in my revision group who knocked me clean onto my little lovestruck ass. Her name was Elizabeth. She was blonde and beautiful with a hint of Moira Lister, and the old ticker tape began spewing orders to fall in love post-haste, straight away, and with immediate effect.

But courting techniques had moved on from those innocent days when a girl expected nothing more than a Harry Worth impression and a quick game of Mousetrap. So, Friday after school, I walked Elizabeth home while serving her a triple helping of Harry Worth, Tommy Cooper, and Blakey from *On the Buses.* By the time we got to her front gate, I sensed a definite green light coming from the end of my flared loons. As Jack Hargreaves said when he came across Dame Barbara Cartland pre-baiting a swim on the River Thames:

'Cor … who would have thought it?'

I spent Saturday night by a lake in Harold Hill, planning how to get my fragrant Elizabeth to join me in payer for a big carp as we held hands under a fishing umbrella. She needed to share my experience of looking up at the wondrous myriad of stars above this ancient priory pond, while local rats stole our Cheesy Niblets.

Sunday morning, with the mist still lingering over the lily pads, I had a go on a mate's 50cc scooter and fell straight into a crop of stinging nettles. It was a sign. A sign that life's too short to sod about on a friend's scooter. I vowed right there to visit Elizabeth that very afternoon and ask for her hand in marriage. Failing that, perhaps she would care to join me over the park for an hour?

I bicycled home and after eating enough roast pork and potatoes to get through to tea-time, I showered and gave the old Barnet a blast with Mum's Pifco until it looked like a Bobby Charlton comb-over with a touch of bass player from Chicory Tip. Then after a quick swig of Aramis, like Mr Froggie, I went acourtin'.

She lived down Carter Drive and as I hurried past the Ascension Church, a small brown dog appeared from the car park and began trotting alongside. Was it another sign? Oh, sweet baby Jesus ... I fucking hope so!

Five minutes later, I took a big breath, opened her front gate and strode towards her front door just as a sweet cockney voice floated out from the downstairs window:

"Oh no ... it's that boy I told you about! I'm not in ... tell him I'm NOT in!"

Ah, now I understood. My little fluffy guardian angel was trying to warn me that Elizabeth batted for the other side.

Dear reader, I was growing increasingly accustomed to these kicks in the courting bollocks, so I executed a perfect Cruyff turn, and retraced my steps. When I got home, instead of sticking my head in the toaster, I finished off the pork crackling and spent the rest of the afternoon listening to *Ogdens' Nut Gone Flake* while playing darts. Then, after a session of *Highway* on ITV, a tinned salmon sandwich and a slice of cake and some cold roast potatoes and a glass of milk and a chocolate biscuit ... I went to bed with a cheese sandwich and a good book.

Kids ... books are the perfect antidote for any setback, always guaranteed to wash away the worries of a world-weary wanker. The choice that evening was *War and Peace* by Leo Tolstoy, about the French invasion of Russia and the impact of the Napoleonic era on Tsarist society. *Mr Crabtree Goes Fishing* by Bernard Venables which is about fishing on a flooded River Avon. Or *The Exorcist* by William Peter Blatty which is about bouncing beds and green vomit projectiles. I plumped for *The Exorcist*. Don't know why. Perhaps the power of Christ compelled me?

I'm not ashamed to say that book scared the crap out of me, and to this day I have never used an Ouija board with anyone called Captain Howdy.

Fashion Part II or The Next Boy to Arrive on Platform Shoes

Girls who like girls who like boys who like girls who like boys in olive-green jungle hats are a rare and happy breed. I knew it and more importantly... the bloke in the army surplus shop knew it. So it was time to stop being half man, half spare-bedroom carpet, chuck out my old parka and get with the fashion beat.

First was to swap my old school trousers for a pair of grey Oxford bags, perfect for wrapping themselves around a bike chain and bringing any journey to a shuddering halt. Bicycle clips would've been the answer but as my clap-o-meter was hovering between Berk and Twat, I arrived at school every day with greasy chain prints on the Oxfords and blood trickling from my nicely proportioned ankles.

Once a month I visited Mr Byrite's in Romford, and returned triumphantly waving another badly chosen fashion monstrosity. Two-tone platforms raised my profile but my best item was a black sleeveless tank top with a sexy purple horizontal band which looked surprisingly elegant when paired with a two-tone brown cowboy shirt.

While my contemporaries were tuning guitars and having unprotected sex, I spent Saturday nights either fishing, or shaking a leg to Tony Orlando at the Collier Row Community Centre. These were family affairs and highly enjoyable apart from moments of sheer terror when aunt Dolly would drag me onto the dance floor for a dose of *Hi, Ho, Silver Lining*. And it was always me who had to slope sheepishly up to the compère with a pair of green knickers (two one pound notes) to claim the Spot Prize (a tin of Ye Olde Oak Ham).

During these family gatherings, I began pondering a few of life's eternal questions. Like, why do girls look perfectly normal jigging around to *Ballroom Blitz*, yet Uncle Derek looked like a crazed serial killer? Also: why do ladies disappear to the toilets every fifteen minutes? I heard whispers about knickers riding up ... but where were they riding up to? *That* was the question.

Yep, that sullen pansy in a black tank top and two-tone platforms sitting outside the ladies' toilets picking over a basket of chicken was me, and something needed to change if I was to fulfil my pledge to the girls of North Romford.

The cavalry arrived in the form of Cousin Jeff, taking a break from robbing sweet shops along in Green Street to show me his new brown bomber jacket. He did this by standing on a chair and turning slowly around like something in a kebab shop window. Apparently, it was doing him no harm down the knocking shops along the Barking Road.

Oh Jesus, Holy Mary Mother and Child Reunion ... I needed a leather bomber jacket too.

Washing cars for money is one thing but top-end items meant making an appointment with my bank manager, and I couldn't have chosen a better time because Tom Jones had just had surgery to correct his sexy crooked nose, and my mum was fumbling for gas mark 4 with her head in the oven.

I set out my business plan to prove that leather was the new tweed, and my rousing finale of *My, my, my Delilah'* must have done the trick because we set off for the Sheepskin and Leather Shop on North Street roundabout where a thousand residents from the Black Mountains of Wales hung lifelessly from steel coat hangers.

The place smelled expensive with the faint whiff of rip-off, and when Mum's X-ray eyes spied the price tags, she dragged me another hundred yards to Romford market to try on a three-quarter length green leather monstrosity with large flapping lapels, four big front pockets and matching green belt. I think the stall holder was leaving it hanging like a side of venison, hoping it would somehow improve with age.

"What do you think?" she said.

"I'm not sure …" I said.

"How much?" she asked the stallholder.

"A score to you, darling," said the stallholder.

"We'll take it," she said.

"But Mum!" I said.

When we got home, I put on the green leather jacket and trucked up the hill to see if the lady in Woolworth's would stop work and give me a good seeing-to.

It quickly became obvious from the concerned reactions of strangers that my green leather jacket was treading a fine line between fashion faux pas and making me look like Jason King's backward younger brother. And when a group of Brownies (collective noun: a shroom) burst into tears, I knew it was time to leave this fashion malarkey to the big boys and give my army surplus jacket a fresh dose of mosquito repellent.

What happened to those two-tone platforms? Well, I sold them to Lynda's then husband, who fancied himself as Romford's equivalent to both Starsky and Hutch, but who in reality was a prematurely balding postman who delivered the royal mail in the style of an out and out wanker.

Careers, Exams and a Peace Protest with Yoko Ono

If I were to join the 1st Battalion of the Royal Dental Technicians, I needed to start brushing up on my oral hygiene. Fortunately for all the gummy people of Romford, I never did get to tinker half-heartedly with their porcelain teeth, and it was all thanks to a game of three-card brag.

A normal Saturday night. At one end of the front room sat the Moffatt sisters and sisters-in-law, *oohing* over the contents of baby Louise's nappy. At the other end were my uncles, playing cards through an assault course of peanut bowls, ashtrays and tumblers of Johnny Walker. It was the briefest of glances but I saw my old man look over his shoulder towards his only son dressed in a magician's cloak neatly sawing his cousin Nicola in half.

Next morning, he told me about a job offer where I could learn dirty jokes, make tea in galvanised buckets, and listen to *The Carpenters Greatest Hits* pretty much every fucking day. To clinch the deal, I was promised my own set of wheels. All I had to do was visit 44 Lodge

Lane and ask for someone called 'Uncle John'. By Sunday lunchtime I was signed up to become a labourer on John's building firm. A few months later and true to his word, John gave me a brand new set of wheels – a builder's wheelbarrow. More from Old Wheelie later.

With a job in the bag, the chances of me knuckling down for some decent qualification was as likely as that traitorous Nigel Farage getting caught leaving the Ecuadorian Embassy with a dodgy memory stick. Mum and Dad still travelled back to Newham each day, so with nobody to make me breakfast I decided to stay in bed for peace, like John Lennon. But instead of sharing my bed with a Japanese lady in white pyjamas, I was gonna share it with assorted members of Pans People who would keep the magic alive by wearing baby doll nighties.

And it was after one particularly frustrating night, squabbling over a single quilt with a troupe of women dancers, that I awoke to the sound of urgent knocking. It sounded like Morse code so I jotted down the dots and dashes. The message read: GET UP AND ANSWER THE FUCKING DOOR. It was the school inspector, who suggested I give up my bohemian lifestyle in return for him not telling my father. It made perfect sense and I went back to school to collect a clean sweep of exam certificates, useful only for making Robert Harbin's origami swans.

For Art O'level, I set out to produce a piece of conceptual art that even Yoko would've been proud of. It was the rear view of Paul McCartney in his Sergeant Pepper uniform, facing a large mirror. Reflected in the mirror was the rear view of McCartney. Yep, a brilliant homage to A Bar at the Folies-Bergère by Edouard Manet, with a nod to René Artois from 'Allo 'Allo! And like one of Yoko's events where audience members snipped away items of her clothing, my A2 masterpiece was whittled down over the next 24 hours by paint-splattered sabotage until it lay before me an undistinguished A5. About the size of a small envelope.

For someone with the speaking skills of a half-cut Arthur Mullard (an *Art Mull*, if you will), English Oral was another big ask. It consisted of speaking for five minutes on any subject, in front of your peers and two bearded examiners. The standard was high. Tammy Whitesnake had opened proceedings with an enthralling five minutes on The History of Top Shop Cardigans from £15.99 to £18.99. Each oral was received with a cursory nod by the examiners until only two candidates remained – a long thin boy with a guitar case, and a long thin boy with a pencil case. Thin Boy One walked to the front, produced a gleaming white Stratocaster, and began an enthralling five minutes on the life of Jimi Hendrix. At least I knew the size of my task. In fact, I knew it so well … I nearly soiled my Oxfords.

Stratocaster Boy returned to his seat to the sound of cheering while Thin Boy Two trudged to the front like he was collecting horse droppings after the Lord Mayor's Show. The room quietened, the examiners nodded, and my little pooper opened up the throttle as I began a rapid verbal tour around John and Yoko's peace protests, with particular regard to acorns and the use of electronic feedback and high-pitched screaming.

Ladies and gentleman; it was like the lights going out over London, as one by one my audience laid their heads on the desks while I ploughed through five minutes of unprepared drivel. Was I way ahead of my time or just a pretentious young Herbert? I'll let you decide because I'm going upstairs to listen to Yoko wailing from inside a large white bag.

School's Out, or, The Moon Age Daydream is Over

The night David Bowie played the Romford Odeon, I was queuing at The Chop Suey Centre for some delicious Chinese chips (only two menu places below the legendary Pineapple Fritter Hong Kong

Style). And when Bowie's disciples ran towards the slender man with a 12-string acoustic slung across his shoulders, he spoke four simple words he was destined never to repeat:

'Goodbye, Romford … it's been great.'

Okay, five words.

Like the great man, I was also saying farewell. To school. My parents bet everything on me providing some decent house-keeping, and now the manager of Collier Row William Hill was having a new kitchen extension. My old school blazer was handed to Cousin Mark and I walked out of North Romford Comprehensive with no fanfare, no qualifications and bent double with sexual frustration. Ten years of schooling and nothing to show for it apart from one love bite and two spare tickets for an Andy Warhol film.

A Rite of Passage or The Outing of the Herbert

Sir Izaak Walton died on December 15th 1683. I was born December 15th 1957. He wrote *The Complete Angler*. I wrote a tall story for a *Magpie* badge. Coincidence? I don't bloody think so.

In the old days, nothing could've kept me from being bankside at the start of the fishing season apart from a Las Vegas hooker offering free pie and mash. So please join me, back in 1973, on a pavement outside Chadwell Heath Police Station.

It was midnight, Saturday 16th June, and forty pairs of thigh-high rubber waders, otherwise known as the Wangye Angling Society, were psyching themselves up for the first trip of the season. Amongst the cigar smoke and rampant sexism, as quiet as a mouse and as thin as a pin, stood a lanky teenage werewolf in a tartan cap.

The coach arrived and the speedy boarders were quickly setting up camp on the back seat, just like those old school coach trips. The language was a bit choice with a hint of ripe, and by the time my forehead rested against the cool glass I had learned more about ladies' undergarments than from two Littlewood's catalogues and five seasons of *The Generation Game*. One particular discussion was about ladies' tights being worn as a thermal layer on a cold winter's morning by the River Thames which quickly evolved into Bruce Forsyth wearing Anthea Redfearn's fishnet stockings and ended with him using her frost-covered knickers to land a 10lb barbel.

Above me, floating serenely in the luggage rack, was the ghost of Emily Pankhurst fanning herself furiously with *The Angling Times*.

Four hours later, in a gravel car park in Norfolk, forty olive-green figures hurried from the coach to accompany the dawn chorus with a pleasing descant of trickling brooks, two sexist farts and one heavy waterfall courtesy of the coach driver.

After collecting their rod holdalls, nets and baskets, each member paid a 50p sweepstake and trudged off into the mist. My number was one of the last, so I had difficulty finding somewhere on the lake not already occupied by an angler peering grumpily over his shoulder and in no mood to help a distressed virgin dressed as a Bay City Roller.

I eventually found a place under an overhanging tree facing a weed-clogged section of the lake. It was a few yards along from two senior members: the famous Bullock twins. Famous for being miserable fucking bastards who could've easily moved up to allow a young member to dangle his size 14. They fancied themselves as a Chadwell Heath version of the Kray twins, but you would never catch Ronnie and Reg screaming like a pair of schoolgirls when a large swan came ashore to gobble their sweetcorn. Shagged out and downhearted, I popped open a can of Sainsbury's cola and wept over the loss of my 50p sweepstake and the departure of Susan Stranks from *Magpie*.

Then a miracle occurred. The angling equivalent of Jesus beating Birmingham match angler Ivan Marks on the Sea of Galilee. From this most uninviting of swims, the ghost of Izaak Walton pushed three heavy roach my way before continuing around the lake to scare the shit out of sleeping anglers. Those three fish were enough to collect £5 from the sweepstake and cement my place in angling folklore.

Next day, after one final lap of honour around the garden, I rushed up to Woolworth's and used the fiver to buy John and Yoko's *Unfinished Music: Two Virgins*. It's the one with the infamous brown cover hiding a picture of my hero throwing his pyjamas to the wind and his wife standing with great dignity alongside her husband's knob. I loved that Granny Smith Apple label spinning around the turntable, scattering electronic warblings around my bedroom, and it soon became a firm favourite alongside *Chirpy Chirpy Cheep Cheep*, sung by a blonde lady who wore hot pants and thigh high suede boots, if I'm not mistaken.

Fast forward nine months and we're at the function suite above the Co-op on Stratford Broadway for The Wangye Angling Society Annual Dinner Dance and Prize Giving. The ladies wore elegant evening dresses, the men wore black bow ties, and I wore a Bruce Oldfield creation comprising of a green leather jacket, floral shirt with collars the size of two windsurfing sails, all complimented by a magnificently poncy silk neckerchief heavily influenced by the necktie killer in Hitchcock's *Frenzy*. When every dining tablecloth was strewn with lettuce and Thousand Island dressing, I stepped on stage to collect a pewter tankard for being Junior Champion.

Fifty years later, it still stands proudly alongside a 'Best Granddad in the World' mug, and an Advanced Scaffolding certificate.

Charles (Chas) Smith

So how come we never got a car? Well, it wasn't my father doing his bit to remain carbon neutral, because his flatulence was causing more holes in the ozone layer than a chest freezer in Iceland. Nope. For years, Mum pleaded with him to learn to drive so that she could lord it up in the back of a Ford Escort, waving regally like Princess Margaret. But he never delivered. The closest we came was during the 1967 Eurovision Song Contest when his brothers-in-law somehow cajoled him into an impromptu driving lesson during a game of strip cribbage. The omens weren't good. The Germans had just pulled off a strong performance denting Sandie Shaw's chances of giving the UK back some pride after last year's dismal showing by Kenneth McKellar.

Aunts, uncles, cousins and neighbours piled out into the street while my old man took a last-minute slash. When he appeared at the front door and strode through the crowd, they cheered like he was a Roman gladiator:

"Charlius, Charlius … Go, go Charlius!"

His chariot was a Winchester Blue Ford Zephyr, and while Uncle Derek showed him the rudder controls, Mum gathered all available infants to her bosom like a protective coat of many cousins. Finally, my old man's grinning face appeared at the driver's window.

"Chocks away!" he called. I was so proud.

Ladies and gentlemen, it was like the Hindenburg disaster.

Cheers turned to stunned silence as the Zephyr inched from the kerb and ploughed slowly into our neighbour's Hillman Imp, crushing its wing with a heavy crump. Grim-faced, the old man climbed out and walked calmly back through the – now silent – well-wishers.

"You alright, Charles?" Mum asked.

"Fuck that!" came his reply as he went inside for a well-earned drink.

There was more than a whiff of the intentional about that Eurovision catastrophe but it stopped my mother's pleadings and proved once and for all, that he was nobody's (drum roll) *Puppet on a String*. I thank you.

He shared many Herbert traits, like never speaking on the phone longer than ten seconds, and kipping between meals without ruining his appetite. He was also happy to keep a low profile, apart from when discussions turned to the merits of the royal family, when he would suddenly squeeze in an explosive storm of expletives that would've left Prince Philip blushing like a potty-mouthed schoolgirl.

He had his favourite phrases, like *dot on the card* (a dead cert), *one for the pot* (an unhinged individual), and *You're all on top, mate* (a one-minute warning to the unhinged individual). A win was *a bit of mozzle*, and his comb was a *strawberry* (Strawberry Roan, a horse breed favoured by gypsies). His socks were *almonds* and for Sunday tea he always enjoyed a nice bit of *stand at ease* on his *Holy Ghost* with a dollop of *piccalilli* (piccalilli). House keys were *twirls* (from prison officers twirling theirs). Numerals were *deuce, nevis* and *roof* (two, seven and four), and wind problems were *Lionels*, or, when in mixed company, *D'Oylys*. His favourite motto was *Nolite Confidere Quis Bastardus*, and his bedtime stories were always from the *Thomas the Tank Engine's Guide To Never being Last up the Bar*.

The only book he ever read was a Roy Rodgers Annual in 1940, but he consistently got the *Countdown* conundrum. He was generous man. Other men liked him, ladies adored him, but he never mastered the Sky remote. Fiddles were actively encouraged, but when I found a £10 note outside our house in Stratford, he told me to first check with our elderly neighbour if it was hers. A noble gesture, remembered mostly for the speed in which her greedy, wrinkled little hand grabbed the note before slamming the fucking door in my face.

He was a no-frills man with a good sense of humour and a stubborn sense of decency, and if I was forced to choose, I'd say he was a Herbert with Geezer tendencies. Somewhere between Rooster Cockburn and Tony Soprano. He would, of course, dispute that because he was also an argumentative bastard who never *blows his own trumpet.*

Biggles Goes to Work (part 1)

Nowadays you can't visit a building site without wearing a hi-visibility safety helmet, welders' gauntlets and knee-high, lead-lined diver's boots, but in 1975 the Health and Safety Executive were more laid back than Andy Williams on a Zen Master refresher course. So, on my first day, I wore a padded navy-blue anorak and some rubber goggles from Mum's RAF dressing-up box. And that's how I came to be standing in a cobbled builder's yard alongside a bright yellow skip, dressed like Captain Biggles' eager young sidekick, Lord Bertie Fokker.

Around me were forty men in flat caps, suit jackets and mud-covered wedding shoes, each saying morning prayers to the mighty god, Woodbine. Many had fought during WWII, heroes one and all who would spend the next five years telling me exactly why they wish they hadn't fucking bothered. It was a man's world alright, and the only thing missing was a teensiest improvement on their personal hygiene so I made a mental note to bring in a spare Andy Capp Talc Dispenser to leave in the outside toilet.

Around the yard were piles of sand, stacks of bricks and racks of scaffold poles propped against walls that were topped with broken glass to keep out the taxman. Timber was kept in an old stable, along with a straw manger for men to lie down on when they saw how much tax they had paid.

When all the jobs were allocated and lorries loaded, those battle-hardened Tommies walked straight out of the gates while I sat in the back of a blacked-out Commer van like a little button mushroom. So far so funky.

There followed a five-minute drive careering through the back streets of Plaistow before the van stopped outside a café in Balaam Street where we were met with a warm blast of congealed ketchup and low-flying expletives. And once the old Joe 90s had de-misted, I saw those very same British Tommies who moments before were sharing tearful goodbyes to the general foreman, now ordering Overlarge-Greedy Bastard-Fuck-Off-Builders Specials.

I found a corner table and watched men wiping Mother's Pride around their plates like they were trying to erase the delicate Delph pattern. The experience was like being back at school really. Same characters, same knob jokes. I even struck up a conversation about Lyndsey De Paul's new single ... no, honestly... I did.

Ninety minutes later, the lady proprietor was slumped behind the counter taking a well-earned pull on her oxygen pipe as the van sped across the Bow Flyover towards a large two-storey factory in Hackney. It was empty apart from some one-legged pigeons in the rafters, four-legged rats in the toilets, and a two-legged gentleman who was to spend the next five years teaching me all things slightly dodgy in the British building industry.

His name was Ted Greaves. An intelligent man able to resolve any building, sexual or financial problem in the time it took to snap his tobacco tin shut and surround himself in sweet smelling Golden Virginia. After a brief introduction, he set me to work mixing concrete and pouring it into holes while he looked on. Finally, I was a working man! Come to think of it, I was the ONLY working man.

It was a knackering introduction to a forty-year career and when I got home, I collapsed into bed and slept like a captain's log (*drum roll*) and woke up in the fireplace of the Starship Enterprise. I thank you.

Biggles Goes to Work (part 2)

Next morning. Up early – bus to Romford – train to Mile End – bus to factory for the final leg. Only one problem: yesterday I was delivered in a blacked-out van so had no idea where the toes were on the final leg. Fortunately, I had three summers experience of tracking Baloo to the chemical toilets, so I jumped on a bus and began looking for signs. I found one. It read CUBITT TOWN. I was going the wrong way, and heading towards the Isle of Dogs where even the old ladies wore Millwall scarves.

I jumped off the bus outside the Poplar Baths which wasn't easy because the bus didn't stop there!

SFX – *We hear an embarrassed cough and the faint rustling of a Raspberry Ruffle.*

Lost behind enemy lines. I rang the office to tell them the good news.

Herbert: *Hello? I'm lost.* (actually thinking: *It's not my fault. I was delivered in a blacked-out van.)*

Uncle John: *Not to worry, son.* (actually thinking: *Oh for fucks sake!)*

I eventually found my ball bearings, and one hour later fell crying at Ted's feet. He listened sympathetically before telling me to start ripping down a large pile of asbestos sheets ready to enclose some metal columns. Lost in a toxic cloud of white asbestos, I went at it like a four-eyed whirling dervish until eventually collapsing like the ghostly white figure of Anne Boleyn.

But Ted was a wise old owl and, recognising a flagging spirit, offered the following advice which I still adopt whenever I have successfully completed a full hour's work:

"Alright boy … let's have a nice cup of tea."

Indiana Jones and The Ancient Tea Ceremony

Ted was the custodian of a battered metal box about the size of a coal bunker, which looked like the Ark of the Covenant and got transported between sites using two scaffold poles like a sedan chair. Apart from the ten commandments, it carried assorted scaffold clips, shovels, slate roofing hammers, drain rods, pick axes, old cardigans for the winter mornings and dog-eared copies of *Penthouse* for the winter lunchtimes. It was also home to a large enamel kettle, a gas bottle and a portable stove.

The stove was always placed in a position of great importance, usually along ancient ley lines, but always near a cold-water supply. Then an assortment of make-shift seats were placed around it in a broken circle like Stonehenge before the mighty god Typhoo could be summoned. The sound of hissing butane prompted a stampede comparable to twelve Ian Duncan Smiths racing towards the nearest camera (collective noun: a cunt), before those working-class druids could settle down for a well-earned cuppa.

There was never much conversation, just the excited rustle of tin-foil followed by disappointed sighs as another cheese and pickle was revealed. What were their partners thinking? Did these men not deserve a bit of variety? Like a chocolate Penguin, a peanut covered Joker, or even a marshmallow Riddler? The answer, of course, was to make their own fucking sandwiches.

Tea breaks increased in duration and jollity until mid-afternoon when, almost hysterical from half-a-day's work, my comrades began planning their evenings. A few were brushing up their racial stereotypes with an ITV sit-com. Ted was going to The Flying Scud for a bar billiards match, and Jimmy Cox, short and stout like a well-loved teapot, was taking his wife to the Dennis Drew dance studios in Manor Park. Me? I was gonna check the Romford Recorder to see when Joan Jett was appearing at the Queen's Theatre, Hornchurch.

These teaspoon time-outs were also the perfect opportunity for a young man to analyse the readers' letters in *Penthouse*, and compare the thrupennies (bits) and raspberries (ripples) in *Fiesta*. Not forgetting the advertisements! What was a buzzing black stallion, and what woman needs a gold-tipped vibrating lipstick? And who in their right mind would try and smuggle an inflatable lady into Beckton Lido?

One particular advert prompted many heated discussions. It was for the Chartham Method: Penis Enlarger. Ted pooh-poohed its new-fangled suction method, but there was a general consensus that wives always appreciated the lengths their men would go to for an extra inch or two.

The Silvertown Way

Like 'Dig for Victory' or 'Careless Talk Costs Lives', Ted's work ethic was based on the wartime slogan 'Make do and Mend'. If it was near home time and one vital piece of the building jigsaw was missing well, let's just say, what Ted could do with a bucket of fresh urine and twenty feet of twin and earth cable would've left that prat Laurence Llewelyn-Bowen having a litter of ginger kittens.

Some of his finest work was in the factories of Canning Town. Gigantic industrial monoliths like Tate & Lyle or Spillers, once the lynchpin of the British empire. But even monoliths need to recharge their batteries and at weekends those factories became ghost towns, empty apart from one-legged pigeons and local builders doing maintenance work.

And there wasn't much that could tempt a young man to leave warm, crumpled sheets on a Sunday morning apart from the offer of unregulated overtime (street name: double bubble) so after an exhausting night watching Babs and Dee Dee rehearse what should've been a straightforward dance routine to *The Hustle*, I set off one Sunday, using Cranes, Trains and Batmobiles, for Canning Town. By 8am, I was peering through a hole in a factory floor.

It was the size of a large car and the job was to fill it with reinforced concrete, ready for a new piece of heavy machinery. Ted had detailed plans to see the lunchtime stripper at The Flying Scud so we weren't hanging about. First some shuttering ply was fixed to the ceiling below and held in place with an array of ladders and props perched on canteen tables and chairs. Then it was up to the floor above using the factory's vertical one-man conveyor belt. I'm not sure those things would be allowed outside of a North Korean Vibrating Lipstick Factory, but getting on and off one was like jumping from a speeding rocket as it travelled through a concrete black hole. Anyway, in the mid 1970s it was the only way to travel.

When we were all on the floor above, I got to grips with two metric tonnes of concrete as Frank, a former RAF pilot, informed Ted of the bad news.

"Some blighter's forgotten to send the bally reinforcement!"

Translation:

"Some cunt's forgotten to send the bally reinforcement!"

Nothing for it. Make do and Mend.

Ninety minutes later, Ted was trowelling smooth the new floor.

Inside the fresh concrete lay a selection of gas-barrels, a scaffold pole, a few lengths of electrical conduit, a bicycle frame and a Tony Jacklin 3-iron, all tied together with wood and string. Quite honestly, a gangster in a concrete overcoat and a starched white shirt would have offered more structural stability but who cares when you're eating roast pork with two members of Pans People and a time-sheet proving you were still in Canning Town. Hooray!

For a few weeks, I kept an eye on *Nationwide,* expecting Sue Lawley to announce The Great Sugar Refinery Tragedy of 1976 but I needn't have worried. The great British worker had triumphed once again and was now celebrating with a feather boa in The Flying Scud.

Mrs Robinson, just off Mare Street, London E.1

Opposite that factory in Hackney was a row of council flats with neatly dressed window boxes and polished steps. One was home to a big-bosomed lady never without a smile for the hard-working men standing behind the factory windows doing fuck-all. There was never any sign of a husband so it was concluded that he was either in prison or lying dead on the shag pile, exhausted by her sexual appetite.

Once a week she got out the Red Admiral and polished her front step vigorously for a full ten minutes, encouraging those bosoms to dance around like two naughty puppies. It was very public spirited of her, and my colleagues started taking bets on which of those two strikers (Mike Summerbee on the left, or Sylvestor Stallone on the right), would be first to *Escape to Victory.* One chap even brought in a deckchair and some ivory opera glasses so he could watch in comfort! For me, she was just a pleasant distraction while clocking up the miles with old Wheelie.

My colleagues must have known she was a man-eating cougar but never thought to tell the baby antelope they strapped to the rain water pipe on that day when those Hackney skies turned a dark shade of carnal.

She had locked herself out and was interrupting our tea-break to borrow a set of ladders to access her bedroom window. Like I've said before, many of those men were hairy ex-commandos who had once thundered up the beaches of Normandy. But that day those heroes fucked off, leaving Private Go-Lightly following the swaying backside across the road like Jim Dale in *Carry on Doctor*. The net was down. I was trapped. Did I escape? Did I fuck.

Actually, it was neither. I did what any well-mannered young foot soldier would, and positioned the ladder under the window and began to climb.

Mrs Robinson was having none of it:

"No, sweetheart," she commanded. "You hold the ladder. I'LL go up."

Come in Herbert ... come in. Of all the Joe 90 impersonators this side of Mare Street, she had chosen me to deflower.

Two old ladies stopped and looked on while Mrs Robinson re-enacted the storming of a Norman castle in a low-cut dress and red high heels as I stood below her, gripping the ladder like a nervous Sherpa Tenzing. She was wearing the skimpiest of drawers for modesty, but if Roy Castle had happened along at that exact moment and plugged me into a heart monitor, I would now be the official Roy Castle Record Breaker for the most rapid heartbeat of a British worker during normal working hours.

With one final legs-akimbo flourish, she climbed inside, leaving me standing at the bottom of the ladder like an emotional Wreck of the Hesperus. My hands were shaking and my knees were weak. Bloody hell, I could hardly stand on my own two feet.

You've seen *Confessions of a Window Cleaner,* right? So, you know she was about to appear at the window and beckon me up the ladder to join her on a quilted bedspread where I would die with my boots on in a blur of wispy pink nightie? Did it happen? No. Instead, she opened the front door and handed me a pack of Cadbury's Fingers before blowing a kiss towards the factory and going inside for a towel down and an Embassy while I carried the ladder back towards my cheering colleagues.

One of the old ladies jabbed me with her umbrella.

"Oi, you dirty little bleeder! You should be bloody ashamed of yourself."

Ah … the self-righteous indignation of an old bag from Hackney.

Lunch with Steve Harley and Cockney Rebel

Work was good. Being paid £17 a week to sod about like schoolboys on Pleasure Island. It never stopped. Firing balls of putty from copper tubing, bouncing on shovels like pogo sticks, throwing sledge hammers like Olympians, or urinating from the top lift of a scaffold. And I can assure you there's nothing like being chased with a loaded nail-gun to keep one warm on a cold winter's morning. Even elder statesmen joined in the fun by nailing a young Turk's sandwich to the ceiling. These shenanigans would inevitably end with one aggrieved party shouting: '*Oi … fuck off, you cunt!*' which was voted No.1 riposte by readers of the KNOCK UP ANOTHER LOAD, YOU SEXY MOTHERFUCKER trade magazine.

I worked with a good cross-section of British winkles. Valiant, humorous, dodgy and dangerous. There was Terry Thomas who could charm an extra sausage from the lady in the café, even when covered in plaster. There was a painter who looked like Dr Crippen and carried a *How to Murder Your Wife* book in a leather doctor's bag. There was an Albert Steptoe whose skinny malnourished torso spent each day stirring tin baths full of Carlite bonding. He also finished every sentence with a chirpy '... *tell your mum*'. For example: '*I'm as mad as a box of cunting frogs, I am ... tell your mum*'. There was a Scotsman who wore terrible toupées but nobody thought to tell him because he was holding a pickaxe and showing every sign of being a complete fucking nut-case. A gentleman from Billericay who wore a sombrero and identified as a Spanish plumber called Pedro. And there was a labourer who regaled everyone with his stories of valour in the Malaysian jungle; pretty impressive considering he had a club foot and spent most of the day face down alongside the spilled contents of his wheelbarrow.

Yep. *Monday, Tuesday, happy days!*

But on Monday, I had Friday on my mind because Fridays were when we went in search of a pub selling hot pies and where a lady was willing to dance naked before us. Who said romance was dead?

In those days, the décor in most pubs was a grim brown, chosen from the Dulux Nicotine Nights Range. However the landlords did provide a dartboard, a pool table, a Jokers Wild slot machine, and the occasional Space Invader machine.

I was nineteen. Instead of an après school Nesquik, I copied my comrades drinking light and bitter. When Ted sipped his, his face lit up like he was savouring the blood of Our Lord Jesus Christ. Those taste buds must have been traumatised during the Normandy landings because it tasted like wallpaper paste and flat lemonade ... without the flat lemonade. Its only consolation was the cooling effect it had upon the scorching hot meat pies now burning their way through the counter towards the centre of the earth like a scene from *The China Syndrome*.

Talking of pies. The following joke is the property of Barry Cryer and was first performed on Jokers Wild, ITV, circa 1973:

Man: *I'll have a steak and kiddley pie, please, lady.*

Barmaid: *Sorry, darling? Did you mean steak and kidney pie?*

Man: *That's what I said, diddle I?*

At 1pm, the clock struck Freddy Garrity on *Pebble Mill at One*, and a lady would emerge from the toilets and step onto a small stage with a simple PA and a couple of spotlights. Without further ado, she started disrobing to *Mr Soft* by Cockney Rebel, which lit the touch paper on a rapid and strategic manoeuvring among the pub's clientele to ensure (a) they didn't get trapped anywhere near the fucking stage, and (b) they didn't get trapped anywhere near the fucking stage.

You see, there is a very old American Indian proverb:

'Never fuck with a partially clothed lady and her feather boa.'

Of course, as a fledging twerp, I got myself cornered and the stripper removed my Joe 90s to use as some kind of humorous prop, and judging by the loud cheers she wasn't using them to read the bar snacks menu. I got them back needing a bloody good clean and Mr Dolland and Mr Aitchison would have been rightly appalled.

Most punters knew those ladies didn't really want to be parading amongst them waving an empty pint glass, and dropped in a few coins. But there were always a few mean-spirited bastards who, when the music stopped, disappeared quicker than the perspiration on Joe 90's forehead after he had successfully cut the wire of a UXB hidden inside his father's attaché case.

Safety in Numbers

I made it perfectly clear on my first day that my fear of heights was second only to my fear of being left alone in a room full of strippers, yet still they had me hanging grimly onto bisexual scaffolds (those that swung both ways), sliding down wet slate roofs, and shuffling along narrow parapets with a 30-foot drop on one side and a glass roof on the other. God knows what conditions were like during the construction of those great London Cathedrals, but in 1976 the building game was comparable to a tour of Vietnam, including hookers doing unspeakable things with ping pong balls and spectacles, but without Apache helicopters. The average age of a soldier in Vietnam was nineteen. The average age of a labourer in East London was thirty-five. That's why I decided to go to college and get me some qualifications.

I started a sandwich course and after a glass of milk to wash it down, set off to an Open Day at one of Havering's finest red-brick education establishments: Barking Technical College. A thoroughly modern building where prospective students were already milling around the chrome and glass reception before sweeping into the main hall to enrol upon any course from throwing a potter's wheel to laying bricks in fluent German. The state-of-the-art facilities did it for me, and I handed over £60 in exchange for an ID card and an envelope with directions to a crappy annexe in Dagenham where I was to spend the next twelve months getting basic science and maths. It seemed this was the price I was paying for staying in bed with Pan's People before being allowed to ride the sexy chrome elevator towards City & Guilds Building Construction.

A week later, I'm breezing through the annexe grounds like a young executive, swinging that old imitation leather briefcase from Rathbone Market. Gone was the woodworking apron, now it carried a *New Musical Express*, a Texas calculator the size of a house brick, and a compass set with a Hare Krishna sign scratched into the lid.

Talking of Karma.

What happened next, left my Gordon Gekko power braces twanging like a Duanne Eddy G-string.

Out of the blue, a girl pulled up alongside me:

"Hello … what course are you doing?"

She was slim, gorgeous, with strawberry-blonde hair tumbling around an enormous pair of turquoise eyes. It sounded like an innocent question but those eyes definitely reached down to give my testicles a playful tweak.

Thanks to all those Sunday afternoons with Cary Grant and Leslie Phillips, I had enough ammo to keep up the banter until we got to the main entrance, where I took the bull by the Goldie Horns and suggested we meet in the canteen for lunch.

Years later I realised she may have forgotten her dinner money, but that day, and to my great surprise, she agreed.

Fucking hell. I'd only been Martin Sheen for five minutes!

Morning lessons flew by as I swotted up on basic algebra and Einstein's Theory of Inactivity. Lunchtime arrived and I found the canteen. Unfortunately, the girl with the killer smile didn't. It seems that lunch breaks were staggered so as not to overly exert the miserable old trout in charge of the chip fryer. Bollocks.

It would be another six months until I saw those turquoise eyes again, during a visit to the Newham Building Control offices. There she was, surrounded by a barrow load of suitors. And as I watched from behind a rubber plant, I could see she was way out of my price range, and if we had of sat down six months earlier, the odds of me keeping her interest were longer than a Ravi Shankar sitar solo.

So imagine my surprise when those turquoise eyes caught mine and she carried them across the office carpet with a smile that, yet again, crushed my testicles in its vice-like grip.

"Hi, you all right? Weren't we supposed to meet up?" she asked beautifully.

She was laying it on a plate and all I had to do was summon a response from the 007 play-book. The play-book where James Bond was played by a staggeringly useless 18-year-old with his knackers caught in the lift doors as he travelled downwards to the Knotty Ash Jam Butty Mine.

"Yes, please, thank you very much," Bond replied in a high-pitched squeal.

That was it! That's all Ian Fleming could fucking muster before he had me skip away to make daisy-chains over West Ham Park.

According to the O'Jays, people all over the world were joining hands, but there I stood watching this *Love Train* disappear down the District Line carrying with it my one true love and my faith in Hare Krishna.

I would visit those pyramid shaped council offices a few more times over the years, but those turquoise eyes never spoke to me again, even though I clearly saw them hiding behind a filing cabinet.

The Pipes, The Pipes are Calling

Paul Cook showed his by squaring up to Bill Grundy, and Glen Matlock showed his by doodling on the bald pate of Robert Robinson, but I showed my Punk credentials by becoming the reincarnation of the much-loved naturalist and television angler, Jack Hargreaves.

From inside three walls of shiplap cladding, Jack taught us how to repair herring nets or scatter Hooray Henry's by carrying a sawn-off shotgun through a Hampshire gymkhana. What a man. Could Stephen Hawking fill a pipe one-handed while landing a 20lb pike in a force 8 gale? I don't bloody think so. With a freshly sharpened scythe and his trademark pipe, no one fucked with Jack.

There was an old pipe tucked away in Dad's trophy cabinet, so one night it joined a half ounce of tobacco and tin of sweetcorn in my tackle bag for an evening's fishing over Berwick Ponds.

The car park was empty and everywhere was quiet as I cast out two grains of sweetcorn, fired up the pipe and surrounded myself in the sweet smell of Nescafé and Golden Virginia. There was magic in the air as I drifted off to evensong under a balmy Rainham sky.

After an hour, and almost hidden against a crop of Norfolk reeds, rabbits and inquisitive little birds began edging closer like a scene from *Snow White*. Do you want to know a secret? Do you promise not to tell? With the pipe clenched between my teeth, I serenaded those little bunnies with my own version of Art Garfunkel's *Bright Eyes*.

'How can the light that gurned so grightly guddenly gurn so gale … Gright Eyes.'

And as a family of rabbits nibbled the juicy grass by my boots, an evening mist rolled in off the lake like the dream sequence from *Watership Down*.

Told you it was magical.

Next morning, virginity fully intact, I set off with H.R. Pufnstuf for some filth and fury refurbishing a series of Victorian town houses in Mile End. The job was plaster-boarding ceilings and entailed dancing across scaffold boards balancing 8' x 4' sheets of plasterboard on your head and hammering nails in faster than Popeye. With both hands occupied and the pipe burning steadily in my mouth, I soon felt a bit *I Claudius**, with beads of perspiration *onsk* me forehead and a waxy sheen *onsk* me chops. *Uck uck uck.*

Yep. Smoking a pipe is harder than it looks and, on behalf of punk impresario Malcom Maclaren, I rushed outside and brought up the contents of my stomach across the hot asphalt roof, I then sat there for a full ten minutes while my chums sang Harry Champion's *Boiled Beef and Carrots.* How we laughed.

Today those town houses are worth millions, especially with a cleaned-up Regents Canal at the bottom of the gardens. But in 1976 the canal was dirtier than a carrot picker's fingernails so I did a Geoff Capes and lobbed the pipe towards the canal where it landed with a sad little plop in the murky green water.

I wasn't a happy bunny. I'd let Jack Hargreaves down, I'd let Captain Sensible down and more importantly I'd let Richard Adams, author of *Watership Down*, down, down, deeper and down.

I thank you.

*I Claudius – niche rhyming slang for *nauseous.*

A Black & White Minstrel v Catherine Deneuve

After a long day pulling down ceilings and showering under cascades of Victorian dirt and dust, I arrived at Mile End station with a soot-blackened face and two white eyes ready for the 5:00pm Liverpool Street to Romford Filly Handicap. In those days, apart from walk-in showers (rainwater), handmade soaps (Fairy Liquid) or expensive oils (white spirit), there were few opportunities for a young gentleman to freshen up before journeying home, so what looked like a BBC Black & White Minstrel was now waiting on platform 2 to collect his reward for spending the day being covered in shit.

The reward was a train packed with fragrant princesses travelling home to their castles in the east. Pretty, plain, sexy, dour, blonde, brunette, Indian, Irish, fierce, gentle, plump, slim, tall, short, each firing pheromone-soaked arrows straight into my throbbing, but nicely proportioned, little heart. Tired and shagged out I slumped into the disabled seats and cast out a few enigmatic stares. Ten minutes later I got a bleep on my Efgeeco Optonic bite alarm.

A middle-aged woman sat opposite me. She was wearing a powder-blue cashmere jumper and a knee-length grey skirt, and was definitely from the Catherine Deneuve School of Commuting. With a glance she ripped out my heart and drop-kicked it straight into the litter box.

Now I can see she may have had a bladder problem, but Catherine began crossing and uncrossing those legs and I could hear a definite murmur of silk ... even above the noise of the Flying Scotsman now flat on his face after tripping over her briefcase.

From behind an *Evening Standard* her eyes were smiling. Bloody hell! This was uncharted territory and I began praying to the Head of London Transport that my inexperienced pooper wouldn't give me away.

We exchanged the occasional glance until we pulled into Goodmayes and she reached down to her briefcase and showed me around the gentle slopes of her cleavage before sitting back up with a Cadbury's Flake which she nibbled seductively while reading an article about Pat Jennings and the Galloping Gourmet sponsoring some new goalkeeping / oven gloves. One by one, she licked her fingers clean. What did it all mean?

Jesus, Mary, Holy Mackerel and Josephine.
Come in, Herbert, come in! Are you receiving me? Over.

What would West Ham goalie Mervyn Day have done except send an internal memo to Buster & Little Jocky telling them ALL LEAVE WAS CANCELLED.

At Chadwell Heath, she let the newspaper fall to the floor, so, being a gallant young officer of the 1st Battalion of The Gay Lancers, I reached down to return it, expecting her hand to be offered by way of introduction. Instead she pulled me close and planted the biggest, deepest, sweetest kiss on my soot-blackened lips. Was this where my boyhood ended? Hurtling towards Romford at 50 mph? Within seconds, my dirty little hands were disappearing up the back of her cashmere sweater as the station announcer at Romford Station woke me from my dream.

The train now standing at Platform 8 will call at:
Gidea Park, Shenfield, and all stations to Southend.'

Yes, folks, that last bit was a cheap cinematic ploy to keep the reader interested during the notoriously difficult third quarter of any book.

But I'm not lying about Catherine and the pale blue cashmere which was now bobbing along the platform in a sea of grey like that little girl wearing a red coat in *Schindler's List*. I jumped off the train and joined the crowd washing up the steps towards South Street.

When I got outside, she was gone and had taken those laughing blue eyes with her. I'm not kidding. I was more deflated than a Tory peer with a punctured lung going down on the Lord Privy Council while holding a Christmas balloon in February.

An old lady selling flowers recognised the signs.

"Say it with flowers, darling ... say it with flowers," said the old flower seller.

"Bollocks," said the dishevelled Black & White Minstrel.

Looking on the bright side, a beautiful woman had given me a free lesson on the dangerous world of public transport courting. A lesson that would ultimately pay dividends some forty years later on the Central Line near Hainault.

In the meantime, standing under the shower after being fully debriefed, I sent a memo to Buster and Little Jocky, apologising for any misunderstanding, and giving them the evening off to play snooker.

Yards of Bunting and Cans of Kestrel

After buzzing around the 1964 FA Cup, the 1965 European Cup Winners Cup and the 1966 FIFA World Cup, the moths in the West Ham trophy cabinet were coming up for parole. Manager Ron Greenwood had left for the England job, leaving the club's directors with a decision. Who to fill Ron's boots? The big money was on Sherpa Tenzing but they took a gamble on John Lyall.

Within six months, all Bunny girls were banned from the team coach, and high-stake card schools were replaced by traditional board games such as Coppit and the incredibly tactical Mousey Mousey. It was Johnny Lyall's master stroke and his team strolled into the 1975 FA Cup Final triggering an immediate world-wide shortage of claret and blue ribbon. Within days, every home in Newham had the official West Ham team photo from the *Stratford Express* sellotaped to its front room window ... and don't get me started on Baco Foil replica FA cups along the Barking Road.

At that time, I was part of a crack team of decorators working on a pair of terraced houses in Plaistow so I wrote a motivational message across the front windows using the soothing pink medium of Windowlene. From outside it would read UP THE HAMMERS and COME ON YOU IRONS in three-foot capital letters.

But writing backwards is tricky, and an elderly neighbour pointed out that my apostrophes were wrong and both the Ss were back to front. I was six foot two with eyes of blue, and wasn't having a five-foot octogenarian bossing me about so I left those messages uncorrected as an indictment of the British education system and a testament to the versatility of Windowlene (which, like Milk of Magnesia, is consistently voted the most delicious household product after a kebab on a Friday night).

Know what happened?

The 4-4-2 window cleaning formation did the trick, and by 5pm on Cup Final day, despondent Fulham fans were trooping home while West Ham fans tipped out the claret and blue jellies. On a sadder note, Bobby Moore was now the defeated captain of Fulham, and as he left the pitch, he acknowledged the West Ham end like the true sportsman he was.

Mum and her sisters never acknowledged him leaving West Ham and still called him '*Our Bobby*'. What made them love him so? Was it those powerful thighs and steely blue eyes? Was it his bow-legged gait and the way he held the match ball to his hip when leading out the team? Or was it because he starred alongside Sylvester Stallone in *Escape to Victory*? Who knows.

He died in 1993, and a sea of memorials stretched along the front of The Boleyn before heading off down Green Street. He played a blinder in so many people's lives and there were flags and messages from all around the world. A teddy bear wrapped in a Rotherham scarf did it for me, and I cried my bleeding heart out.

They don't make heroes like that anymore.

The Thriller in Manilla

It was the most important and over-dramatic decision of my young life.

Nineteen quid in a manilla wage packet. Take away housekeeping, fares and shares in Rotham's International left five pounds to donate to one of my two favourite multi-millionaires. Would it be Lennon's *Mind Games*, or McCartney's *Band on the Run?*

A record collection is a valuable peek up a young gentleman's keyhole. Carefully compiled and guaranteed to charm the knickers off any girl caught hiding in the wardrobe. Mine included Dylan (Bob), Marley (Bob, not Jacob), Clarke (Cooper, not Kenneth), Elvis (Costello and Rhinestone). The Jam (Weller not strawberry) and Pistols (Sex not water). There was some comedy, country, Crimson and Cohen. Soul, Sinatra, Stewart and Streisand. I even shelled out for the Quadrophonic version of *Dark Side of the Moon*, which lost none of its magnificence coming from a pair of crappy two-inch speakers.

But nothing, absolutely NOTHING, compared to unpacking new Beatles music.

For example, I once walked out of Romford Our Price with Lennon's *Live Peace in Toronto*, and an hour later was found slumped unconscious between two bus seats. So, choosing between two grandmasters was never going to be easy. The fiver eventually went to *Mindgames* because, like Lennon, I was also a short-sighted only-child with a tendency to support lost causes.

On the bus home I read the sleeve notes, committed the art work to memory, and listened for the faint crackle of static while inhaling a lungful of mint Apple vinyl. Marvellous. Life couldn't have got much better unless Suzi Quatro's white leather jump suit got itself caught on Sally James's black leather boots as they romped together happily in a bath full of Bird's custard.

Collier Row looked magical that Christmas. Lamp posts were decked out in Christmas lights and a baby Jesus, sponsored by 7 Eleven, laid serenely in the middle of the roundabout. It was Friday night, and as I strolled down the hill with stars overhead and a Christmas tree in every window, I thought of those thousand of Romford bedrooms where all the young dudes were making plans to go out in search of an obliging old bag. But oh no. Not me. I never lost control. I was face to face with some saveloy and chips watching *The Goodies*. And by 9 o'clock, I was tucked up with a mug of tea and *The Rats* by James Herbert (no relation).

And in the corner, Lennon was singing those *Mindgames* forever.

Only Six Strings Away from a Bunk-Up

It was just past midnight on Sunday morning and I was this close from getting laid. Unfortunately, 'this close' was a lake five nautical miles from where sweaty girls were dancing around their handbags (collective noun: a clutch). Dear reader. I was between a rock eel and hard plaice, because there's not enough Andy Capp talc in the world to entice Brooke Shields to join me shivering by a lake in Harold Hill, yet I came out in a rash anywhere near a glitter ball and strobe light. Time for a new hobby? You bet your sweet ass.

Since being gazumped by white Stratocaster boy with his polished maple neck, I had been keeping my eye on a shop in North Street where all kinds of guitars were strung out like a butcher's shop window. Honey coloured spruce tops, mother of pearl inlays, 12-string Rickenbackers, and solid gold, easy action Les Pauls. I bet even David Cassidy's ratio of lipstick coverage went up when he had a Gibson Jumbo slung around his neck.

The next step was obvious. I needed to become a guitar maestro, and nothing was gonna stop me except talent, skill, and a complete lack of musical ability.

A friend with a grubby neck gave me an electric guitar with a warped neck which I part exchanged with a man whose neck I couldn't see because it was covered with long greasy hair, and before you could say '*I saw a pentatonic scale sitting in a pentagram circle*', I was the proud owner of a second-hand Eko jumbo acoustic and Bert Weedon's tutorial book *Play for Today*. One set of tuning pipes later and I'm adjusting my Roy Orbison clip-ons.

SFX – To the soundtrack of Rocky II, there follows a three-minute montage showing Herbert strumming that jumbo resting between his thighs. Dates fly from a calendar as his handsome young face changes from a strangulated George Formby into Carlos 'The Jackal' Santana, via a brief stop at Herman Munster. To the dying notes of *Eye of The Tiger*, the screen fades to black …

Until then I had been keeping my left hand for best … now it was covered in painful blisters. On the bright side, I could sprint through *Michael Row* the Boat Ashore like Jake Thackery with his knackers trapped in a Fender guitar case. I even wrote a song using the three major punk chords of the time: Gob Major, Spit 7th, and Wanker Minor. It went something like this:

'No, I ain't sniffing glue, see, I'm sniffing back the tears I cried for you.' (Repeat twelve times.)

I posted a demo to EMI and waited by the letter box until they sent back a telegram telling me to fuck off.

Just as well really. Supporting Clodagh Rodgers at The Rainbow was gonna have to wait because I had concrete to knock up, a wheelbarrow to push and some fresh insight into British politics to be gained from some genuine working-class heroes.

Two Teas, a Lion Bar, and some British Politics, please

When they weren't purloining picnic baskets in Jellystone Park, Yogi Bear and Boo Boo liked to watch *Old Faithful* send clouds of hot water spewing into the air. A similar process was taking place in Hackney where, every hour on the hour, Ted's kettle would splutter and hiss while an old geyser held court about the merits of large Bristols. Occasionally, these conversations swerved spectacularly into the unforgiving waters of British politics.

Apart from the John Lennon album *Sometime in New York City*, I got my political information from Alf Garnet, Mike Yarwood, and the home-spun philosophers sitting in a circle around me who were about to take part in an argumentative Mexican stand-off.

Confucius: (a plumber, sucking on a cheese straw) *You know what? I reckon old Winston Churchill lumbered this fucking country.*

Immanuel Kant: (a skinny labourer covered in plaster) *What the fuck you on about... tell your mum.*

Confucius: (jabbing the air with a cheese straw) *Well, thanks to fucking Churchill, we're now supposed to trust any cunt who went to Eton!*

Karl Marx: (a scaffolder folding a crisp, white paper doily) *Fascinating.*

Bertrand Russell: (a roofer, holding up a copy of *The Sun* with a picture of the Tory Party Impropriety Committee) *Here, have a look at the tits on that!*

I tried to steer clear of politics but there's nothing more dispiriting than a young Conservative on *Question Time* so I started dressing to the left, and kept a look-out for anyone draping themselves in the Union Jack. Like our Tory MP in Romford for example, who conned half my family before taking a huge patriotic dive into the pot during the expenses scandal while leaving most of his constituents practising the forgotten art of retrieving coins from gas meters.

Marches, meetings and leaflets? Being a realistic Herbert I knew if I did get involved, I'd soon be packing it in. I mean, they never found that little Chinese student who threw himself under the king's tank in Tiananmen Square, did they?

So, from beside a bucket of used teabags I decided to give Buster and Little Jocky at least one decent aerobic workout per day, and leave those old geezers spouting and erupting at regular intervals like my forebears … or two, if you discount Yogi and Boo Boo.

This is the Captain Speaking, or, Do You Want Ice With That?

After shortening the examiner's life by five years, I ripped up those L plates and got to work selling the idea of a £1000 lime green Ford Capri sitting outside our house. Dad put his hand in his pocket, Mum put her heart in her mouth, and together they shelled out £165 for a 1966 Cortina MK 1. In return, I swore on the Highway Code to drive them wherever they wanted from here to eternity.

The Cortina was beige with rust-coloured highlights, and wipe-clean imitation leather seats. After pimping it up with a Paddy Hopkirk steering wheel cover and a traffic-light air freshener, I took it out for its maiden voyage.

Down the A.12 we sailed towards Ilford. Captain of my own ship with Rod Stewart's *Sailing* on Capital Radio. Twenty minutes later, I pulled into an empty Methodist church car park… empty that is apart from an anti-parking pole which sliced a horizontal gouge down the driver's door like the Titanic iceberg. It was *A Night to Remember* alright and after trudging the final fifty yards, I waited gloomily on my mate's doorstep while he laughed his fucking head off.

Apart from a wife called Annette, and a set of Stanley chisels, he also had a Ferguson VHS cassette recorder that was so big it took up most of the front room and half the kitchen. Ladies and gentlemen, this was the moment I'd been waiting for since 1973. Earlier that day I had popped into a video shop in Plaistow and handed over my passport, the deeds to my mum's house and a £15 deposit for a copy of *The Exorcist.*

Turns out that even on the small screen the demon Pazuzu is perfect for making you forget the gut-wrenching damage done to your first car. Looking back now, I suspect that rusty slash on the driver's door may well have been a supernatural payback for parking on holy ground.

Anyway. Having my own set of wheels meant the casual thrill of cancelled trains had been replaced by the casual thrill of a temperamental Ford engine. The 'Super Funky Mk I Cortina' was now known as 'That Fucking Bastard'.

Dolly's husband Bill taught me to check the camcorder belt, clean the sparkly plugs and shit in the carburettor, but I still spent Sundays looking at the underside of an oil sump. When it failed its MOT, I started looking for a place to dump it until a chap in a cowboy hat offered me a once in a lifetime opportunity and 'The Bastard' was back on the road.

But no matter how many times I shat in the carburettor, my stuttering journey home from Hackney always led to a spluttering capitulation opposite Ilford Police Station. With a dodgy MOT and twenty yards from the local CID, I had to become a one-man Formula One team – popping the bonnet, unscrewing a tube from the 'carbonara', and sucking petrol up until it spewed into my mouth and reassembling the lot before gunning the engine like Niki Lauda. It worked every time but did mean sitting down for my tea like a New Romantic with a white face, bright red six o'clock shadow, and puffy swollen red lips. The old man looked over his pie and chips and shook his head sadly.

Our on-off romance was severely tested during the winter of 1976 when, like a highly strung child, it was put to bed with old carpet laid under the bonnet, and woken at 6am with a cup of tea and a kettle of boiling water lovingly trickled over the engine block.

"Well, are you gonna start?" asked Herbert.

"Well, that depends, motherfucker!" answered the stroppy Ford Cortina.

With the bonnet up, the choke out, and exactly two and a half pumps on the gas pedal, it either coughed like a sick child or screamed like a cat with its bottom on fire.

The only good thing was its heating system because there's nothing better on a cold winter's morning than a Ford heater going full blast, with the orange lights on a Tandy graphic equaliser bopping along, and Mary Millington sitting beside you singing old English folk songs.

Which brings me to one of the funniest things I've ever witnessed, apart from any last-minute winner against the Spuds. It happened one winter's morning in 1976, somewhere between *Hey Nonny Nonny No* and *Blow the Wind Southerly*.

I pulled up near East Ham Town Hall to let a city gent use a zebra crossing. With a polite nod he stepped from the kerb, lost his footing on the icy surface, and did a tremendous Freddie Flintstone leg blur, before falling flat on his back. His forward momentum then carried him across the road, feet skywards and briefcase gliding smoothly alongside him like a loyal curling stone. With a gentle bump, he reached the other kerb, climbed to his feet and gave another brief nod before continuing on his way.

And that, my dear devoted foreign reader, is why the British never buckled during the Blitz, and why Nobby Stiles never resorted to repeatedly kicking the Portuguese striker Eusebio on our way to World Cup victory in 1966.

The 1977 Queen's Jubilee

Aside from two Mohicans haircuts outside the Romford Our Price and a build-up of day-glo fluff around my stylus, there were few signs of anarchy in this part of the UK. I was 19. The perfect age to go full punk. But no matter how many times I ripped my jeans, Mum always stayed up all night repairing them like something from *The Elves and the Shoemaker*. Anyway, what is so special about dressing up like a cunt? I've been doing it for years.

The day of the jubilee, I went to a street party in Harold Hill where Lynda's kitchen looked like a British field hospital at Rorke's Drift, with women buttering enough bread to feed the Zulu hordes while men stood around doing fuck-all. There was a bonny baby competition and a fancy dress parade where Eileen (dressed as Britannia) and Dolly (dressed as Queen Boudica) bickered over a cardboard trident while uncle Derek dehydrated inside a Womble costume. A good time was had by all.

At exactly 5pm, Lynda cruised to second place in the 'Partially Frozen Trifle from Bejams Competition', and good-looking girls began roaming the estate looking for anyone with a winkle and a cork screw. Yep. That night's firework display would be the perfect opportunity for Joe 90 to get jumped by a beautiful girl in an off-the-shoulder Union flag. Sadly, I had made arrangements to celebrate twenty-five years of our monarch's reign by going night fishing over Berwick Ponds.

My partner that night was an old school friend whom I quickly realised had forgotten the first rule of Fish Club which is to move around the lake with the stealth of a cat burglar in Battersea Dog's Home.

By 10pm, he was hopping from foot to foot and talking complete bollocks like Bill and Ben.

It got worse.

By 11pm, he was cartwheeling around my brolly, cackling like

Basil Brush and showing absolutely no respect for the royal family and, in particular, Princess Anne.

At midnight, he unscrewed the butt of his fishing rod and out dropped a packet of red, white and blue sweeties. Bloody hell. Alone with a drugged-up cowboy, and all I could do was unwrap a cheese sandwich and stare grim-faced into the darkness.

By 2pm, he had calmed down and we sat pontificating about the genius of Stanley Unwin, pointing our cockney fore fingold at the heavenly bode and moon and dangly, until dawn when bubbles exploded across the pond like royal navy divers were hoovering up our kernels of sweetcorn.

And by lunchtime, covered in tench slime, totally happy and happily fucked, we snoozed lazily under the warm summer sky as the Red Arrows screamed passed towards London, knocking my partner clean off his chair and onto his little drugged-fuelled arse.

Far out man, I thoughkus, far out.

Ahh, So We Meet Again? The Mysterious Girl From the Prefabs

While studying the ancient art of City & Guilds Building Construction, I met someone who (a) looked like Phil Lynott of *Thin Lizzy* (b) played guitar like Carlos Santana of *Santana*, and (c) did a better impression of Jim Callaghan than Mike Yarwood of *The Mike Yarwood Show*. His name was Jeff and he was a cool motherfucker, so I started following him around until he let me be his friend.

One lunchtime, instead of sitting in the college cafeteria doing lines of smoky bacon crisps, we drove to Cliff Owen's Music Store in Seven Kings to pick up his new Sunburst Gibson Les Paul, which was waiting for him safely cocooned within its own velvety coffin. He plugged it in and immediately began bending strings like Bunny Wailer while his fingers scampered up and down the guitar neck like

Squirrel Nutkin. This boy could play. Two girls buying sheet music looked over towards us so with great presence of mind I edged closer to Carlos and, with a serene smile like the Maharshi Yogi, basked in the talent of my young disciple.

That night we went to The Green Man in Leytonstone where the resident band were going to give Jeff's new Les Paul a test drive. There was a decent crowd and it was during an incredibly emotional version of *Dreadlock Holiday* that I saw her … The Girl from the Prefabs!

Taller obviously, and without her bike, but she was unmistakeable. Her blonde hair was now platinum and shagged up like Debbie Harry, and her jeans were so tight I could still see those dirty knees. That's right, folks, she was (*drum roll*) … a Dirty Harry!

And that's when the fourth wall collapsed, and the director shouted "CUT!"

Director: *Okay everyone, clear the set. Someone get Herbert onto the dance floor, please. Hurry now, chop chop!*

Chop Chop, the Chinese floor manager, positioned me under a giant mirror ball, where a meteor shower of glittering lights danced across my rounded shoulders to reveal a sexy dusting of working-class dandruff.

Director: *Okay, start the dry ice – Cut studio lights! Best of luck everyone, run cameras … and ACTION!*

Ding, ding, ding. The landlord rang the bell, pulled the plug, and touched up the barmaid.

She was gone. Only moments before, Little Miss Platinum had been strutting her stuff. Now she was everywhere and nowhere, baby. I checked the car park but the closest I came to a fairy tale ending was a drunk footman leaning against an Austin Princess.

I suppose you think this 'girl disappearing thing' is just another literary ploy ... except it's not. She really was there and I found out later that Cinderella had broken the heel on her glass slipper and had left early to hop home along the Whipps Cross Road towards Walthamstow.

She didn't know it. I didn't know it. But we were destined to meet again some sunny day.

The Bridge House, Canning Town, or, Rod Stewart's ex-Missus

Beatle Fact 1: in 1964, as the Beatles toured the hotel rooms of America, Paul Simon was living above a carpet shop in Hornchurch. Beatle Fact 2: in 1977, as John Lennon scrambled around an archaeological dig in Cairo, I was in Carlos Santana's house watching a video about roller-skating pizza delivery girls, an enjoyable task made difficult by Carlos' mum bursting in just as a pizza girl was going the extra mile with a large margherita.

Things were moving fast. Carlos got himself a black leather jacket and was now planning a wider assault on the entertainment industry with an electrician called Steve, another excellent guitarist who could also rewire your house. I was an honorary member, not because of my stuttering mastery of *The Harry Lime Theme*, but because I had a van useful for chasing down equipment in the Exchange and Mart.

And that's how I came to meet Rod Stewart's ex-missus.

It was a wintery night. Me, Carlos and Steve were driving back from Catford with a second-hand Marshall amplifier, and stopped off for a quick one at The Bridge House, a live music venue in Canning Town.

The place was buzzing, so while Steve checked the fuses, me and Carlos joined the audience bobbing up and down to a band whose lead singer was prancing around with a white electric violin. Watching from the back was a glamorous blonde in a sheer blouse, leopard print trousers, and driller killer heels. A rare and beautiful thing, lost alongside the sensuous curves of the Canning Town flyover. She was holding a handwritten sign:

"Don't – whatever you fucking do – come over and talk to me."

Would a handwritten sign stop Frank Sinatra and a tumbler of Jack Daniels from sidling towards her singing *Luck be a Lady Tonight*? Nope. Pumped full of lager shandy, I bounced across the floor, like Jason King doing a gymnastic floor routine, to offer her a Scampi Golden Wonder. She declined, and so, with bravado hissing from a dagger-shaped hole in his green leather jacket, Jason King checked his rear-view mirror and reversed back into the crowd.

It turns out she was Dee Harrington, model and former girlfriend of Rod Stewart, and it was her current beau prancing around with the white violin. Too bad. We were thrown downstairs. Two hours later, I'm pulling in a gentle rhythm on my bullworker, while Dee touched up her lipstick in a chauffeur-driven limo outside a kebab shop near Rathbone Market.

When the coast was clear, she went inside.

Dee: *Evening. Can I have a large donner with chilli sauce, but no red onion please?*

Kebab Shop Owner: *Certainly, madam, that'll be seventy new pence.*

Dee: *Thanks. I don't suppose you've seen a bloke in a green leather jacket, have you?*

Kebab Shop Owner: *No, sorry.*

Dee: *Phew … thank Christ for that!*

Skin Trouble

Me, Carlos and Steve were getting along swimmingly, but two accomplished guitarists and one set of aluminium ladders do NOT the new Chicory Tip make. To get on *Top of the Pops* and bask in the wealth of Noel Edmonds we would need a steady back-beat, and not from me banging two coconuts together. Carlos knew a drummer living near Wanstead Station so we paid him a visit. He answered the door like Mr Universe in a bulging T-shirt, fake tan, and cut down jeans. He would have looked at home on a Californian beach, but here he was rippling away fifty yards from the Central Line.

Compared to Mr Universe, we looked like two deathly white runner beans and a five-a-side goal post, but Noel Edmunds waits for no man so we followed him into the attic where stood a drum kit bigger than Lord Cozy Powell's, Ginger Bread Bakers, and the entire Romford Drum and Trumpet Corp. Without warning, he began a drum solo, beating those skins, the pedals pounding against two bass drums. He was good but he fancied himself, and we already had two of those so we left him knocking one out and went to a café for a decent hot meal.

Carlos and Steve were crestfallen. So crestfallen, they almost stopped playing excruciatingly long guitar solos.

I vowed there and then to find them a drummer who would make this band complete. No matter where it took me. North to the snowy Scottish Highlands, down through the Welsh valleys, or east to the land of the Angles where warring tribes once stretched Roman foreskins to make snare drums. Climbing aboard my valiant steed, I wound down the window and bade farewell to those two merry minstrels. Five minutes later, outside Argos in Romford Market, my journey was complete.

Beatles Fun Fact 3: did you know Ringo Starr's first drum kit was bought by his step dad from a shop in Romford? Beatles Fun Fact 4: did you know the person I met in Romford Market was also called Ringo?

Actually, it was his mates who called him Ringo; his real name was Steve and I met him on a building site near the Old Ford Road where, while the rest of us got to grips with thoughts of Samantha Fox, Steve 2 spent his tea-break playing drum solos on an array of mugs, buckets, paint kettles and tins of undercoat. I asked if he wanted to meet Noel Edmunds, and agreed to bring along Carlos to a party in a block of flats in Manor Park.

Like many of his friends, Steve 2 was West Indian, and judging by the pigeons fluttering lifelessly to the pavement, most of them were stone fucking deaf. As we stepped from my van, *Rastaman Vibration* hit us in the chest like the crunching ordnance of the American military. Then, after following a trail of dead pigeons, I introduced Carlos to Steve 2 using semaphore before bouncing across the dimly lit room to sit on a Rastafarian's lap. Oh how we laughed.

One hour later, with my eyes oscillating like Raggedy Anne, and Buster and Little Jocky deflated like a worn-out pair of Scottish bagpipes, I went down to the van and spent the rest of the evening with some jerk chicken and a picture of Debbie Harry.

Abbey Road Studios E.15

Remember my medieval ancestor, Herbert the Unready? The one who sat on a wooden bridge looking into the River Lea? Well, in 1177 that bridge was washed away so Queen Matilda, wife of Henry I, ordered a substantial stone replacement. With the new bridge's distinctive bow shape, the area became known as Stratford-atte-Bow.

The bridge was a strategic link between London and Essex. Alongside it was the largest Cistercian Abbey in Britain where Kings and nobles were entertained. That bridge was still there when peasants stormed across it to pin King Richard inside the Tower of London. Thirteen people were burnt on it for heresy. Battles were fought there during the English Civil War, and in 1967 it became the final resting place for local villains when the GLC built a concrete flyover allowing commuters to speed across the River Lea towards London before getting caught at the next set of lights. In 1978, a pair of size 12 cowboy boots stood in the shadow of that flyover, unloading a drum kit from the back of a Ford Transit. We Herberts have sure come a long way.

The band recruited a bass-playing Goth with black fingernails, and were away like Boomtown Rats out of Teddy Boys' drain-pipes. Rehearsals were held every Sunday where the band practised songs from Thin Lizzy to Chuck Berry. To add a South American vibe to a few Santana numbers, I got some bongos from the G60 music shop opposite The Ruskin Arms in Manor Park, where Ronnie Lane met Steve Marriot. A week later I went back and bought some roto-drums, a pair of size eleven Chad Valley drum sticks, and a microphone so my softly spoken percussion could be heard above Rocky Racket and the Fucking Rabblerousers. Rather than petrol money, they gave me lead vocals on the Beatles *Come Together* and a song called *Get Out of My House* by The Business, a rocking little number about a father challenging his daughter's boyfriend.

It went something like this. Ahem …

"Out, out, get out of my house … you better take your trench coat too … cos no daughter of mine's going out with a hippy or a scruffy looking bleeder … like you."

My singing style was somewhere between John Lennon and Johnny Rotten, with a hint of the stylish yet drippy Conservative MP

John Selwyn Gummer.

Every Sunday rehearsal, the air was thick with glowing substances (possibly Kryptonite, more likely Gitanes, the cigarette of choice for chesty young rock musicians). Harmonica and keyboard players came and went as we searched for that elusive ingredient to catapult us to the lucrative Sunday lunchtime gig at The Queens Theatre, Hornchurch.

The special ingredient arrived one Sunday morning on the arm of Steve 1, who looked decidedly ashen (white faced, not Chinese) from whatever they had been doing (possibly Monopoly, more likely Battling Tops). In her tight blue jeans and leopard skin ankle high boots, she looked like Cherie Currie from The Runaways. Her voice was like low-tide on Southend beach (dirty, gravelly and a little rocky), and when she sang *Stormy Monday*, the band played with an intensity that until then, had been decidedly lacking. And when she caressed the microphone and began swaying her hips, I started beating the crap out of those bongos like a man possessed.

Afterwards we went to The Cranbrook Arms where Carlos and Steve (1) swarmed around the new singer like Gibson Flying Vs around a Bee-Bop-a-Loofah. I left them to it and went into the other bar to play darts. Five minutes later, Southend Cherie followed me. After some initial sparring – she put her dirty hands down my pants, took all of my crisps and left me naked by the silvery moon. Me, the Fifteenth Earl of Herbert, necking with a fully paid-up rock chick!

Man alive. All it had taken was a quick game of Round the Clock and some lyrics from a Rod Stewart song, and my life was about to change. Instead of mixing plaster in a tin bath, I was gonna share a hotel bath with Cherie, and have unprotected sex in The Cliff's Pavillion while the band went head-to-head against some of the biggest acts in showbiz. With a love bite the size of a blood orange, I waved goodbye to Cherie. Stay cool, motherfucker, I thought. She'll still be there next week!

The following Sunday, Dick Whittington buffed up his cowboy boots, kissed the cat and set off to begin a long-term relationship with a dirty woman in the back of a Ford Transit. The plan worked perfectly, apart from Cherie not turning up.

"Bollocks," said Dick Whittington.

"I did try and tell you!" said his cat.

This band was going nowhere. Punk was the future. A bit of vitality and imagination. A touch of the old Dunkirk spirit … know what I mean?

So, like Ziggy Stardust, I broke up the band. To be precise, they fucked off and left me. I sold my gear to Steve (2) and bought some seafood from a stall outside The White Hart. By Monday morning, I was back on the chain gang. Wheeling my wheelbarrow, through the streets broad and narrow, crying cockles and mussels with a can of Five Alive-O.

Romford Snooker Hall and The Lanky Ginger-Haired Twerp

Aunt Bertha was one of the earliest settlers to load her wagon and head east. With her hubby, Prospector Pete, they journeyed through Indian country (Manor Park), watered the horses at The Best Little Warehouse in Redbridge (Ilford Palais), and by-passed the knife-wielding Turks in Kebab Canyon (Chadwell Heath), before staking a claim on a plot near Boot Hill (Romford Cemetery) in the shadow of a large cylindrical drum known as the spiritual home of the Romford Gas Works.

Living wasn't easy and every morning Iron Horses shook the greenhouse and unsettled the tomatoes. But sharing an outside toilet with five brothers gives a girl something, so Bertha simply boiled some water, threw a cloth over the budgie cage, and set about delivering my two country cousins, Little Pete and Stevie Boy.

Little Pete was a bit older than me and spent his days in a Genesis T-shirt, fiddling overtime at Romford Brewery. So, I used to hang out with his kid brother. Steve was a good-looking boy who had obviously inherited our grandfather's good looks, because his wanted poster was on every telegraph pole in Romford.

There were few places where two emotionally backward crisp rustlers could avoid female bounty hunters but one was a gravel pit in South Ockendon and the other was a snooker hall in Romford, famous for a ginger-haired teenager who could build a hundred break in the time it took me and Steve to find a cue that wasn't shaped like a fucking banana.

The club's smoky half-light and the smell of Carlsberg was overseen by a man called Spiny Norman whose job was to scare off young women and flick the table lights when your toasted cheese sandwich was ready. With his deathly white pallor and hang-dog expression, Norman was a true International Man of Misery.

Every Friday evening, while local costermongers shut their transit doors on unsold knock-off transistor radios, and Havering cowgirls were queuing for buses into Romford, me and Stevie were already cocooned behind the heavy black curtains of the Luciana Snooker Hall where the only thing to break the hushed silence was the gentle clacking of balls as Buster and Jocky practised their Spanish flamenco routine.

By 11pm, with every night club rammed with girls in tight sparkly dresses, it was finally safe for me and Steve to head home for a cup of tea and a Hammer Horror on ITV, and the only evidence of our stay was a small deposit of blue chalk outside the kebab shop.

Steve is now a respected pillar of the community who graciously does the honour at family funerals. He retains the looks of a self-assured Ralph Fiennes, but we all know that having grandfather's genes is a double-edged sword and it's only a matter of time before he waves goodbye to those gleaming white choppers.

Tony Jacklin and the New Rock and Roll

I was halfway through my transition from teenage loafer to adult loafer. I knew what a bunk-up was… just not fully *au fait* with all the ins and outs. According to the chaps at work, young women want nothing more than loyalty, humour, and a large portion of helmet.

Yet I was still confused.

One day, while ripping the guts out of an exquisite Georgian House for the last ounce of scrap metal, I asked Ted when he had first stepped into his father's hobnail boots. He rolled one and puffed for a moment, before offering the following advice which could so easily have been lifted from that old master baker, Mr Rudyard Kipling.

Ted: *Well, Grasshopper, it's like this …*

IF you can meet with triumph and disaster
And treat those two impostors just the same;
If you can make one heap of all your winnings
And risk it on one turn of pitch-and-toss,
And lose, and start again at your beginnings
And never breathe a word about your loss;
Then yours is the Earth and everything that's in it,
And what's more, you'll be a man my son when your balls touch your bum!

Wise words indeed.

As well as dragging bags of lead to the scrap metal merchants, I was also in the middle of an Open University course: Basic Courtship Level 2. The first assignment was some heavy petting with a girl from school. This was followed by a heart-stopping encounter with a middle-aged lady outside the Joker's Nightclub in Seven Kings. I then did a four-week stint with an Indian nurse in Hornchurch before she realised the benefits of a nice Indian doctor rather than a labourer with a David Essex waistcoat and calloused hands.

But throughout my studies that little foil envelope had remained firmly *in tacto*, and Buster and Little Jocky were growing increasingly uppity. I needed a way to release some of this pent-up fury, and it arrived in the form of one of Britain's finest golfers.

Since Tony Jacklin showed what an Englishman could do with one leather glove and a roll neck jumper, working-class men had begun whacking off over some of the finest golf courses local councils could offer. And why not? Tell me a better way to grab some fresh air and chat with your mates while urinating against a variety of spruce trees?

Apart from swearing at Eamonn Andrews on the telly, my old man didn't go in for hobbies, so it was a big surprise when he agreed to join his brother-in-laws (collective noun: a flatch) over at Risebridge Municipal Golf Course.

Come Saturday morning, I loaded him into my car, pushed home a Frank Sinatra cassette, and set off. Ten minutes later we're looking at a long line of golfers already waiting at the first tee, and I sensed some hesitancy from Charlie, Champion of the World. He hired some clubs, joined the queue, and spent the next hour watching complete strangers make overly jolly conversations while taking huge extravagant practice swings. The reason for this enforced jollity? Each condemned man knew they were about to be judged, and quite harshly, by at least forty of their peers.

At ten minute intervals, a Pringle jumper climbed the gallows and waved a Lee Trevino 3 wood around like a mad axeman. If he stuck the golf ball first time, that gentleman was awarded due reverence. If he missed it, he was silently judged to be a complete cunt. After much huffing and puffing, Isaac Newton's Law of Probability inevitably took effect, and another Four Golfers of the Apocalypse were set free to spend five hours searching for lost balls.

Throughout these goings on, my father was chain-smoking and doing a decent impression of Mount Vesuvius as each brother-in-law imparted golfing knowledge gained from at least three previous rounds.

"Okay, Charlie, head still, arse out, breathe in, arm straight, chin up, eyes closed, trousers down."

Eventually he got his call-up papers, and, resplendent in brown roll neck jumper, work trousers, slip-on shoes with slip-on soles and a battered 3 iron in his vice like grip, he stepped forward.

With an upper body capable of lifting a full-grown grizzly, he gave one almighty swing at the little white ball sitting invitingly on a bright red tee peg. He missed of course, and a nervous fart slid down his trouser leg before falling limply onto the dewy grass. He took another swipe, but just like the unsympathetic customs officer listening to a young man explaining a rucksack full of 1969 Liberty desk diaries, the ball remained unmoved.

Dad's patience was about to head off towards the bus stop when, with an almighty crack like a bottle of Asti crashing against the hull of the Titanic, he sent the ball sailing over one hundred and fifty yards. A magnificent shot apart from the ball arrowing straight in to the pro shop where it came to rest inside a large bucket of second-hand balls.

"Blimey, that's unlucky, Charlie," said Uncle Gordon.

"Bollocks," said my hero.

By the third hole, after losing four balls and most of his self respect, the old man muttered those five motivational words only heard from determined Olympians at the peak of their game:

"Fuck this for a game of soldiers."

With that, he threw me his clubs and headed back to the café.

Forty-eight hours later, I'm in the 'Sports and Pastimes' section of Collier Row library, leafing through *How to Play Golf with Lee Trevino*. I read it from back-to-front and was soon taking huge back-to-front divots from my mum's carefully manicured lawn. I was hooked alright, and a few weeks later Dad came home carrying a large cardboard box. Attached to it was an address label:

Mr Wilbert Trumpington Esq.
Still Waiting
Some Hope
Little Hampton
Sussex

It was a full set of golf clubs, and for the next three years I spent every Saturday morning covering myself in mud and crying with laughter at the antics of my sporting uncles.

In their own fields, they were successful members of society. In this field, they were fucking useless. Wearing increasingly luminous clothing, they turned into foul-mouthed threshing machines, debunking Gary Player's wise old maxim: *'The more you practice the luckier you get.'* Each week, in a fresh wave of optimism, they would purchase expensive new golf balls, carefully unwrap the cellophane wrapping, and instantly dispatch them straight into a pond.

wrapping, and instantly dispatch them straight into a pond.

I watched Derek's cheap mail-order clubs snap in half and fly through the air like arrows at Agincourt. I saw Gordon traipse after his ball into a copse of trees, heard a rifle crack and a strangled cry of '*Oh ... for fuck's sake!*' before emerging holding a bent 7-iron which looked like it had come second in a violent altercation with Uri Geller. And I almost soiled my plus-fours watching John follow his ball into a green side bunker and disappear in a sand storm, while his brother-in-laws made jokes about John Mills in *Ice Cold in Alex*.

But the 1978 BBC Sports Personality of the Year award must go to my uncle Bill (he of the notoriously short arms and asbestos-lined trouser pockets). Rather than lose a ball, he would calculate every shot like Sir Barnes Wallace, checking yardage and wind speed. Then, after adjusting his boxers to allow a full shoulder turn, he addressed the ball and coiled like a mud-covered spring before unleashing his immense power ... only for the club to screech to a halt inches from the ball. Yep. Fear of forking out for a new ball had given him the yips. Six times he would repeat those deliberate practice swings, and each ended with a wrist-wrenching full-stop. This wouldn't matter if the ball eventually flew in a graceful arc towards the horizon. But no. It only ever skittered forward forty yards and waited sadly in the mud for the process to be repeated.

Yep, a round of golf with Uncle Ebeneezer could take well over six hours, but his battered old golf ball became such a loyal and faithful companion that we sent it birthday and Christmas cards.

I Once Knew a Lassie, a Bonnie, Bonnie Lassie, or, The 1975 European Cup Winners Cup

If I had to choose between chipping a golf ball from the glove compartment of a burnt-out Ford Escort on a par 3 in Romford, or

Moira Lister tugging my trolley along a lush green fairway in Perthshire, well, let's just say I'd seriously consider swapping my collection of Swedish erotica for a Bay City Rollers scarf.

It turns out that all I needed for that Argos golf trolley to join me on an overnight train to the Highlands was a coupon from *Golfer's World* magazine. In the next sleeper was Uncle John dreaming of malt whisky, and further along was John's mate, Fred, dreaming of shifting a stubborn backlog in his colon. As we hurtled through the mist and rain towards Perthshire, I didn't know I was about to lose my heart to a beautiful Scottish girl, and damage a significant amount of muscle tissue overdoing the old Shermans.

We stayed in a nice little hotel in Crieff where even the local golf course had lush fairways, perfect greens, and snow-capped golden eagles. The experience would have been a golfer's paradise if not for the incessant fucking rain. When the sun did pop out, it was only to look down and laugh, before it began fucking raining again. It didn't matter to me, though. It could've been raining Datsun cogs for all I cared because my thoughts had already turned to the young hotel housemaid preparing our soup of the day.

Her name was Mary and she blew me away with her soft Scottish lilt and shapely Scottish legs. Every morning I slipped into a bright yellow roll neck with elegant blue and white checked golf trousers, and rushed down to find Mary McHousemaid waiting with her freshly steamed kipper. Her fresh-faced beauty and short tartan skirts made for some long nights under the Perthshire moon and I got through so many leather golf gloves that the pro-shop had to order fresh supplies from St Andrews.

Two days in, and Mary was taking long, languid back-swings at my heart, sending it spinning into the long grass. Dear reader. I was in love, and I can honestly say I hadn't felt this way since the time before last. The only thing spoiling our breakfast love-ins was Fred's colourful bulletins about his battle with constipation.

Wednesday evening, I went down to the empty TV lounge and watched West Ham in the European Cup Winners Cup Final. Just me, David Coleman, and Hamish McBartender. Until then I was feeling a definite connection with the swirling pipes and shortbread biscuits, but Hamish put a tremendous strain on this relationship by dancing around like Andy Stewart as West Ham went down heroically to Belgium side, Anderlecht. I went to bed one thoroughly cheesed off young Herbert and even thinking about Mary's head resting upon my thigh as she sang *Donald, Where's your Troosers?* couldn't raise my flagging spirit.

The last day found us at the world-famous Gleneagles Golf Club. Three holes from home and Fred suddenly dropped his clubs and rushed into a green side bunker where, overlooked by a forest of mighty Scots pines, he emptied his bowels. Two pounds lighter, he kicked the sand over his doings and walked triumphantly back onto the green to putt out for a two over par seven. Result.

I never got to say goodbye to Mary Queen of Scots, and when we got back to Romford, I spent the next week looking sadly out of my bedroom window towards the garages while playing romantic laments on a 12 string medieval lute. Unrequited love is a bastard, so I wrote her a letter, promising to return and enjoy her freshly steamed kipper by a babbling brook in the Trossachs. Then, in my role as the 'Jinty Annual Teenage Fantasist Award Winner,' I sketched out plans for a wedding at Gretna Green with Buster and Little Jocky looking very smart in tiny tartan trews.

A week later our letter box clanked and a pink envelope postmarked Perthshire floated onto the mat. It contained a single piece of delicately perfumed pale pink paper, and written in beautiful feminine script was a message from my Sweet Lady Mary:

"Dear Herbert ... of course I noticed you ... incredibly well-mannered ... your sense of style... very mature, like a young Val Doonican ... John and Fred had us

all in McStitches ... I could tell from your crispy bed sheets that you have the stamina to become a golfing legend ..."

She went on, very kindly and considerately lowering me down to earth before signing off with one final kick in the Dunlop 65s. Blood that only moments before had been pumping around my body like red hot lava, now slowed to a trickle as she wrote that her boyfriend, Hamish McPrick the barman, also sent his regards.

Och Noooooooooooo ... the McBastard!

The Girl from Romford

Becontree Heath. Once the biggest social housing development in the world. Twenty-six thousand homes with enough indoor toilets and privet hedges to house 100,000 people, 10,000 dogs, 1,000 cars, 100 corner shops and 10 pubs.

One of those pubs was The Merry Fiddlers and in 1978 I was recruited to play for its darts team. Back then, darts was like international football, with league tables and opposition players swapping sides. Reputations to be won or lost. One night you're *The Crafty Darty with a Shafty*, next you're *The Choking Smoker* walking home with a tungsten dart up the jacksie. Me? I was a 'ten goal a season' player. Nice and steady, and known as *The Ravi Banker,* after the Indian Sitar virtuoso.

Anyway, it was during an away match in Gidea Park that I met a young woman who would not only take my innocence but also relieve me of a brand new set of Union Jack dart flights.

She was working behind the bar and I noticed her laughing at my crappy jokes and waving a big green flag. A few days later, I went back and she had written big white letters on the big green flag. It read: FOR CHRIST SAKE, ASK ME OUT. So I did, and she agreed ... which came as a complete shock.

On the way home, I prayed to Our Lord God Jocky Wilson that I wouldn't cock this one up. On the contrary.

When I got in, I rushed upstairs to retrieve something I had been keeping hidden inside an insurance-approved fireproof Quality Street tin. It was *The 1947 Observer Book of Courtship*. A bit old-fashioned I know, but if it was good enough for Jack Hargreaves ...

Chapter One: Show The Lady a Good Time.

I've always liked 3pm but we settled on 7:30 pm, which gave me enough time to iron my Levi's and catch the first half of Larry Grayson on *The. Generation Game*. The choice of venue was critical so after considering a visit to the Savoy in Park Lane, I settled upon a working man's club in Enfield where a mate from college was playing a gig with his band. Yep, that should do it.

Chapter Two: Collect Your Lady in a Horse-Drawn Carriage

As Jack Hargreaves was on holiday, I sent a message to John Lennon asking to borrow his psychedelic Rolls Royce. A day later I received a telegram telling me to fuck off; especially charming as I had shelled out six quid on *Mind Games*. Anyway, I borrowed a Ford Transit with *G & A Carpenters* on the side, and, after hosing down the seats, I loaded the cassette player with Dr Feelgood's live album *Stupidity*. So far, so funky.

Chapter Three: The Big Night

After a quick one-two with the Ronco Brush-o-Matic and a final dusting from Andy Capp, I set off. Ten minutes later, I'm pulling into the pub car park where The Girl from Romford came out looking like a million dollars ... that's a white trouser suit, not a wad of bank notes held together with coloured elastic bands.

Her mother also appeared at an upstairs window and looked down proudly at her only daughter climbing into a Ford Transit. Seconds later, the grandmother appeared at another window, her face also a picture (possibly *Whistler's Mother* though more likely *The Scream* by Edvard Munch). We set the controls for the heart of the sun, and ninety minutes later we're pulling up outside the prestigious Ponders End Allotment Club where the band were already giving it plenty.

Something was wrong. Apart from two little girls skipping around to *Smoke on the Water*, the dance floor was empty, and dark clouds were gathering by the fire exit. It seemed the audience wasn't fully on board with heavy rock music and mutiny was in the air. And when the new electronic bingo display crashed to the floor, we could only watch as the function secretary got dragged outside to be tarred and feathered.

Luckily, a riot was prevented by the arrival of a one hundred and fifty scampi and chips caught that very morning from a Bejam's in Grimsby. They gave everyone a chance to cool down and me the opportunity to regale my date with sparkling repartee memorised from a 1968 *Jackie* annual. That massive injection of salt and vinegar worked its magic, and when the drummer started kicking his bass drum with a steady beat, the audience were on their feet, sensing their moment had come to step in time.

'Knock three times on the ceiling if you want me ...'

Yes folks, Tony Orlando and his wife Dawn had done it again, and the dance floor was quickly awash with ladies doing the twist, grannies showing their bloomers, and middle-aged men doing a complex fusion between ballroom dancing and the Harlem Shuffle.

Chapter 3: Coming in to Land

Apart from the sad demise of the function secretary, the evening was a roaring success. The transit found its way back to Romford where Wilko Johnson rocked up a storm as we kissed under the dim courtesy light, and all those years of holding my breath in gentlemen's lavatories finally paid off. When we came up for air, The Girl from Romford produced a clipboard, licked her pencil, and began marking off a tick sheet. A minute later she turned and said:

"Congratulations, you've passed!"

Man, I was living the dream!

When I told the old man I had met a pretty girl who lived in a pub, he immediately commissioned his very own gold-plated jewel-encrusted bar stool. Man ... HE was living the dream!

Her parents came from a long line of professional boxers and bookmakers, but as the line was so long, they had bought a pub instead. They were a lovely couple and I was introduced to the family on a Thames river boat. The women were glamorous with diamonds and sparkly bags, and the men had a selection of gold cufflinks and broken noses which made my dad and his brothers look like the cast from *Bugsy Malone*. Unperturbed, I talked them through the intricacies of sparring with a Freddy Mills punch bag.

Dear reader, I finally had a fully paid-up girlfriend with all the perks that came with it. Every Saturday night we borrowed her father's Audi and tore down the A127 with Lennon's *Rock and Roll* on the eight track to spend the evening inside a pair of warm bowling shoes on Southend Pier. After practising our fingering techniques with a large pair of heavy balls, we held hands under the coloured lights of Peter

Pan's playground before sharing a tub of Rossi's ice cream as moonlight danced across the Thames Estuary. Like millions before us, it was a Southend Love Story. Wonderful, innocent, and beautiful.

Yep, those Southend nights were really something. It was during the week when our courtship took on the guise of a long-running British stage farce …

I usually spent the evening swanning around the bar like James Bond in *Casino Royale* copping complimentary drinks and discounted Golden Wonders. Then it was last bell, and our cue to disappear upstairs while the parents stayed in the bar rounding up the stragglers. This left thirty precious minutes to complete our mission.

SFX – *A match strikes. A fuse is lit, and the Mission Impossible theme tune begins, closely followed by a copyright warning from Paramount Pictures.*

The first fifteen minutes were spent discussing the NHS with the grandmother, followed by another fifteen minutes heavy-petting without the grandmother. Then, what sounded like eight large men running up the stairs turned out to be two Great Danes who would sniff my nether regions, making Buster and Jocky go in-and-out like two little figures on a weather barometer.

Yep. I was getting the perks all right, and most nights had to walk to the bus stop like Herman Munster and pay extra for the puppy jumping around under my sheepskin.

As you can tell, I was a young man in a hurry. Unfortunately Major Tom was still stuck at Cape Canaveral with no sign of him blasting off towards Cloud 9.

Then, thanks to a Ladies' Night at Romford Dogs we got the flat to ourselves. Curtains drawn. Beatles *Love Songs* on the turntable. Lights down low.

SFX – There followed a period corresponding exactly with the length of *Norwegian Wood, Long and Winding Road* and three quarters of *You've Got To Hide Your Love Away*.

Downstairs, a Joker's Wild fruit machine played Handel's *Hallelujah Fanfare* as it pumped out a fistful of dollars. Upstairs, Buster and Little Jocky shared a post-coital cigarette while me and The Girl from Romford shared an Indian meal.

Yes, folks *(drum roll)*… I was finally a young man in a curry!

SFX – *Rapturous applause interspersed with cries of 'Bravo' as the author bursts into tears and joins the crowd in an impromptu Mexican wave.*

Saturday Night Fever with Barry, Maurice, Robin and (to a lesser extent) Andy

Living with the perks was great. We went to see *Saturday Night Fever* and while she tapped her feet, I lost my soul in that disco inferno. Then we strapped in for *Close Encounters of the Third Kind*, and while my jaw hung wide open, her eyes stayed wide shut while working through ten quid's worth of ice-cream. I went night fishing – she took disco dancing lessons. After six months, we were talking about dressing our kids in matching white suits. And although she was beautiful and kind, I knew The Girl from Romford could never be Anne Zeigler to my very insecure Webster Booth. To tears all round, I fired up the Golas and continued my search for The Girl in the Prefabs.

Meanwhile, the old man had taken delivery of his jewel-encrusted bespoke bar stool, and when Mum told him I was no longer going out with a pretty girl who lived in a pub, his response was typical in its sympathy and understanding:

*"Bloody hell, Jean! You know who's to blame, don't you? It's that bleedin'
John Lemon, filling the boy's head with fucking peace pipes!"*

Well, Pop, now you know.

Don't blame it on the sunshine, don't blame it on the moonlight,
don't blame it on the good times, blame it on the Bee Gees.

Collier Row, New Year's Eve 1979

Since that time when Adam stood quietly beside Eve as she bought
yet another fruit tree from the Eden Vale Garden Centre, men have
instinctively known when it's not worth arguing with a certain
contingent of womankind. The contingent who would happily pop
their partner's testicles into the toaster just for forgetting to bring in
some milk. I refer of course to the beating heart of every nation.
Working-class women. Every hour of every day a little battle of the
sexes will take place somewhere, and you can bet your bottom dollar
that the gentleman won't emerge victorious … even when they're
celebrating victory.

Appearances can be deceptive. Take my two grandmothers, for
example. Sweet old ladies who thought nothing of squeezing the
equivalent of a dozen bowling balls from their vaginas while the
German Luftwaffe bombed the shit out of their washing lines. If Flo
Smith had negotiated with Hitler instead of Chamberlain, we would
not only have had peace in our time but Flo would've also had
Hitler's other ball in a jar next to her wooden penguin. And if
Matthew Hopkins had tried his luck with Polly Moffatt, then I reckon
the old Witchfinder General may well have found himself tied to a
ducking stool, and being dunked in the River Lea like a Rich Tea
biscuit.

Suffice to say, it's much easier for a gentleman to hand over his genes in a tadpole-shaped baton, and take out any frustration on a bucket of golf balls over the driving range.

This was especially true around December when family discussions inevitably turned to the venue for that year's parade of Christmas jumpers. My uncles could only listen helplessly as it was decided which one of them would be blowing up balloons on Christmas morning instead of watching Laurel and Hardy with a fried egg sandwich.

The Moffatt ladies didn't fuck around when it came to the Festival of Cranberry. Meticulous plans were made to provide an uninterrupted stream of turkey, presents, games, cold meats, crackers, pickled walnuts, trifle, cheese and Dubonnet, through to midnight when a squadron of vacuum cleaners was unleashed against any man brave enough to stretch out on the floor with a pot belly and a Baileys.

On Boxing Day, the venue changed but everything else remained the same like a festive Groundhog Day. Full roast dinner, games, cakes, the lot. In fact, everything except my uncles were allowed to sleep through Disney Time.

And it was on Boxing Day 1979, with little cousins reduced to cutting out the puzzles on the back of the Cadbury's selection boxes, that it became my old man's turn to look heavenwards as Mum invited everyone to our house for a New Year's Eve fancy dress party. Yay.

I now had a new girlfriend who thought it would be nice to meet my family, so as the alternative was spending New Year's Eve standing outside by the bins, I began filling up some sandbags.

By New Year's Eve morning, the Christmas tree had already disappeared, leaving a trail of lonesome pines through the house and ending abruptly outside the back door. Mum was making good use of her three feet of oak-effect worktop to prepare 150 sausage rolls, while the old man crouched over a gold-effect drinks' trolley and cracking his knuckles like he was breaking into the Bank of England. This was serious fucking business. Polishing peanut bowls and emptying wood screws from his 'Drink Canada Dry' ice bucket before lining up lager cans and stacking reinforcements and boxes of wine on the patio. Then, after replacing his decent whisky with a bottle of cheap Johnny Walker, he lifted the smoked plastic lid of the music centre, allowing Al Martino to fly in from Las Vegas. Mum, now stirring a bubbling cauldron of West Indian chicken curry, shouted to him through the serving hatch:

"Oh, Charlie, I love this one... can you turn it down a bit?"

At 7pm the portcullis was raised and in they all strolled.

First was Lynda dressed as a St Trinian's schoolgirl. Aunt Dolly was next, in a chamber maid costume. Aunt Pat ran inside chased by a brother-in-law dressed as a yokel and lifting his smock to show an oversized stuffed appendage. Derek was a clown with a big red nose and tortoise shell glasses. Bill Godfrey was in full British Rail uniform, and having a quick one before seeing in the New Year in a goods' shed in Ilford with a set of playing cards. Nan was sipping a Mackeson and giving Gordon a tantalising view of her Christmas bloomers. Aunt June was dressed as Shirley Temple and having a heated exchange with the back of her husband's head. Aunt Jean, in a glittering flapper dress, was sharing a can of light ale with an overweight Chewbacca (possibly a Bungle), while our terrified cat got chased upstairs by a posse of young cowboys and a twinkle of little fairies.

In the middle of the room, spinning his bloody awful Honky Tonk piano records, stood the abandoned love child of Tony Soprano and Jimmy Clitheroe. It was my old man, dressed as a schoolboy in short trousers, school cap and a blazer bursting at the seams and a Curly Wurly poking from the top pocket. The entire ensemble was finished off with a pair of size 12 brown Hush Puppies. It certainly finished off the distressed Punk Rocker standing in the corner under a lamp shade offering smelling salts to his new girlfriend.

Midnight arrived, Big Ben bonged, and Andy Stewart swung Moira Lister around his head like a tartan lasso. Eileen led a conga into the freezing night air before doing a quick 180 and coming inside to hear Christine and Lynda perform a heartbreaking duet to Connie Francis's *Where The Boys Are*. By 1:30am they began drifting away like crazies from a Cronenberg movie, some carrying sleeping cowboys, some carrying knackered princesses, but all carrying a tin-foil package of left-overs issued by my mother dressed in her Red Cross outfit.

And while the Red Cross emptied ashtrays into a black bag, the old man retrieved his 20-year-old malt and joined Frank Sinatra singing along to *In the Wee Small Hours*. At 2am, the cat came down wearing a tiny, elasticated policeman's helmet, and it was time to disappear with my shell-shocked girlfriend.

Britain has a proud tradition of men acting like schoolboys. Fine actors like Harry Fowler, Charles Hawtrey and Gerald Campion. Not forgetting Ian Duncan 'Punch the Air' Smith, who was filmed eating his own bogies in the House of Commons. It's on YouTube. Yay!

But for me it will always be that image of my father, three sheets to the windy pops, conducting Frank Sinatra with a Curly Wurly, that is forever burned onto the photographic paper in my mind. It's also why I am still seeking help from the Terry Scott Appreciation Society.

Collier Row 10th May 1980 – The FA Cup Final

Remember the start of Chapter 2? When we moved in and how our new neighbour was going to make me the happiest boy in Collier Row? Well, it turns out she was a cousin of Trevor Brooking and after bribing her with a Cadbury's Flake wrapped in a ten-pound note, she agreed to pass on my letter:

"Dear Trev. Can you fix it for me to see West Ham win the FA Cup? It's

been five long years and I'm beginning to think we might be fucking useless! God Bless. Tim Smith, aged 22 ½."

It worked. West Ham, now in the Second Division and with a kit more ragged than Boris Johnson after a weekend in Italy with a KGB agent, sailed through to another Wembley final to face the mighty Arsenal and their magnificent goalkeeper, Pat Jennings, whose hands were like bananas and whose haircut came straight from the cheese counter at Fortnum & Masons.

Bookmakers had stopped taking bets on an Arsenal win, but they had reckoned without one thing: English Spunk and London Pride (*two things*), and more importantly – our neighbour's cousin (*okay, three things*).

The big day arrived and to settle any pre-match nerves, Papa and I went across to The White Hart to watch Dickie Davies compère *The All-Star Secrets Cup Final Special* on a fat old telly perched precariously on a tiny shelf over the pool table. Quite honestly, it looked like it was about to jump down and make a run for it back to Rumbelows.

Anyway, it was an hour well spent, and after watching Fred Dinenage interview Alf Garnet, it was time to sup up our beer and collect our fags.

Dear reader. Since my pre-school training at the Forest Gate Winkle and Shrimp Academy, I cannot pass a seafood stall without stopping to cast an expert eye over the display and take a lungful of the seaside aroma. That day was no different and we polished off some whelks and a bowl of sad-looking prawns.

If I had known King Neptune was that most rare of things, an Arsenal fan with a sense of comedic timing, I might've done a Dionne Warwick ... but I didn't and we soon realised those little blighters were on the turn.

Now, my old man had done his National Service playing cribbage in the Middle East so he simply shrugged off the Salmonella/E. coli combo. Not me. By the time we got home my face was the colour of a crab stick and my legs were more wobbly than a tub of jellied eels on a ghost train. Honestly, I felt like the last cockle swimming in a bowl of its own vinegar as I clung desperately to a yellow washing up bowl. The rest of the family thought it was hilarious so, to the dying strains of *Abide With Me*, I issued each of them with a series of foul-smelling penalty notices.

At 2:50pm exactly, the Second Division warriors emerged from the Wembley tunnel towards flashing bulbs and a world-wide television audience. Alongside them strolled the swanky mascara and lipsticked-up First Division favourites.

The ref had hardly wet his whistle before the West Ham captain began swashing and buckling like Billy-O, putting Arsenal to the sword. And when wing commander Devonshire popped one into the box for midshipman Brooking to nick the only goal, I rose from my death bed like Stan Lazaridis and looked down from the Artex ceiling at my family going absolutely fucking NUTS! Ninety minutes later, Billy Bonds filmed a ten-second cameo of him lifting the FA Cup that would be shown on BBC's *Match of the Day* for decades to come.

Next day, the Cup was paraded through the streets of Newham. Beginning at Stratford Town Hall, it travelled past the barbers who did my billiard ball hair cut, past the pie and mash shop, past the bus shelter roof and the last resting place of my old football boots, along the Barking Road past Jeff's house, past the Granada building where the Beatles played in 1963, and over the zebra crossing where a city gent slid like a curling stone. The parade ended at East Ham Town Hall where, with my new girlfriend and 100,000 others, we watched the Lady Mayor goose Phil Parkes (British record goalie) on the Town Hall balcony.

West Ham supporters are used to getting kicked in the nuts but that Sunday we all jolly well got the day off. Many times I've considered giving up the heartache but like Al Pacino in Godfather

III, *'just when I thought I was out, they pull me back in'*. Anyway, what other team can count Barak Obama as their biggest fan, have appeared in The Simpsons and Harry Potter books, and have the most recognisable anthem in the world born in my dear old primary school? I may be a Mr. Softee but *I'm Forever Blowing Bubbles* can reduce me to a blubbering hammer-shaped wreck. There are a few others, too. Like *Easter Parade* by Judy Garland because it was Mum's favourite, and *Let Me Call You Sweetheart* sung by Chas Hodges, because I sang it to my daughter every night for five years. Not forgetting *Underneath the Arches* by Flanagan and Allen for all those suffering with their feet, and *Puppy Love* by Donny Osmond to remind me there's always some other bastard worse off.

And as the Lady Mayor led away 17-year-old Paul Allen (youngest ever player in the FA cup final) to her private quarters, we set off for my girlfriend's flat near Abbey Road studios NW8. She was from the mystic East and would spend the next 30 years making me a happy and enlightened Herbert. But back in May 1980, we were just going steady through Islington with claret and blue ribbons fluttering from the van's aerial.

Nobody told me there would be days like these.

Collier Row, Tuesday 9th December 1980

Where was I when I heard the news? I was in bed with the cat (not Peter Bonetti).

Beside me was an ashtray and a travel clock. Opposite was a bookcase loaded with horror novels and Milligan war memoirs. The woodchip around the dartboard was peppered with tiny holes, and on the window sill was a set of Eric Bristow tungstens nestled in a puddle of condensation. On the carpet was a Pye music centre and a stack of albums. An EKO acoustic guitar leant against an MFI wardrobe containing a blue velvet jacket, a pair of Levis, a West Ham scarf, two pairs of tartan house slippers (one mint, still boxed), and a green leather jacket from the 'Department S' special effects wardrobe. Sellotaped to the chimney was a 40 x 30 inch poster of John Lennon wearing a 'People For Peace' armband.

At 7am, Mum brought in a cup of tea and told me he had been murdered.

SFX – The Utopian National Anthem. (*Silence*)

Nobody's perfect BUT he was in THE Greatest Show on Earth, and now some deranged Yank had shot him. It was like losing my beast friend. I went to college but no one seemed bothered by the news so when a lecturer started making jokes about the murder, I went home, made a sausage sandwich and watched the crowds gather outside the Dakota in New York.

So, it wasn't just me then.

Lennon used to say we could all do something for Peace, no matter how small:

'Grow your hair for Peace. Stay in bed for Peace. Do something they can't get. Something they can't smash.'

Which was all very well, but not much help to a 22-year-old, light-fingered labourer from Romford.

ACT 3

A WORKING CLASS HERBERT

IS SOMETHING TO BE

(2022)

A spaceship hovers over Gallows Corner roundabout on the busy Southend arterial. Coloured lights chase around its underside playing the same five musical notes like an intergalactic ice cream van. Commuters stare in disbelief as light spills from the underside. Car engines die, street lights flicker, as figures descend ...

First out was a man in a WWI uniform, followed by a Pearly Queen and a lady in a 1960's mini-skirt pushing a psychedelic Rolls Royce. Bob Moore was there. Jack Hargreaves and Susan Stranks too. Last out were a pair of Gola trainers blinking rapidly behind a pair of Joe 90 glasses. A man in a white coat told us we had all experienced a Close Encounter of The Cockney Kind.

Dear reader. When the stork with the postman's hat opened his bomb doors over a chimney in Gladstone Road, I hit the jackpot. Delivered into a happy family, protected day and night by a host of beautiful, funny women who were feminising their asses off before Germaine Greer had sandpapered her first pair of nuts. One moment weeping over *Gone With The Wind,* next, scraping a Cocker Spaniel from under a bus. Pound for pound, the most impressive of their species.

So, when I'm not dreaming about DCI Jane Tennyson, I like to imagine working-class ladies like them, running things. They'd be some bloodshed, obviously, but I'd love to see my aunt Alice kicking Trump's sorry ass around Hainault Golf Club, or watch a teenage Alexander Boris de Pfeffel Johnson dare to set fire to a twenty-pound note under the nose of my aunt Queenie. What say you, ladies? Keys to the kingdom in return for having your purses ready at the supermarket checkout?

My Forest Gate nan died in 1986. Another matriarch buried in West Ham Cemetery. She and her son Bill were estranged at the time, but I remember him coming smartly to attention and saluting as they lowered her into the ground. Around the grave stood her boys. Wide shoulders. Dark suits. Holding back tears.

As far as the Moffatt family is concerned, most are now in a heavenly through-lounge reading a Catherine Cookson or playing three-card-heavenly-brag. However, they did leave thirty or so doppelgängers dragging their grandchildren around every B&Q in the South East. Bill Moffatt is still going strong, and for his 90th birthday rearranged his own bedroom furniture. John Adlam still charges around like the Duracell bunny, and Lyn and Christine are both doting great-grandmothers. Cousin Den hasn't changed a bit since I killed her goldfish, and Jeff became a multi-millionaire who apart from making luggage for the royal family, supplies anglers around Britain with top quality tackle at low, low prices at robbostackle.com.

What about Buster and Jocky, my two little counterfeit Gucci handbags? Well, in a moment of weakness I got a vasectomy which did cause a little friction. However, they still bump into each other at weekends, usually when I'm doing that bow-legged dance routine to *Crazy Horses*.

Like the Mississippi River, my old man keeps on rolling along. A year after Mum died, he had a stroke which left him in the same rehabilitation ward as football legend Jimmy Greaves. Both in the same boat, both surrounded by distraught relations. During one visit, and bearing in mind my father couldn't walk and had lost the use of his right arm, he whispered to me in his booming voice:

"That's old Greavsie over there. Poor bastard."

We shake hands every birthday and Christmas, and the only time I can ever remember embracing him was the day his wife died.

I kissed Jean Florence Smith goodbye on the evening before the 2012 Olympics, not knowing it would be our last. Even in her eighties my mum could've handled the entire Olympic catering contract with a phone under her chin. It would've been nice to climb onto our old shed in Stratford and hold hands as the Olympic fireworks burst over our heads and tell her she was everything a mother, wife, sister, grandmother and great-grandmother could ever be. In 1955, her fiancé gave her a musical cigarette lighter bought from a tobacconist near West Ham Library. It was shaped like an old gramophone and played *Smoke Gets in Your Eyes*. She polished it every Saturday morning for sixty years and it now stands safely between a picture of them both.

So, what about The Girl from the Prefabs? Was she real or a figment of my overactive thyroid? I am glad to say that she was real, and while I was learning the ropes in Stratford, she was pedalling her bike around the streets of Walthamstow. Like comets, we orbited some of East London's top attractions like the Green Gate at Leyton, the ice flows of Whipps Cross, and pushing pennies off Southend Pier. The closest we came was in Manor Park when I was buying drumsticks and she was two doors down above a sari shop, ears packed with cotton wool as the drummer of Iron Maiden smashed the daylights out of his kit in The Ruskin Arms.

Not destined to meet until the gravitational pull of an aluminium building in Hainault proved too strong and we collided in an explosion of rubber plants and tea cups. A kindred spirit with dirty knees and kind eyes. The glass slipper fitted perfectly and in 2015 she became my beautiful wife, Georgie.

I never found *The Eye of the Tiger* but as I stand before you with a face like it's done twelve rounds with Apollo Creed, allow me to grab the microphone like Rocky Balboa and say one last thing to my Girl in the Prefabs …

"*Yo, Georgie … WE DID IT!*"

THE END

Cue music: *Puppy Love* by Donny Osmond

One final tracking shot of smiling people waving goodbye like the end of *The Railway Children*.

CREDITS ROLL

Infant Herbert …Baby Caligua

Young Herbert … Boy from *Flipper*

Teenage Herbert … Frankie Abbott (*Please Sir*)

Jean Smith … June Whitfield

Charlie Smith … James Gadolfini (*The Sopranos*)

The Girl in the Prefabs … Georgie Samantha Smith

John Winston Lennon … Himself

William Moffatt. … Lord Mountbatten Admiral of the Fleet

Polly Moffatt … Dame Peggy Mount

Flo Smith … Dame Margaret Rutherford

Bert Smith … Sir Anthony Hopkins / Ralph Fiennes

Lynda Moffatt … Barbara Windsor

Derek Moffatt … Stan Laurel / Matthews

Bobby Moore ... Himself

Sandy the Stingy Lodger ... Gordon Jackson

Jim Smith ... A very large Charlie Drake

Buster ... Bruce Willis

Little Jocky ... Uncle Fester

Eamonn Andrews ... Himself

Jeff Vaughan ... The Artful Dodger

John Adlam ... Sir John Mills (*Ice Cold in Alex*)

Charlie Vaughan ... Charles Atlas

Bill Smith ... Sean Connery (*Dr No*)

Bertha Jackson ... Pat Coombs

Bertha's Budgie ... Joey

Steve Jackson ... Bert Smith / Ralph Fiennes

Theresa Smith ... Marie Osmond / Adrienne Posta

Dolly Moffatt ... Mother Christmas

Eileen Moffatt ... Princess Margaret

Alice Moffatt ... Delia Smith

Bill Moffatt ... A young Tom Courtney

My First Love ... Susan Stranks

Gordon Milne ... A Bespectacled Lee Trevino

Bill Godfrey ... Ebeneezer Scrooge

Brian Jupp ... Bernard Bresslaw or a giant Postman Pat

The Cat ... Peter Bonetti

Howard Woolly's dad ... Dr Phallus

Donny Osmond ... A Dairylea cheese triangle

Denise ... Sally Geeson

Jeanie Moffatt ... H.R.H Queen Elizabeth II

June Moffatt ... Dame Margot Fonteyne

Pat Moffatt ... H.R.H. Hylda Baker

Christine Moffatt … Nanny McPhee

Alfie Bumble … Popeye

Reg 'Uncle' Whiteman … Deputy Matt Dillon

Mr Perryman … Capt Mainwaring / General Montgomery.

Thirty cousins … 9th Battalion, Regiment of The Coldstream Guards

Girl in Off-Licence … Goldie Hawn

Rayleigh Chopper … Moulton 'Shopper'

Adult Herbert … Tim (Leader of Utopian Popular People's Front)

Executive Producers

Jessica, Joseph, Alec, Leanne and Sophie

Directors

Oscar, Casper, Bella, and any future grandchildren who have the inalienable right to put Peppa Pig stickers on any freshly painted walls.

(Music ends, screen fades to black, stage curtains close.)

ACT 4

AN ACORN RUNS THROUGH IT

'Take this, brother, may it serve you well.' The Beatles. Revolution No.9

We hear the dull thump of theatre seats springing upright as the author appears on stage wearing a velvet smoking jacket. After blowing a few kisses and with tears in his eyes, he motions for the audience to sit ...

So, there you have it. The evolution of a bonio-fido working-class Herbert, no different from those charmers in the Bullingdon Club, apart from a sense of decency.

I'm sure their mothers must be very proud but does anyone believe men like Cameron and Johnson ever consider the rest of us while plotting with their chums? With the information available, I'd say NO and we must look to President George W. Bush, who said this about the 9/11 attackers:

"There's an old saying in Tennessee ... that says, fool me once, shame on – shame on you. Fool me – you can't get fooled again."

No nonsense, our George.

I've had a few heroes. Moore. Tenzing. But the man who could sing *Mr Moonlight* faster than Pinky and Perky was always No.1. In 1969, John and Yoko sent acorns for peace to world leaders. The Malaysian president planted his in the palace gardens. Queen

Elizabeth sent a letter of support, and President Richard Nixon chucked his out of the Oval Office window before ordering the FBI to dust off their phone tapping equipment.

Like *Jack and the Beanstalk*, that little acorn bounced around for a few years before landing in a bedroom in East London where I picked it up and placed it to my ear.

Stay in bed for peace. Grow your hair for peace. Do something they can't get. Something they can't smash.

For forty years, that little acorn rolled around my dashboard between crisp bags and a Screw-Fit catalogue, while I hid from strippers and amused my children. But old Tricky Dicky had reckoned without one thing: Lennon's legacy and the stubbornness of a British Herbert (okay, two things).

This book has been my own 'Little Acorn for Peace'. It won't threaten the legacy of Adrian Mole, but it will be stored in the British Library so future generations can read about my gloriously ordinary family, and find out the names of the miserable self serving Tory politicians who screwed up our country. Who knows, it might stir a few memories of a time we all sang *Power to the People*, and at the very least remind Ian Duncan Smith that he's never more than ten feet from a Herbert.

Today I am one content old paddle steamer, floating along the slow-moving rivers of Suffolk. On the top deck, my grandsons are gobbing over the rails, and following behind, pedalling like crazy on her unicorn pedalo, is my granddaughter, carrying with her the genetic benefits of a whole host of badass women.

Kids. You get one go on this merry-go-round so play music loud, read books quietly, fall in love, dance like nutcases, hang upside down from trees, create happy memories, and use your vote. And if you ever need me, I'll be in the British Library, right here in Granddad's

Magic Memoir.

Bloody hell ... just *Imagine*.

*

Postscript:

Charles (Chas) Robert Smith

After my mum died, Dad lived alone in their flat, doing his own shopping and cleaning. Of course, the old shyster coped perfectly. I visited him every day and Georgie became the latest woman to fuss over him. After his stroke, Braintree Council arranged for a team of wonderful carers to park him on a commode in front of the football with an Iceland ready meal. He made a few visits to Broomfield Hospital but, thanks to the NHS, always came home to cheering crowds.

In January 2019, something changed.

"I've had enough, boy," he said.

His grandchildren spent the day at his bedside in Baddow Ward but by tea time it was just me and him. His breathing was laboured as his giant hand covered mine. And as staff began serving the evening meals, he took one long, satisfying yawn, smacked his lips, and closed his eyes. For five minutes he breathed easily and looked for all the world like his mum. Then he stopped squeezing my hand and I realised Lennon wasn't my hero after all.

My parents did some of their courting over West Ham Park so I have sprinkled a portion of their ashes around Dr Fothergill's Maidenhair tree (*Gingko Biloba*), where this story began. It's peaceful there.

Bye bye, everybody. Bye bye.

Jean and Charlie Smith 1973

Dr Forthergill's Maiden Hair (Ginko Biloba) West Ham Park 2021

THE REAL END

ABOUT THE AUTHOR

- ✓ He's a 64-year-old ex-builder with two metal knees
- ✓ His mum shares a birthday with Paul McCartney.
- ✓ His daughter shares a birthday with George Harrison.
- ✓ Ringo Starr got his first set of drums from a second-hand shop in Romford
- ✓ Like John Lennon, he's a short-sighted, only-child with a tendency to support lost causes (in his case, West Ham United).
- ✓ He also believes women are our only hope.

Printed in Great Britain
by Amazon

24822510R00165